# NEW INDIA

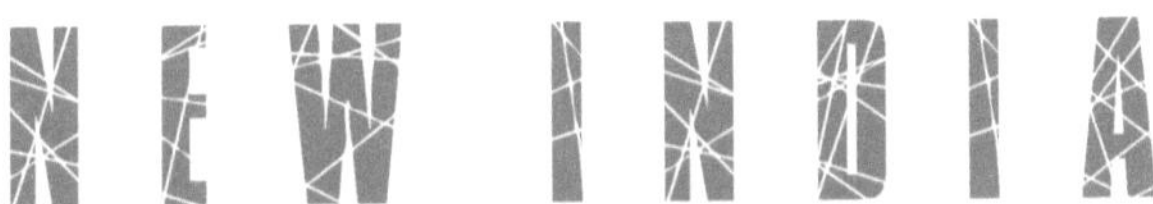

*Ancient civilisation
in tragicomic phase*

अजब देश की ग़ज़ब कहानी

INTRODUCTION
I
Old Land, New Miracles
II
India of Nightmares
III
Creative Resistance

FANTASY

OPINION
REPORTS
POEMS

## L K SHARMA

### EDITOR

*Many Indians feel distressed
by the New India.
This Guide tells them they are
not alone.*

———————

The Editor expresses immense thanks to the
contributors. Articles included with the
permission of writers or publishers and
of the Swiss Charles Veillon Foundation
for Arundhati Roy's lecture.
Cover image by studio4rt on Freepik
factionbooks@gmail.com

# CONTENTS

## REPORTS



## POEMS

# INTRODUCTION

L K SHARMA

## I

# Old Land, New Miracles

The New India, like the old one, is a land of miracles. Western visitors admired Indians for walking on water and the rope-trick. Now, they love its Nonbiological Being (NB) who claims in human voice that he is not human! Moses split the sea. Prophet Muhammad split the Moon. NB split society, a feat no less than splitting the atom.

Indophiles, who come to explore exotica, find that the New India is not beguiled by modernity. They interview spiritual saints, criminal saints, and the Political Baba. In their countries miracles do not happen anymore but in India anything is possible. They know that *Modi hai to mumkin hai.* They see a child narrating his past life and a Baba producing a golden necklace out of thin air or talking to Lord Hanuman on the mobile. They record a first-hand account of cancer cured by milk or urine. India is far ahead of Africa in the number of faith healers. The demand for Godmen has shot up. Godwomen had always been there but now children appear as appropriately dressed miracle doers, attracting large audiences. Those shocked by this development point out that while China is training children in robotics, India is training them to be Godmen! The BBC does a TV report on a woman who calls herself "*Chamatkari Mata*" (Miracle Mother). She is followed by the poor and illiterate as well as by educated rich Indians. She gets donations for fulfilling the wishes of the devotees. The BBC report says India is a home to many such figures who claim divine powers – some of whom face allegations of misconduct, corruption and even sexual assault. Yet, they continue to draw massive followings. The BBC points out that during 2024, over 120 people lost their lives in a crush at a religious gathering led by a self-proclaimed Indian 'Godman'. The Government did not mind this report but raided the BBC office when it released a documentary on Modi.

Godmen prescribe miracle remedies to their devotees. One "spiritual" discourse covers 'inappropriately dressed' women and the women in live-in relationship, whom the Baba calls "prostitutes". This Godman spares the men who go to the prostitutes. He prescribes a drug for the women who cannot conceive. "Feed wheat to a cow and from the cow dung, pick up the sprouted wheat and eat it!" Another saffron-clad Godman claims that for 14 years, Lord Ram's brother Bharat had porridge cooked in cow's urine! Many new Godmen have appeared and dozens of Ashrams have come up. Many Godmen enlighten devotees through virtual sessions. Some commit crimes as per complaints by the women molested by them. They are arrested and then released on bail before elections.

While the ruling establishment moves to turn the secular India into a Hindu nation, a Godman announces a plan for a real estate project named Hindu Village for 1000 Hindu families! Non-Hindus would not be allowed entry into this village. The Godman says a Hindu district and a Hindu state would follow eventually leading to the establishment of the Hindu Nation! A wag says that unless the Hindu Village has at least one mosque, its Hindu residents would not know what to climb on during their religious festivals! A recent Hindu religious procession on the Ram Navami had loudspeakers bombarding the roadside masjid with the dirtiest abuses.

With the fusion of religion and politics, a Godman with divine powers dominates the political scene, supported by a giant meme factory run by the Troller-in-Chief assigned to intimidate non-Hindus. Prime Minister Modi vowed to transform India. He has been helped by social media, inexpensive mobile phones and cheap data! As a political tool, the mobile phone instantaneously conveys hate messages to millions of people. The mobile is also having an effect not planned by Modi. It now spreads messages of sanity, peace and love. As a tool of illicit love, the mobile generates strange stories every week – an elderly woman runs away with the prospective son-in-law and a twice-married Muslim woman marries a Hindu student years younger to her! The mobile has hit the nursery schools in which the teacher has to pull away a student kissing a girl in the class!

The New India is a happening place. Bharat Mata reawakened by a politician; Hindus reawakened by the BJP's shrill call. Muslims stay awake day and night, guarding their bodies and belongings. Awakened Hindus recite the prayer: "*In a country where the mind is without reason and the heart without love, and from where others are banished, into that land of servitude, Dear Leader, let my Bharat awake.*" "We are proud of being Hindu", they shout while marching on streets. They blame nine generations of their somnolent forefathers for not fighting the foreigners and take a vow to demolish the graves of those foreigners. In their homes hangs the *Akhand Bharat* map painting the world saffron.

Many Indians wade into a toxic ocean of sectarian hatred. Awakened Hindus are running a National Digging Festival to find a mandir below every masjid and attack the archaeologists and historians questioning them. Hindutva warriors achieved a huge success by demolishing the Babri Mosque and building a Ram Temple on that very spot. They identified four other major spots for repeating the same operation. Then in March 2025, the Hindutva Strategy Group realised that the disputed mosques are limited in numbers while many elections will have to be won in the coming decades. So, it hit upon the idea of digging up the graves of the Moghul rulers, beginning with that of Aurangzeb in a BJP-rule state. It has yet to decide with what should the grave's contents be replaced! So, after lying in peace for 318 years, Aurangzeb is turning in his grave. Aurangzeb's Hindu relations belonging to a princely family of Rajasthan have not protested. The first stone was thrown at Aurangzeb by Prime Minister Modi himself during his 2024 election campaign.

The current national obsession with Aurangzeb should not give the impression that India lives in the 17th century. India lives in several Ages simultaneously. The Age of Ram, Age of Anger, Age of Surveillance, Age of Unreason, Age of Stupidity, Age of Aggression, Age of Assassins, Age of Idiocy, and Age of Fantasy. Citing false promises and deceptive rhetoric, some call it the Age of Cant! 'Age of Monsters', some mutter under their breath. The Leader calls the new era *Amrit Kaal* This Amrit (nectar) produces more billionaires every year in a country that is placed in the "serious" category by the global Hunger Index and Freedom Index. This strange India elates many, frightens some and amuses observers.

Awakened Hindus have destroyed the cradles of reason by targeting premier universities. They plastered every university campus with the signboard: *Dissent is Treason: Thinking Prohibited.* Rationalists have gone into hiding. Misologists and misogynists have outed themselves. The Hindutva warriors barred Bollywood from promoting inter-faith harmony through films and turned a macho film hero, Mahanayak, into a lapdog. They killed a TV ad applauding inter-faith marriage. The ad showed a Hindu daughter-in-law excited by her Muslim in-laws having a Hindu ceremony for her! The jewellery company was attacked for promoting "love jihad". Awakened Hindus forced another company to kill the ad that "de-Hinduised" a Hindu festival. They punished a shoe company misusing a Hindu God's image to sell shoes. The right to feel hurt takes precedence over the right to life.

Strangeness that marks the political and social ethos is also reflected in the country's new physical features. Real India lived in villages but now lives in gated colonies in the Whiteland where the 31st floor penthouses have private swimming pools and lawns. From the apartment block, one steps out on the Harley Street, walks in the Hyde Park, crosses the Covent Garden, and goes via the Hackney Street, Tooley Street, Kings Cross Road, and Baker Street to reach the consumers' paradise near the Wembley Estate. It is called the Eros Mall where international branded restaurants serve an infinite variety of exotic cuisines. "Little London" has come up on the ruins of a village. This 'Luxury Living' is showcased just 30 km. from Delhi. Travel on a pot-holed road and see gigantic "English Wine" stores sparkling with Christmas lights round the year besides dark, dismal slums and heaps of broken bricks of demolished houses. One runs into a lathi-laced, saffron-wearing group of young men protecting the Mother Cow from humans and reverentially letting her eat polythene bags and kitchen waste in the company of diseased dogs. The men come charging to sniff your car to detect if it is carting beef. Vigilante groups feel empowered by the nexus of religious fanaticism and political power.

New India's tragic state is analysed by scholars while satirists highlight its comic aspect. Imagination has ended, so, satire is not read as satire but mistaken as the narration of a real event. A cultural revolution has ushered in the post-truth age. Whatever is true about India, its opposite is also true. Confusion is now confounded by a national charade, with the political performer playing double role to entertain two sets of spectators. For the corporate kings in the Balcony, he plays the role of Manager, and for the poor souls in the Stalls, that of Saviour. The clown show makes feeling supreme, thinking irrelevant. It attracts millions of blind devotees. Innumerable social media posts praise the Vedic wisdom of the one who says ancient Indians transplanted heads. All see the wizard transplanting brains without touching a surgical knife. Just by words, he remotely conducted multiple brain operations in one go. The Leader knows cosmetic surgery and reproductive genetics. He tells doctors at a Mumbai hospital: "We all read about Karna in the Mahabharata. If we think a little more, we realise that the Mahabharata says Karna was not born from his mother's womb. This means that genetic science was present at that time. That is why Karna could be born outside his mother's womb." He goes on: "We worship

Lord Ganesh. There must have been some plastic surgeon at that time who got an elephant's head on the body of a human being and began the practice of plastic surgery." The Leader does not keep his scientific knowledge to himself. He guides scientists, declaring that the climate is not changing, we feel it because we are getting old. He claims that clouds blind the radar so bombers should attack when it is clouded. Being fair, the Leader also gives his political warriors the freedom to make 'scientific' statements (bizarre claims). BJP's Tripura Chief Minister claims that the internet was invented lakhs of years ago and satellite communication was used in the Mahabharat era. That is how Sanjay reported to Dhritarashtra the war from Kurukshetra. Ancient Indians forgot to get their invention patented!

A Union Minister of the BJP claims that Darwin's theory of evolution was wrong and should not be taught. Humans appeared on Earth as humans from the very beginning. The Science and Technology Minister tells the Science Congress that the Vedas contain theories much superior to Einstein's Law. He tweets: "Each and every custom and ritual of Hinduism, is steeped in science; every modern Indian achievement is a continuation of our past scientific achievement." A BJP minister of Rajasthan claims that cow is the only being that inhales as well as exhales oxygen. The malady has affected non-politicians also. A Rajasthan High Court Judge announces his theory that peacocks do not copulate. The peahen does not indulge in sex but gets pregnant by "swallowing the tears of the peacock".

Cow urine research is a major scientific project and more such initiatives are in the pipeline. The director of an IIT held an elaborate ground-breaking ceremony for building a cowshed on the campus. Someone posted on social media an image of the invitation card for the cowshed ceremony attaching the reports of successful scientific projects of foreign institutions.

A Government lab should develop a gadget to remotely detect beef in the Muslim refrigerators. Some Muslims who had stored meat and not beef were murdered wrongfully. Such mistakes will be prevented by this gadget. The lab is more likely to be asked to develop a thought detection gadget so that the anti-nationals can be rounded up for the crime of thinking. Modi makes anything happen. Modi announced demonetisation and the TV channels reported that the new currency notes have a miracle chip that will send signals to the income-tax inspectors to enable them to recover hidden wealth from under the deep sea or earth! The panic lasted till it was reported that the notes were chip-free.

Scientific approach has been banished from the only country whose Constitution mentions "scientific temper" and whose first Prime Minister devoted public speeches to promote it. In such a country, the Leader's silly unscientific statements are believed and silly statements are lapped up by the masses. The Science Congress now needs to be covered by mythology experts, not science reporters. A scientist claiming that he has transplanted an elephant's head on a human body will be applauded.

In this atmosphere of make-believe, the population of ghosts has grown abnormally while dubious figures of the rising population of Muslims are circulated. India has ghost citizens, ghost pensioners, ghost teachers and ghost employees who draw salaries without coming to work. Ghost entrepreneurs run ghost companies. Ghost history is manufactured by ghost 'scholars' sustained by the Government busy demolishing credible institutions. It is written as per official guidelines and purveyed by the WhatsApp University.

Ghost documents circulate on social media. Ghost Aadhar cards, ghost ration cards, ghost caste certificates, ghost birth certificates and ghost university degree certificates are manufactured per order and sold. Ghost voters appear on the polling day. A man goes to the polling booth to meet his wife on the polling day to find that she had already voted and gone. He cries, saying that he would have to wait for another five years to meet her at the polling booth. The perplexed booth officer asks him whether he does not meet her at home. He says his wife died 14 years ago but comes down to earth on the polling day to exercise her democratic right! Some ghosts never appear in public. Ghost writers, masters of rhetoric, reside in the

Leader's office, making him eloquent. The Ghost Media Manager supplies ghost stories to the TV channels. The channel owners never see him; only hear him on the phone, ordering them to kill unfavourable reports filed by recalcitrant journalists. Newspapers and TV channels are sanitised before release.

Politicians run misinformation campaigns to get votes. Godmen do it to get followers. Godmen give discourses that are videographed. The viewers are warned that their future will be endangered if they did not pay for the Hindu religious ceremonies. Millions take a holy bath in the sacred river water to wash off their sins even as a laboratory finds that the water is not clean enough for bathing. Water companies are selling the sacred water in bottles for drinking. Those unable to go for the holy bath can use a service offered by an entrepreneur. Send him a digital photo of yours; his company will print it, take it to the river, bathe it and send you a video of "you" taking the holy dip!

Mythology is invoked to promote patriarchy. The State Women Commission of U.P. proposes that no woman can engage a male tailor, male hairdresser, or a male gym instructor because that would lead to "bad touch". It wants to protect women from "bad intentions" of men. The right-wing vigilante groups raid gyms and hair salons in search of unmarried couples who face violence in public places and cannot find shelter even in a safe hotel room. In Yogi's U.P., a hotel has barred unmarried couples from getting a room, leading to a brisk sale of false marriage certificates. Most married couples have no document certifying their marriage. The Hindu Purity Sangh (HPS) may insist on virginity tests before marriage. Its president is going to the UK to learn from the British immigration officers who were once asked to check out women arriving at the British airports. That scheme had to be dropped because of protests.

"Live-in relationship" has been turned into a term of abuse by the Hindutva vigilantism. The state of Uttarakhand has made it mandatory for the live-in couples to register with the government under the new Uniform Civil Code. Perhaps its violation will be checked through midnight knocks at the doors demanding the Registration Certificate! What is more, the official measure is approved by a very large section of the people as revealed in a sample survey. Most of them disapproved of liaisons without the permission of the parents! So, patriarchy still rules the minds of men and women in this state. The issue also got clubbed with the inter-faith marriages resulting from "love jihad" by Muslim men!

## From Light to Darkness

India's journey from light to darkness has been long. Centuries ago, the marriage of a Rajput princess to a Muslim emperor was celebrated by the Hindu masses, not condemned as 'Love Jihad'. The principles of Hinduism were contested and debated in public.

Criticism was considered necessary to maintain the purity of a spiritual tradition. Some 150 years ago, Swami Dayanand Saraswati founded the Arya Samaj to turn Hindus towards spirituality based on the Vedic culture. His campaign against fake religiosity attracted a large section of Hindus who took to the reformist path. But in the past few years, empty rituals, idol-worship, and blind faith increased their hold on the mass psyche.

Seeing the extraordinary results of the fusion of religion with politics, marketeers unleash Hindu gods and goddesses to promote their goods and services. Many videos are interrupted by a God's image with the video-maker urging the watchers to say "Jai Sri Ram". The watchers are told the benefits that its chanting would bring and the tragedy that not chanting will inflict on them. With that the commercial break ends. One woman asks the reel-makers to recite a spiritual hymn to increase their viewers, bringing more money to them.

Mass hysteria over a manufactured non-event grips the Land of Dope and Glory every now and then. The people are fooled easily because rationalism has declined. Millions of *"Andha Bhakts"* show their blind devotion to the Leader who calls upon the people to ward off Corona by clapping and beating metal plates *(Tali* and *Thali)*! Thousands of Indians heed the Faith Healer and shout: *"Go Corona, Go!"* The virus ignores the call but the Leader's credibility is not diminished.

The weird political, social, and religious events show that India is passing through a tragicomic phase. It makes one cry as well as laugh. Many do not know whether to cry or laugh. Has India become a nation of idiots? Was this the India envisioned in the 15th century by mystic poet Kabir?

## How do you?

How do you,
Asks the chief of police,
Patrol a city
Where the butcher shops
Are guarded by vultures;
Where bulls get pregnant,
Cows are barren,
And calves give milk
Three times a day;
Where mice are boatmen
And tomcats the boats
They row;
Where frogs keep snakes
As watchdogs,
And jackals
Go after lions?
Does anyone know
What I'm talking about?
Says Kabir.

Kabir's poem translated by<br>Arvind Krishna Mehrotra

# India of Nightmares

Fusion of religion with politics has adversely affected both spheres. A Leader won power in 2014 to protect Hinduism and Hindus. Ironically, bombarded by politicians with the warning that they are endangered, Hindus lost self-confidence. The Polarisation Project which split society on religious lines also divided Hindus between the Hindutva warriors and liberal Hindus. The differences among the Hindus based on caste, subcaste and language got exacerbated. Ghettoisation increased. There are places where it is not enough to be a Hindu, one must be a Tamilian Brahmin! In a modern metropolis like Mumbai (once called Bombay), the Hindu must speak Marathi to avoid problems. The Hindu fish mongers in a Bengali colony in New Delhi are threatened because their shops are close to their temple! A couple of Hindu rationalists have been murdered. So, Muslims are not alone!

Hinduism has become an intensely contested faith and lost some followers. Its brand value in the international faith market has come down as incidents of intolerance get reported abroad. The idea of India is diminished. India is no longer well-known for its multi-cultural traditions. While Hindu nationalists sloganeered, an external enemy grabbed some of India's territory. The Leader could protect neither India nor Hinduism.

The impact of the Modi years on Hinduism is yet to be analysed by historians of religion like Karen Armstrong who may focus on what politics and the state did to Hinduism. One recalls how Christianity declined in the West. The 'migration of the holy from church to state' has been highlighted by western scholars. Paul Kingsnorth attributes the decline of Christianity to the failure of the faith to live up to its own traditions. He discusses the trend of the "church leaders cosying up to earthly rulers or attempting to become earthly rulers themselves". An interesting observation in the current Indian context! He cites the schism within the Western church as another factor. In India, Hindus are hotly, at times aggressively debating who is a true Hindu. The campaign to make Hinduism muscular and militant has caused a sharp division within the faith. The current conflict between Hindutva warriors and 'liberal' Hindus would have lasting repercussions, distorting the concept of spirituality.

Religion infuses politics with undesirable fervour, making political rivals more aggressive. It makes the state dominate spirituality. Since the market dominates the state, religion becomes a handmaiden of the market. The new Ram Temple of Ayodhya is sold to the masses by projecting the huge revenue to be earned by Ayodhya. Some traditional priests protested but their voices were ignored. In India, the state cannot replace the temple as the locus of life, so the Prime Minister hit upon a novel idea. By projecting himself as NB, a Nonbiological Being, with some of his ardent followers describing him as God's incarnation, Modi has claimed for himself spiritual loyalty – "the primary, deepest allegiance and mandatory obedience of the citizens". Fake religiosity has become more popular.

The political scenario looks equally grim. India is now called a 'failing democracy' or an 'elected autocracy'. India's credentials as a secular democracy are questioned in India and abroad. The Government does nothing to improve the situation. It has perfected a three-pronged response to such criticism. It ministers cite examples from mythology of India's ancient democratic traditions! They discredit the international agencies monitoring democracies and issuing adverse reports on India. And above all, with the help of some *sarkari* intellectuals, the Government sets its own standards of democracy by which it should be judged. The situation on the ground related to civil liberties and democratic rights gets worse and worse.

A German character in a novel by Nayantara Sahgal tells an Indian: "Our past is your future". If he were to analyse dreams of Indians in 20025, he would say, "it is your present". In his country, journalist Charlotte Beradt had compiled *The Third Reich of Dreams* from 1933 to 1939. She transcribed the nightmares of citizens and analysed them. Many dreamt that it was "forbidden to dream". They felt dreaming was illegitimate. She smuggled the manuscript to the US and it was published in 1968. This analysis was recalled by British columnist Zoe Williams when Donald Trump began to rule America.

The word "fascism" now figures prominently in the political discourse. Many Indians hesitate to utter the word fearing that it would only embolden the fascist or that for saying it, they would be punished by the state. British academic Prof. Michael Rosen wrote the poem "fascism arrives as your friend..." He fears people think that fascism arrives in fancy dress worn by grotesques and monsters as played out in endless reruns of the Nazis. They think it will restore their honour, make them feel proud, protect their house, give them a job. By a sheer coincidence, Prof. Rosen published this poem in 2014, within a few weeks of Modi coming to power.

To understand our present, we must peep into our recent past and the past of others. The comic scenes in India portend a tragic future. Comic books made Musk and Trump as the imagined Batman arrived in real life and Gotham town appeared on the physical map. That is the direction India has taken. The Second Coming of Trump in America and somewhat similar political developments in Europe make analysts recall how a selfish hate-filled state was once condoned by the majority. A cruel joke during Hitler's reign said: Germany is filled with 1 per cent. of the population not backing the Nazis in plebiscites. In 1933, Lion Feuchtwanger published *The Oppermanns*, the novel being read as 'a warning from history'. It shows the destruction of a civilised, literate, upper middle class, Berlin Jewish family as the Nazis take power. This novel was written even before the extermination camps were set up. *The New York Times* calls it a classic novel of the Nazis' rise that holds lessons for today. Reading it is like staring into the worst of next week, says the critic. *Kirkus* writes: "It is hard to imagine 90-year-old book timelier." The novel has today's headlines.

Then as now, fact and truth were the first casualty. A reader says on social media: "This is how fascism will triumph: first with cartoonish politicians saying outrageous things and blaming foreigners and those in need; the rubbishing of experts, intellectuals and so-called elites, the media backing and idolising them so much and so often that their audiences believe them. Sounds familiar in the India of 2025 where faith and fascism have been fused together. This fusion has made fascism not just acceptable but desirable. A kind of religious fervour has been inducted into politics with the adoration of the Leader. Political pilgrims overlook their safety to join in a mass ritual. Some Modi devotees are prepared to die! Consolidation of the Hindu votes generates 'collective effervescence' that energises fascism. Communalism leads to a communal ritual on the polling day!

The democratic secular India has informally been transformed into an unconstitutional Hindu Rashtra and an undeclared Emergency has been imposed. "Contemporary India does not present a pretty picture" will be an understatement. Festivals of different communities used to spread joy. Now every festival is tinged with anxiety and fear. Three lines by noted journalist Rajdeep Sardesai say it all: "The idea of India is built around joyous diversity and richness of our festive traditions, not on threats and muscle flexing. Curbs on meat shops, curbs on namaz, and now a threat to seize passports if 'rules' violated. Did anyone say that those who burst crackers late into night on Diwali in violation of the Supreme Court orders will have passports seized?" An entire community feels besieged. Its poor can be lynched for allegedly carrying or storing beef or for running a love jihad and at times just for belonging to that community. Its well-to-do members face economic boycott and hate campaign on social media. Muslim women feel intimidated and miserable in the present social ethos. Some tweak their names or put a red dot on the forehead. Ismat Ara, a noted journalist, finds safety in hiding her name. She writes: "As an Indian Muslim, I have learned to say many words in whispers. The thought recently struck me when my husband and I were at a McDonald's in Thailand that casually offered beef burgers to customers. The word "beef" felt oddly jarring to me. It had been a long time since I'd even heard the word *beef* spoken freely. In India, I don't say it... I couldn't shake the thought: *What a strange, unnecessary weight we carry back home. How heavy!"* She was among the accomplished Muslim women who were targeted through a novel campaign that "auctioned" them on the internet. Here is what she wrote in January 2022: "As the first day of the new year dawned in New Delhi, I woke to find that I had been put up for auction on the Internet. There it was: a photograph of me with the words "Your *Bulli Bai* deal of the day. *Bulli* is a derogatory term reserved for Muslim women and *bai*, meaning maid, is another derogatory term often used by India's right wing for Muslim women. I was no stranger to trolling. In fact, I am one of the 20 most abused women journalists in India. But being auctioned? There were nearly 100 more women on the list—prominent ones, such as broadcasters, politicians, authors, pilots, and actors. Like me, all were Muslim."

These illustrative examples may not be considered significant in a country where calls for the genocide of Muslims are given openly at Hindu religious conclaves. There is a concerted campaign, blessed officially, to establish majoritarianism. Institutions have been hallowed out, higher education diminished and law and order nearly destroyed. India's ranking in the human development indexes has declined. Toxicity and mental pollution cannot be measured precisely but their abnormal rise is detected by social scientists. Economic indicators too do not look promising.

How did we get here? India of 2025 did not suddenly erupt like lava. The Fool's Paradise wasn't built in a day. The RSS, born a hundred years ago, marches on, waving the saffron flag of Hindutva. In the garb of a cultural organisation, it has become a major political force. The dream of the RSS to wrest political power remained a dream till one of its members demonstrated that an aggressive anti-Muslim campaign could invest him with charisma and let him propagate the ideology that caused tragedies but never lost its appeal entirely. The formula was proven in Gujarat. Years before 2002 and the communal killings in Gujarat, alarm bells about creeping fascism were rung but went unheard in the din created by the demagogue. The RSS noted Prof. Ashis Nandy's diagnosis of Modi as a "textbook fascist" and began to groom Modi as the future Leader. So, in a way, Nandy made Modi. Had he not identified Modi's exceptional quality, the RSS would still be using Modi to serve tea. The communal killings assured Modi's political future. After coming to power in Delhi, the Leader, as per the RSS diktat, is transforming India, freeing it from its old ideals and value system. Having remade himself, the Leader is busy remaking India and Hinduism, reorienting institutions and getting history re-written. He wants to make Hinduism muscular and militarised. A new term 'Hindu Terror' has come into vogue. 'Hindu Pakistan' and 'Abrahamic Hinduism' are talked about.

In early 2014, alarm bells were rung louder as several commentators were shocked by Modi's election campaign which was a campaign for religious polarisation powered by hateful speeches. Badri Raina, noted writer and columnist, said: "For more than a relentless month now, the Modi campaign has been pegged on familiar hyper nationalism that seeks to bind three totalitarian policy objectives into a single, unified, and altogether forbidding injunction - that there can be no loyalty to India without loyalty to Hindutva, to militarist nationalism, and corporate control of the state, all three to be understood as loyalty to one supreme leader set to function as the only and final arbiter of "Indianness" and "patriotism". Raina cited the BJP leader Giriraj Singh's call to Modi's critics to leave India and go away to Pakistan. This ominous, but entirely anticipated, pronouncement shows that finally the cat is out of the bag, he wrote.

Such warnings were ignored by a majority of the voters. The diminution of democracy and secularism shocks intellectuals and activists but heartens the votaries of the majoritarian state. Democracy is of little concern to a majority of voters who want livelihood and economic growth more than civil liberties. They are enchanted by the tale of a glorious ancient India that the Leader promises to usher in. So, they attribute their economic misery to providence and not blame the Leader. Blind faith rules. Faux religiosity diminishes humanity and empathy. As knowledge society, India keeps regressing. The morality of religious polarisation apart, its adverse impact on internal security is highlighted by experts. But experts are not needed as the ruler has proclaimed himself to be the font of all wisdom.

Many Modi devotees admit the erosion of civil rights but justify the trend by talking of economic progress brought about by Modi. They would like a leader who asks: "Give me your freedom, I will give you prosperity." A wag may perversely point out that the number of cars burnt in a communal riot must be replaced which boosts car production and houses bulldozed help the real estate industry! Many economic experts expose the false claims made about economic growth. They say that the Prime Minister's report card in that area is also not good. They claim the "Gujarat model of development" was false propaganda.

Economists overlook the disruption of personal relationships caused by religious polarisation. In this regard, Modi has done more than the mobile. Families are fractured, fighting over Modi. Many Indians cannot visit their near and dear ones as near and dear ones clash at the dining table. It is common to see political clashes in families and a disruption of personal relationships. A cartoon shows a doctor asking the patient if there is a history of mental illness in the family. The patient replies: "Yes. My uncle still wants to vote for Modi!" A grateful son narrates on social media that his father, a staunch BJP-supporter, has at last started attacking Modi! Peace and harmony has been restored in the house. "Thank you, Papa, I love you."

That India is going through an abnormal phase is believed by all – those who feel distraught and those who feel elated by the new social and political trends. What was initially considered an aberration has become the new normal. The degradation of universities and even Bollywood is there for all to see. Social scientists have warned against the consequences of polarisation, hatred and aggressive behaviour and increased blind faith and ignorance.

Empires do not last. And in politics anything can happen. Modi reoccupied the Prime Minister's office with the help of two regional leaders, his one-time critics who became his allies. Whatever his sins of omission and commission, Modi will not face a rebellion by his party M.P.s who "elected" him as their leader. They are trained by the RSS to follow its diktat. Modi was the gift of the RSS to the nation and he will continue as the Prime Minister unless the RSS dumps him before the next parliamentary elections. Even that scenario does not give much hope to the Indians who worry about Modi's legacy. In his remaining days in office, Modi will not be able to achieve the kind of total transformation of India as he had set to do, but what he has done will have tragic consequences. Prof. Ashis Nandy says, "one generation will have to bear the cost of what Modi has done".

III

# Creative Resistance

The New India is a conjurer's table with secret pockets and hidden crevices that are hard to fathom. The smokescreen of false logic further hides the reality of a strange country. This Guide is written by novelists, poets, journalists, and intellectuals. To understand the New India, one must go beyond learned articles by social scientists and reportage by journalists. Novelists and poets sense and describe the reality better. They discuss populism, communalism, hatred, vigilantism, lynching, autocracy, kleptocracy, mafia state, mafia capitalism and majoritarianism. Their exploration leads them to one man whose populist rhetoric fooled all those who facilitated his astounding rise and feel elated by the dismal present.

On the eve of the 2024 elections, eminent writer Amit Chaudhuri noted with concern Modi's "revelations" about his being God's messenger and a non-biological being. The time of these, he said, "contains a premonition of a Third Coming, a third term in office". Modi became the Prime Minister again. An independent video channel releases interviews with those despairing that India faces an 'existential' crisis. An interviewee points out that the tearing of the social fabric by the majoritarians will increase extremism in the minority. Many confess to having 'sleepless nights', mulling over the future of India.

A society in the throes of sweeping changes caught the fancy of poets and novelists. The polarised India quickened their creative impulses. History will judge how destructive the Modi Years were. That these have been creative is seen by the volume of dystopian literature written since he came to power. Not just accomplished artistes but even simple housewives, folk-singers and unlettered farmers release dramatised anti-Modi satire and songs of resistance on social media. The subaltern can speak. Despite his limited exposure to literature, Modi has promoted literary activism by the common people.

India's tryst with idiocy has not gone unrecorded despite the mainstream media turning a blind eye. The repressive State could not silence all. The creative community defied legal action by the State that considers dissent treason. Poets, novelists, artists and satirists ignore the threats of violence by the state-empowered vigilantes. Together with stand-up comedians and cartoonists, they raise their composite literary fist. Folk singers such as Neha Singh Rathore gained immense popularity by challenging Modi. Writers are moved by the power of nightmares. Papri Sen Sri Raman sees the unmaking of India in a nightmare. Startled, she wakes up and narrates her dream of a Hindu King guided by an organ of his body other than his brain!

Modi gained by ridiculing his opponents. Comedians are giving him the taste of his own medicine. During the farmers' agitation, young women composed and sang protest songs. Audience halls reverberate with songs such as *Sab Yaad Rakha Jayega* (We shall remember it all) and *Kagaj nahi dikhayenge* (We shall not show any document to prove our citizenship). Pakistani poets Faiz and Jalib are recited in small groups and large halls. Ironically, oppression by the authorities made the suffering Indians turn to Pakistan's famous poet Faiz who had challenged a military dictator by electrifying audience with the song "*Hum bhi dekhenge...*" (We too shall see...). A song written in Pakistan against a military dictator became relevant in democratic India to challenge an elected leader. The videos of *Main nahi manta* by Jalib and *Hum dekhenge* by Faiz went viral, calling to fight oppression and live peacefully. One shows the JNU students reciting Jalib.

Contemporary India features in several novels. Journalist Tanushree Bhasin explains: "With human interest stories disappearing from newspapers and television news, personal-political stories have found a home in fiction." She says if the novel is a space where the personal and political meet, it is also where differing voices can be explored. Eminent writer

Nayantara Sahgal finds that political truth can be told better through contrived characters.

Non-fiction carries some fiction while more fiction is based on facts! Writers are "rebuked" daily by reality --the reality of insults, intimidation, harassment, microaggressions, murders and social deformation. Poets and novelists scan headlines to write about things happening around them and to them. Some Indian novelists themselves are undergoing what they are making their character say. Their work promotes intertextuality! While reading a novel on the misdeeds of bankers, one consults Wikipedia!

The Leader has cast a dismal shadow over every aspect of life and learning and influenced literature in multiple ways. The curtailed freedom of expression silencing some writers is only one aspect. The New India has caused a problem for fiction writers by breeding strange people. Novelist Philip Roth identified this problem: "The actuality is continually outdoing our talents, and culture tosses up figures daily that are the envy of any novelist", Roth said. The artist gets overwhelmed by reality, says British dramatist David Hare who wrote a play on the privatisation of the Railways! He is often asked: "Are you the person who makes plays out of what is going on in the papers." Curious times demand curious art. Hare explains that factual work asks questions *for* us and fictional work asks questions *of* us. A work of art can do both. Novelists can and do improve on the facts, contrary to

Hilary Mantel's view. The current ethos has taught artists not to take time to absorb events. Even earlier, poems were written in the heat of battle. E. M. Forster says it is only in a novel that we can know people perfectly, hinting at the intimacy between the world of observable facts and the mysteries of the period. Fiction describes a weird nation well. When a sacred epic text is turned into a political document, novelists start reading political reports. Horror-filled newspaper headlines give a taste of dystopian fiction. Dystopian novels were grounded in facts but they still needed to mix fantasy. Today, novelists living in a dystopian world, do not need to inject fantasy into their stories. Hyperlinks in the novel *Love Jihad* take the readers to videos of the inter-faith couples being thrashed by vigilantes. More political novels are being written and read. The nonfiction novel, fiction based on news reports, has become popular. Even if a novelist does not write about India, her experience of living in the politically tumultuous India seeps into her work.

Poets are called prophets and unacknowledged legislators. Art does not exist in a vacuum. Fiction tells readers what is going on and even antedates events. A novelist intuits the future. Facts follow fiction, as illustrated by Amitav Ghosh's books and the events of major fire and tsunami. Several writers imagined events that did happen later. Science fiction could guide policymaking, it is being said. Journalism has lost authenticity and public trust. "Facts" are not sacred and opinions are not "free". Straight reporting cannot make sense of an absurd situation. Weird India cannot be covered by journalists. They deal in facts but facts have become stranger than fiction. Surrealism rules Absurdistan. The real and the absurd have merged in an infantilised India. This journalist resorted to writing faction – *Aadhi Haqeeqat, Aadha Fasana* (Half facts, Half fiction). His *Number 10 Is Closing Down* envisioned an Indian as the Prime Minister of Great Britain more than three years before an Indian actually moved into No. 10 to live there. *The Twain,* another book of creative fiction by this writer, featured a fictional Indian Prime Minister taking the gift of cows for his host in Great Britain! Some years later, Narendra Modi took the gift of 200 cows to Rwanda. Twitterati laughed and asked him to send a *Gau-Rakshak* (cow sentry) Squad to that beef-eating country.

The writers here guide those wanting to know why they feel so anxious and despondent. Novelists foresaw signs of coming events. Soon after Modi became the Prime Minister in 2014, eminent Kannada writer U. R. Ananthamurthy wrote that Modi's victory is in direct opposition to Gandhi's dream of Hind Swaraj. It has taken India closer to Savarkar's idea of Hindutva. "It seems to me that that the Gandhi era has come to an end; Savarkar has triumphed." He said the people appreciated Modi because he silenced the minorities. Ananthamurthy did not remain with us to see where Modi would take India after 2014. Novelist Kiran Nagarkar wrote a scathing letter to Modi in 2016, asking the Prime Minister to match his deeds with words! Novelist Nagarkar did not live to see what Modi did after 2019.

The real India is revealed in novels. Journalist Aakar Patel has written nonfiction about contemporary India. His 2021 book *The Price of The Modi Years* led to the confiscation of his passport on some other pretext. Within two years, he published *After Messiah,* a novel that, according to a reviewer, "feels very real". It features nameless Big Man. Those who have read about dictators of Africa do not need to know the real name to recognise him in any country. The Big Man has outlawed dissent. He runs an office that dominates all offices of the Republic. He speaks of himself in third person and has a sidekick who does all his dirty work. The Big Man is portrayed as a megalomaniac and narcissist political leader. Patel gives details of his daily engagements to illustrate the point. "The Big Man's content sounded, to some, banal, but his delivery was energetic and often emotional." Or: "Two large screens played out visual of the Big Man' contributions to the nation..." On reading the book, a reviewer says that "political satirists have now the unenviable task of competing with the everyday outrageous reality of India."

Sumana Mukherjee finds the backdrop too familiar. – "in fact, I had only to look up from the book and glance at the newspaper to find developments uncannily similar to a key narrative in the novel".

Another reviewer, Aditya Sinha, says "fiction can often provide greater insights into the Zeitgeist than data and political science, and fiction can be great vehicle to say things obliquely..." Fiction also gives a cover to the writer because by citing *After Messiah,* the best of the Government's attorneys can do any harm to Patel in a court of law. One recalls what famous Urdu poet Rahat Indori had said. Once he was asked by the police whether in his poem, he called the Government corrupt. He admitted that he did but he did not name the government. It was the Government of Pakistan he had in mind!

The number of political novels being published keeps going up. Devesh Verma's novel *The Politician* is about "one man's quest for unbridled power, which warns us not to make politics a matter of emotional calling". What is important, it articulates, in the words of a reviewer, "how the unbridled quest for power is not clinched by brute force alone in a democratic world".

Arvind Adiga's novel *The White Tiger* has Muslims facing discrimination. The protagonist's employers demand to know whether he is a Muslim. A character is blackmailed and sacked when outed by the protagonist for secretly practicing Islam. In New India, Balram Halwai, a rural entrepreneur, gains business success through murder and theft.

A love story is published with the cover showing Lord Hanuman in action! *The Memoirs of Valmiki Rao* reimagines Ramayana in a Bombay struck by violence and bigotry after the demolition of the Babri mosque. The current political turmoil was never far away from Lindsay Pereira's mind while writing his new novel. The love story runs parallel to investigations of the Hindu-Muslim riots. A reviewer says the novel is about the failings of Gods and their fanatic believers who very easily turn into a blood-hungry mob.

Siddhartha Deb's novel *The Light at the End of the World* covers the turmoil of fascism. It resonates with themes of majoritarianism, fascism, fabricated conflict, and official conspiracies, says reviewer Tina Borah. It moves between different locales of India, "mixing the phantasmagoric with real incidents." She points out that "Deb ambitiously melds science fiction with the mundane, spanning not just diverse locales within India but also timelines...The past, present, and future blend into each other, conveyed through hallucinatory fever dreams. It feels like getting trapped inside an insidious Wonderland, one in which the borders between fantasy and reality are blurred."

Neha Dixit's book *The Many Lives of Syeda X* is the story of a Muslim worker. Syeda's religious identity would have been of no great significance had the book been written some other time. December 6, 1992, is the date that figures prominently in the book because it changes the life of Syeda. The current context makes the book popular. Syeda's most significant statement: "I don't get up daily to think about how to defeat the

Hindu Supremacists. I think about how my family and I would survive this day." Following the demolition of the Babri mosque, Syeda, her husband, two sons and a daughter, leave Benaras for Delhi. Modi's India is a key protagonist alongside the titular character Syeda, who has held 50 jobs in 30 years, says a reviewer. The book came about because years earlier, the author did a story on the Muzaffarnagar riots in which women had faced sexual violence. She was shocked to find that the women were forced to go back to work in the farms of the accused against whom they had filed cases. Belonging to a poor weaver family, Syeda lived in Benaras. The worst case of communal violence made her migrate. It was after the demolition of the Babri mosque in 1992. Syeda recalls: The police destroyed so many looms in the weavers' houses that sarees clogged the drains and the area was engulfed in stench. Her natal and marital families suffered violence. Syeda says: "We had known hunger, grief, sorrow, and frustration, like everyone else. But this was the first time we experienced terror because of our religion." Her brother Kashif was attacked in a cinema because he got identified as Muslim due to his beard and clothes. Her thatched-roof home and the pucca room housing the loom were burnt down by uniformed men. Syeda X arrives in Delhi but within a few years, communal violence follows her with the 2020 riots in north-east Delhi. Her son is forced to run away with Babli, ironically a *gau rakshak*'s sister, to escape from the local vigilante who would have murdered him for his "love jihad".

Nayantara Sahgal's novels, *When the Moon Shines by Day* and *The Fate of Butterflies* are published as *The Unmaking of India Chronicles.* Kiran Nagarkar says her novel is a meditation on what is happening in our country today. The brave and hugely readable novel is a telling comment on what may happen when a country's rulers wipe out chunks of its history and marginalize an entire community, Nagarkar says. In Sahgal's novel, Sergei tells Prabhakar: "In Europe we think of wars about religion as belonging to the Middle Ages." Prabhakar responds: "Here we are back to the Crusades. Our Popes have declared war on Islam." The characters talk of the civil war in Yugoslavia in the 1990s, the one that eventually broke up the country... but not before thousands of Muslim women were raped by Christian Serbs. "It's what war does to women but this was something new, Religious rape. Like here", says another character. A woman describes her rape giving testimony in court.

Over lunch in a restaurant, the characters in the novel talk of the Cow Commission that went around making sure that there is no beef anywhere. One says he was thinking of becoming a vegetarian because he was scared as hell that his fridge might be raided and the mutton turned into beef.

The Director of Cultural Transformation, in-charge of racial purity, asks: "Is it not reasonable that the people should do to our tormentors what our tormentors did to us?" In *When the Moon Shines by Day,* a Muslim is forced to move out of his flat because of his religion. Zamir adopts a Hindu name. Rehna says: "Huge ancient megaliths and mountainsides had not withstood religious wrath; what hope was there for a pseudonym?" A foreigner is writing a book with "the climactic event of the announcement of Hindu nationhood, the Anno Domini from whence the new era would date".

Sahgal's description of a meeting of the NRI Hindus is hilarious. "American voices filled the room that was full of Indians. Trays were offering American cocktails among other drinks. In the hall, behind the cocktail bar, the cartographer had fancied an India extending from the Indus in the far north to the Arabian Sea at its southern tip as one unbroken landscape of lustrous gold. No obstruction had been permitted to mar the peninsula between the snows and the sea, no Afghanistan, no Pakistan, no Bangladesh. An amused person says: This artistic vision of the future...summed up everything!" One speaker says: We're VHA, the Voice of Hindu Americans. We're getting a lot of support from the Administration. My Senator is trying to get Hindus in the White category... In racial hierarchy, we belong at the top, to the Indo-European racial category. A PR executive is assigned to "spread the word about a Hindu Kingdom". Indian diaspora lives in two worlds simultaneously!

In the real India, a character tells us: ...There is no Mughal cooking any more. There is no Mughal anything anymore, not even the empire. They've taken it out of history books. Prabhakar says this and Lisette responds: "But that's absolute nonsense". Both agree that this is as ridiculous as the nursery rhyme, she learned when she was six years old:

> *Hey diddle diddle, the cat, and the fiddle,*
> *The Cow jumped over the moon.*
> *The little dog laughed to see such fun*
> *and the Dish ran away with the spoon.*

Sahgal says Hindus in India are "Wonderlanders'. *Hindus-in-Wonderland* is the title of the *Afterword*. "In this environment of violence, vengeance and lawlessness, where law is what Wonderland says it is, India's ancient and flourishing tradition of debate, discussion, disagreement and self-expression has been trashed, yet the over-arching fantasy of *Hindus-in-Wonderland* is that India is a democracy."

Sahgal explains why he took to writing what may be called political novels. "My political awareness became painful as *Hindus-in-Wonderland* made it clear by their speeches and behaviour that violence was a virtue and violence against the Other was perfectly all right.... For me and millions of other Hindus, *Hindus-in-Wonderland* have nothing to do with Hinduism. Religious fanaticism was never part of it. Now it rules the land as we watch the destruction of the secular democratic republic our founding fathers established, and which we built on with pride since Independence." Sahgal says: "I wrote these two novels in an agony of mind to recreate in fiction what India was going through at the time of writing...to bring alive the tragedy of the unmaking of India".

Nayantara Sahgal in 2015 returned her Sahitya Akademi Award in protest the state's failure to safeguard cultural diversity and protect those dissenting from the ruling ideology of Hindutva. Some other literary celebrities did the same. A century ago, Tagore renounced his Knighthood in protest the Jallianwala Bagh massacre. Sahgal's statement *The Unmaking of India* says: "In a recent lecture, India's Vice-President, Dr. Hamid Ansari, found it necessary to remind us that India's Constitution promises all Indians "liberty of thought, expression, belief, faith and worship." The right to dissent is an integral part of this Constitutional guarantee. He found it necessary to do so because India's culture of diversity and debate is now under vicious assault. Rationalists who question superstition, those who question the ugly and dangerous distortion of Hinduism known as Hindutva —whether in the intellectual or artistic sphere, or whether in terms of food habits and lifestyle – are being marginalized, persecuted, or murdered. Eminent Kannada writer and Sahitya Akademi Award winner M. M. Kalburgi and two Maharashtrians, Narendra Dhabolkar and Govind Pansare, both anti-superstition activists, were killed by gun-toting motorcyclists. Other dissenters have been warned they are next in line. Most recently, a village blacksmith, Mohammed Akhlaq, was dragged out of his home in Bisada village outside Delhi, and brutally lynched, on the supposed suspicion that beef was cooked in his home. In all these cases, justice drags its feet. The Prime Minister remains silent about this reign of terror. He dare not alienate evil doers who support his ideology. It is a matter of sorrow that the Sahitya Akademi remains silent. The Akademies were set up as guardians of the creative imagination, and promoters of its finest products in art and literature, music, and theatre. In protest against Kalburgi's murder, a Hindi writer, Uday Prakash, returned his Sahitya Akademi Award. Six Kannada writers returned their Awards to the Kannada Sahitya Parishat. In memory of the Indians who have been murdered, in support of all Indians who uphold the right to dissent, and of all dissenters who live in fear and uncertainty, I am returning my Sahitya Akademi Award", said Sahgal.

Novelist Arundhati Roy describes in powerful prose India's recent descent into totalitarianism. Her *Azadi: Fascism, Fiction, and Freedom in the time of Virus* won her the European Essay Prize. The jury said she "uses the essay as a form of combat, analysing fascism...Her essays offer shelter to a multitude of people." *Jacobin* says Roy embodies humanistic ruthlessness of a public defender, the wit and wordplay of a poet, a comrade who takes no injustice as given. A novelist-activist is the product of our times.

Influenced by strange India, nonfiction writers narrate facts in a literary style, Imaginative touches make it easier to understand the reality. Narrative nonfiction has become popular. Such nonfiction may have no direct comment on the state of the nation but much can be read between the lines. The context matters. Pratap Bhanu Mehta's article *The Battle after Dussehra* does not refer to the state we are in. It is the context that links it to the state we are in. Mehta does not write on the famous battle preceding Dussehra. Mehta writes on what was not there. He touches a topic that writers shy away from for the fear of hurting the Hindu psyche. In New India, every Hindu religious festival is a risky topic to comment on. *Vijayadashmi* is the most important day for the RSS which holds a special ceremony, with the RSS chief performing *shastra puja*, the worship of weapons, symbolizing strength for the protection of *Dharma*. Yet Mehta comments on *Vijayadashmi* and on Ram's conduct.

Poetry too is heavily influenced by news reports. Poets weave in the political into personal feelings. Vigilantes attack lovers physically and the Leader frustrates a lover remotely, as in *The Love Song of K. Anand Kak*. Night after night, Kak, and his girlfriend talk, not of love, but about the Leader destroying India! Day after day, a couple in a closed dark room do nothing apart from talking of the state of the nation! It happens. *Modi hai to mumkin hai*!

Love stories are not set in perfumed gardens or lonely forests, not even in urban rootlessness and chaos. Disturbed by daily events, poets wade into politics. Gulzar says what the blood-soaked newspaper feels and what he feels getting it every morning. Poetry lovers recite Sarweshwar Dayal Saxena's poem which warns that a nation is not a map drawn on the paper. *"If one room in your house is on fire, can you sleep in the other. If corpses rot in one room, can you prey in another..."* Urdu Poet Rahat Indori also pointed out the interconnectedness of the communities that makes it impossible to harm just one single community. Responding to the barbaric times, poets jot down mangled words. Some stop writing poetry! Their faith in poetry is shaken as they suspect artifice in this creative medium. Fortunately, this feeling does not last. The poet resumes writing to exist.

In literature, Hate is clubbed with Love. Juxtaposition between two human emotions gives an edge to a work. Poetry serves a purpose beyond art and entertainment. Patriotic poetry played a significant role in the freedom struggle. Protest poetry rallies people in the fight against sectarian hatred. Urdu poetry sessions attract audiences protesting majoritarianism. These poems portray, not an India of the imagination but an India that has lost imagination. Poetry comes in handy at such times as an antidote to repression and depression.

Salil Tripathi writes a poem on his aged mother's response to the Babri Mosque demolition by the Ram devotees on December 6, 1992. The mother, a freedom fighter, rings the son in Singapore and says: "We have killed Gandhi again." Pratishtha Pandya is silenced as a poet by the burning Manipur. Parul Khakhar, also a woman poet of Gujarat, angers the Modi devotees with her poem *Shav Vahini Ganga*, (Ganges, carrier of bodies). She criticised the 'naked Emperor' and his handling of the Covid pandemic. Her poem on the holiest river swollen with corpses went viral. A satirical sequel to Parul's poem is titled *A Macabre Dance*. Sagari Chhabra wrote poems that could not have been written before the Modi era. She says in Kafkaesque times, poetry and art are the only ways to express oneself. Arts play a significant role in resisting dictatorship. Bob Dylan said: Art is a disagreement; money is an agreement. Artists have not failed the nation in this critical phase.

# FANTASY

## A Marionette plays Performance Politics

PAPRI SEN SRI RAMAN

Vlad

*If it were not for my friend Vlad who came up with this fantastic illustration as soon as I floated this idea of writing fantasy, perhaps this piece of imagination would not have seen the light of day. Vlad got the idea after reading just a few paragraphs, knowing that in my country, the kings always had jesters at their courts to offset the seriousness of the business of ruling.*

*Vlad's image haunted me. It was all hands and legs everywhere... as if there was so much hype that coherence was lost and anything was everything everywhere. It was, of course, before political comedians like Dhruv Rathee started getting the kind of following that they have today, 15 million and growing. In honour of the likes of Dhruv Rathee, Kunal Kamra, Vir Das, Munawar Faruqui, and so many others, in jail and out, it is time to air this story of the* King.

## *King is on the stage. Alone.*

The spotlight is always on him. Social distance glorifies him. He stands holding his head in his hand. Wondering. Wondering what had gone wrong. Gone wrong. Something had gone very wrong. The year 2024 brought problems galore. He had ensured that there were at least a dozen elected Sanyasis and Sadhus in Parliament, yet things had gone wrong. The sums had gone wrong. Not 400 but a measly 241. The priests of the Kingdom of the Brihut Bhikshuka Mahajanapad were furious. Such a long holiday from governing, how could the sum be wrong? Since 2014, King had pushed strongly for the idea of 'simultaneous Lok Sabha and State assembly polls'; it had taken a decade to get the Bill into Parliament. It is appalling that Mahajanapads must contend with Tenali Ramans, Birbals and the likes of official dissenters, the Opposition.

The roof of the new Ram Temple leaked; the 'temple of democracy', the new Parliament House had rainwater dripping from its roof. The King had said, '*Pehle jab tak maa zinda thi mujhe lagta tha ki shayad biologically mujhe janam diya gaya hai. Maa ke jaane ke baad in saare anubhavo ko mai jod kar dekhta hoon to mai convince ho chuka hoon ki parmatma ne mujhe bheja hai. Ye urja biological shareer se nahi mili hai ....*' The King claimed divine birth... but that did not work. In the heart of Ramrajya, ruled by a yogi, Ramlalla's hometown did not vote for the King.

King had no 'thank you voters' speech. The thing was, neither he, nor his near and dear ones, liked this business of voting. And did not like these small federal parts of the Mahajanapad, where satraps ganged up against him. King wanted to shout out loud, 'I want a Tasher Desh', a classical kingdom of cards. The priesthood advised caution. King had to listen; the priesthood was really annoyed. *Saffron News* said the priests had done 'their bit but members of the King's cohorts were complacent'. The writer also said that the King 'did not seek assistance from the priesthood cadre' in the June elections.

King stood with his head in his hands. Confused. The teleprompter screen was blank. No cues at all. Was the priesthood Russian? Was the High Priest an atheist? Did he not believe in Ramlalla? How could he have said, 'the construction of the Ram Mandir in Ayodhya should not lead to further conflicts'. The priesthood's involvement in the movement for the construction of Ram Mandir was an exception and that the organisation will not lead any more movements. 'Under the burden of the extreme past, it is not acceptable to resort to extreme hatred, malice, enmity, suspicion and rake up such new issues daily. ...every day, a new matter (dispute) is being raked up. How can this be allowed? This cannot continue', the High Priest had opined in a public discussion on Vishwa Guru Bharat. 'Ram Mandir is a matter of faith for Hindus. The Hindus believed Ram temple should be constructed. But by doing that one does not become a Hindu leader,' he had opined. A Rasputin? A Lenin? What the High Priest said did not seem to be inspired by Dugin, who called for 'unification of all Russian-speaking peoples in a single country'.

Clearly the High Priest wasn't speaking like a Žižek, who said, 'an Ideology is an unconscious fantasy that structures social reality... political ideologies are successful when they refer to "sublime objects", which are extraordinary things like God, the Führer, or the King. People identify with these objects....' The priesthood wasn't supporting the divine Kinghead, nor a kinghood.

The year was ending on a bleak note. The only good thing was, King's old friend Trump was back in the White Temple. And he had wanted King to extend a hand of friendship to Supreme leader Kim Jong Un. The Guru of the world, right hand holding Trump, left holding Un. And he had visited war-ravaged Ukraine and counted the assault rifles from Russia the Mahajanapad had.

But not knowing what the High Priest was thinking was conflicting; 2025 was thus far a haze, worse than AQI of +450. The year 2023 was the best year. King made a Rs 8,000 crore allocation for the National Mission on Quantum Computing. The budget would enable the private sector to build data centre parks throughout the country. Data on 1.4 billion people would need a lot of servers. Several firms are developing Artificial Intelligence capabilities in India. The Indian Artificial Intelligence market is projected to reach $8 billion by 2025. Hopefully, there won't be too many contrary humans in the future.

So, where had he gone wrong, the Kinghead wondered. The King-voice box, embedded in his throat, had reminded him that he had to memorise his address to **the** summit being organised by MeitY, the Ministry of EIT and NITIA. Now the voice-box was silent, even the peacocks in the palace gardens brooded quietly.

The Kinghead looked for the telephone. In the surrounding darkness, that was not easily spotted. He wished he could take out his mobile from his pocket as easily as Big B did in KBC and talk to the two As, the only ones who could set up the server parks. Things had gone horribly wrong... north of north India had become China.

# King-voice interrupts Kinghead

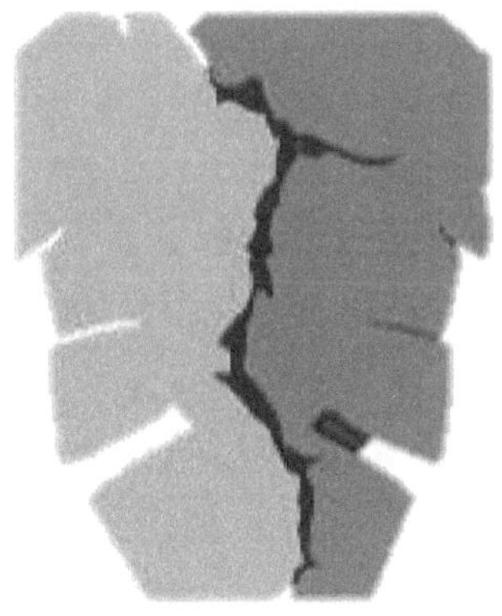

*King-voice:* You need not be nervous. You made a brilliant speech just the other day. At the global virtual summit, *Vaibhav,* you said: 'Through this gathering we sit to form our long-lasting association for empowering India and our planet'. You said, 'these efforts will help create an ideal research ecosystem, merging tradition with modernity to create prosperity. These exchanges will certainly be useful and will also lead to useful collaborations in teaching and research'. You said, 'India wants scientific research to help our farmers'.

*Kinghead:* Farmers! Don't talk about farmers. They only know how to squat on rail tracks and block roads. Don't talk to me about farmers. Even the SAD betrayed us. And now, there is a Haryanvi, storming the social media.

*King-voice:* Wheat stock is good, with buffer stock that stood at 74.6 lakh tonnes for April 2024. In December, a total production of 1132 LMT of wheat was recorded during Rabi 2024. FCI rice stock stands at around 299 lakh tonnes. Farmers produced it. Half a kilo tomato costs Rs 15 and half a kilo onion costs Rs 25 almost, affordable. The Ministry of Statistics and Programme Implementation is a great betrayer. It says, cost of food in BBM increased 9.04% year-on-year in November 2024, following a 10.87% surge in October. Prices of vegetables recorded the biggest increase (29.3%), followed by oils and fats (13.3%) while cost of spices declined 7.43%.

*Kinghead:* What rubbish. Even I know, one kilo of fresh paneer costs just Rs 260, moong dal costs Rs 160 and drumsticks cost Rs 60 per kilogram.

*King-voice:* Farmers are not appeased.

*Kinghead:* Now I know why my Prompt Panel shows that the Global Hunger Index ranks India at 105 out of 127 countries? It indicates a 'serious' level of hunger, says the 2023 report. Even countries like Sri Lanka, Bangladesh, and Pakistan fare better. According to FAO estimates in 'The State of Food Security and Nutrition in the World, 2020 report, 189.2 million people are undernourished in India. By this measure 14% of the population is undernourished in India. Also, 51.4% of women in reproductive age between 15 to 49 years are anaemic. Further, according to the report 34.7% of the children aged under five in India are stunted (too short for their age), while 20% suffer from wasting, meaning their weight is too low for their height'. The data does not appear to have improved much in the last four years, though we have rejected the latest report.

*King-voice:* Stop. Stop. Look, there should be consensus between you and me. We cannot be talking differently. We are one entity. We are a federal democracy, governing by consensus with advisors and a cabinet and a party with an ideology, voted in by the people. Can't appear to be a one-man show with two voices. And you are forgetting the High Priest and the priesthood high command.

*Kinghead:* That would be too much cacophony. All the peacocks in the garden would take flight.

*King-voice:* More than the cymbals and *thalis* that we beat to drive away the Corona?

*Kinghead:* Don't even name it. Remember what that AAP ass said, 'I have never supported lockdown'. Look how much peace it had brought. Almost as good as the Kedarnath caves. No one anywhere near me. I stand under the spotlight and make the pronouncement that comes on my prompt panel. I like that.

*King-voice:* Are you suggesting you are a marionette? All you had to do is make all the bad policy decisions public and take the blame for the 100,842 deaths? And the ten million migrants? And about 21 million job losses that the Centre for Monitoring Indian Economy has said, happened three years ago? About 53% businesses shut.

*Kinghead:* That oaf of a minister of state told Parliament in a written reply that UP and Bihar were the worst-affected. What was the need for disclosure? Bihar at the time was going into elections, and we must always keep the spotlight away from UP.

*King-voice:* True. These rapes did not happen.

*Kinghead:* Look what the *Orange News* had said: 'Ayodhya's Goddess Sita must be worried.' All betrayers. We have no friends.

*King-voice:* Fake news to malign your dispensation. Most things did not happen. Didn't happen: 'Output loss due to demonetisation of a little over Rs 1 lakh crore. The RBI annual report for 2017-18 had two additional statistics that damned demonetisation. 'One, household savings held in the form of currency shot up, from an average of 1.12% of Gross National Disposable Income (GNDI) in the pre-DeMo five years to 2.8% of GNDI in 2017-18. In other words, savings in the form of currency multiplied 2.5 times, not quite the less-cash result the government had hoped for. Worse is the increase in financial liabilities. Liability went up by 83% from Rs 370,964 crore in 2016-17 to Rs 679,349 crore in 2017-18. Worst-hit were small enterprises.'

*Kinghead:* Did not happen. All lies.

*King-voice:* The shortfall in GST collection is ₹ 2.35 lakh crore for fiscal 2021, your government said. The total GST collection in the current fiscal till February '25 stands at Rs 12.74 lakh crore. The Cess will have to be done away with and the repayment schedule of the Covid borrowing envisages payment of Rs 55,104 crore in 2025-26 and Rs 1.36 lakh crore in 2026-27, while no repayment has been scheduled in 2024-25. The interim budget has proposed as much as Rs 1.24 lakh crore collected as cess in 2024-25 to be used for repayment, leaving Rs 67,500 crore to be paid off in 2025-26.

*Kinghead:* Too much complicated computation. Like the Census. Didn't happen. ...those are stories from an old hat. Don't want any discussion or debate. Just imagine if all 1.4 billion people spoke at all times.

*King-voice:* You are truly scientific. But what are we going to do about the 300 million youth who are laughing at us on the internet?

*Kinghead:* We have the science to control it, don't we?

*King-voice:* Don't go that way. Remember Pegasus, the Israeli spyware? It was used on ministers, opposition leaders, journalists, religious and minority leaders, political strategists, activists, administrators including the Election Commissioners and the heads of the CBI and Intelligence Bureau. As many as 50,000 phone numbers accessed by Pegasus were leaked to *Forbidden*

*Stories.* And the Government did not cooperate with the investigation.

*Kinghead:* What about the IT cell? The Fake News Factory? What are they doing? Why are not more terrorists being sentenced? We can do many more such things democratically, without even amending the Constitution.

*King-voice:* Nothing seems to be working. Our Social media has been hijacked. The early advantage we had in 2014 has gone in these ten years.

*Kinghead:* As King I have talked of all my subjects, Muslims, and Christians, urban Naxals, anti-nationals and *ghuspet*s of all hues. I have cried hoarse about Pakistan and China. I have told mothers and wives, their *streedhan,* jewellery will be snatched. I have studiously avoided the economy, joblessness, hunger, and healthcare. How to control the young men on social media? What more can I do?

*King-voice:* Talk about the Mars or the Moon, or the landing of the 'Pushpak', ISRO's RLV technology demonstrator. The *Pushpak Vimana* may resonate with the constituency more than the Ram temple.

*Kinghead:* All are betraying me. ISRO has mapped the underwater natural rock formation of Adam's Bridge, ending the long-drawn controversy that Ram built *Ramar Sethu.* Now, even I am forced to wonder, if Ram was real because of the lack of the Ram temple's impact. I know, its popularity has surpassed Taj Mahal's but temples like Siddhi Vinayaka and Balaji continue to compete on the popularity charts.

*King-voice:* The National Commission for Protection of Child Rights, guided by us, has already begun the process of getting children who will grow to be loyal to the state. It has asked eight State governments to 'repatriate and restore' children from their care homes.

*Kinghead:* Good, the Aadhar Generation. Numbered.

*King-voice:* We don't need Greenpeace and Amnesty. AI can put all figures on the public domain on the need-to-know basis.

*Kinghead:* Scientific. You agree, darkness all around is good, don't you? The spotlight shines brighter. Ethics, morals, rule of law, justice are all creatures of the sunlight. In darkness, what the cabinet and advisers and government and police are doing cannot be seen. What cannot be seen does not exist.

*King-voice:* You are fantastic.

*Kinghead:* What's new? That now-turncoat CB called me Fantastic in 2014.
>   *Fixes the head on the throat, looks at the empty*
>       *theatre, waves, and walks into the darkness.*

So, dear readers, you see, even the *Mahabharata* had Vidura. The scholar, Shruti Sharma, writes in *Dharaa. Maha Subhasita Samgraha*, a compilation of Sanskrit proverbs and parables, is an exciting verse describing a whimsical conversation between God Shiva and Goddess Parvati.

*Panchatantra* is one of the best examples of Indian satire. Over time, satire has become a powerful tool for making fun of politics and pushing back those in charge. The people used satire to criticise religious rules and hypocrisy, and the dominant norms set by the Brahmin class in society. Satire was used cleverly to question and change how things were. In the court of Vijayanagara ruled Tenali Raman (1480-1528), best friend of Raja Krishnadevraya. Witty Birbal (1528-1586) graced Akbar's court. and Gopal Bhar adorned the court of Raja Krishnachandra (1710–1783), King of Nadia. Linguist Sukumar Sen has said Gopal Bhar is a fictitious character, never mind his popularity.

Perhaps subservience and satire go hand in hand. It was Bengal, the richest su*bedari* of the Mughals, that allowed the British to set foot in rich India. And it is Bengal that fostered the first armed struggles, and anti-colonial songs, poetry, and theatre. Tagore was inspired by *Alice in Wonderland* and Western opera when he wrote the dance opera *Tasher Desh* (Kingdom of Cards) – a satirical portrayal of a society ruled by strict conventions and a veiled criticism of the society.

Today, the Kingdom of Cards is not fantasy, but a reality embodied in the present world; the city, society, and the homes we belong to. The intertwined strands of the orthodox and the liberal and our society's continuing failure to separate the two have created a dual discourse – a conflict between the real and fictional – the visible and invisible – the actual and the aspirational', said artist Ali Akbar Mehta, curating an exhibition on the subject.

Another of Tagore's work is *Raktakarabi*. Says Banglapedea: 'The royal ideal of the king of Yaksapuri is exploitation of the citizenry; he has an insatiable greed for money. The coolies of the gold mine get burnt in the fire of that greed. In the eyes of the king, the coolies are not human beings, they are mere tools for acquiring gold; they are only cogs in machines bearing the sign and numbers like 47a, 269f and so on. They have no value as human beings. Here, humanism and humanity are held by the shackles of machine.

There is no expression of life at Yaksapuri. Nandini is a symbol of life's complete expression, love, and beauty. Under the spell of his greed, the king of Yaksapuri does not feel the touch of joy in Nandini; the ascetic does not feel it because of his craving for religious reform; the pundit does not get it due to his scholarly and slavish instincts....' Protagonist 'Ranjan is tied to the bond of machine. This machine delinks his love from his life; the poet believed that this was the characteristics of a mechanised life'. Applicable to corporate government.

In the home of the English language, Ol' King Cole has no historical existence. And they believe it was Charlie Chaplin who demoralised Hitler. Shruti Sharma says *The Hindu Punch*, like its English counterpart, used satire to reflect everyday life, employing caricatures to depict Indian perspectives and positioned itself as a "foremost publication to promote political awareness through humour". She writes the periodical, *Harijan*, 'overseen by Gandhi, regularly carried satirical compositions exposing social injustice, dissembling conduct of the ruling establishment, and the imperative for transformative action'.

In independent India, we had R K Laxman and his exquisite Common Man. We had his brother, the writer R K Narayan, whose *Gods, Demons and Others* is a classic sarcastic interpretation of the Hindu pantheon from mythology. And we had artistes like Utpal Dutt. There were Cho Ramasamy and Harishankar Parsai. Freedom is a word with many meanings! In Bengal, Shibram Chakraborty (1903–1980) is known for his short stories and novels with pun, alliteration, play of words and irony. *Moscow bonam Pondicherry* (Moscow versus Pondicherry) and the play *Jokhon Tara Kotha Bolbe* (When They Will Speak) are among his best political works. His autobiography, *Eeshwar Prithibee Valobasa* (God Earth Love) should not be missed. His most quotable quote: To earn the freedom of a nation, a freedom fighter must sacrifice his own freedom.

*Marathi paper Sakal depicts
Headless King's Road Show.*

Technology has brought the word, the voice, the artist, the art of satire on a common platform with politics. The game of the 21st century is not over yet. That is why *The Fantastic Marionette*, is a work in progress.

Courtesy: *Mainstream*

# Nationalism and the Cult of Bharat Mata

MRINAL PANDE

March 2016

One views India's transformation from a personal angle. In 1950, when India became a secular Republic, I was four and my mother was twenty-five. I grew up hearing how if it were not for an unusually liberal father who packed off the mother and her siblings to Tagore's Shantiniketan (where she spent the next twelve years and emerged a graduate), my mother would have been home educated and married off in her early teens, like most girls from upper caste middle class families. Also were it not for the subsidised university education and western science, my father, a humble village postmaster's son, would never have acquired a first-class master's degree in chemistry. My sisters and I were told repeatedly that our right to a wholesome education and a well-paid job afterwards, was absolute.

They never let on that both within most families and on the campuses of 1930s, the Indian bourgeoisie remained a complex and deeply divided phenomena. We were never told about the ideological divide within Gandhi's Congress or even within our own larger family. Were they faced, as a writer and an educationist setting up a chain of state run schools with local help in a far-off Himalayan region, with inevitable clashes with their Brahminical tradition bound families or the state government? Did they take them on? Or capitulated on various fronts? Was it worthwhile?

As I watched the repeated suppression of writers, thinkers, intellectuals and students, and a string of lies spewed out by our rulers to justify it, I was so upset I could hardly speak. Peace protests, pacifist appeals and a global protest the suppression of free speech, nothing seemed to work as the nation entered a long tunnel of fascism with a domestic face, that of lawyers and Party activists who called themselves proud sons of Bharat Mata and beat up protesting citizens calling them traitors and seditionists.

At that point one began re-reading the literature and popular tracts from the 1920s. It is obvious that back when our parents were growing up, there were two opposing sets of views about the nationalist discourse and cultural identity of the Indian middle classes. On both sides, national and traditionally embedded social values about class, caste and gender fed into each other. So, while our mother and her siblings were enjoying their school years in one of the most liberal co-educational campuses in the country under the benign gaze of Tagore, Nandlal Basu, Kshitimohan Sen and Hazari Prasad Dwivedi, most girls in their age group were married off before they reached puberty to live lives as laid down by Manu centuries ago, as wives and mothers dependent on men.

In the Hindi belt a forty-page monograph on women's duties, *Stri Dharma Prashnottari*, published by the Gita Press was doing the rounds as a bestseller among middle class families. It recorded a conversation between an ideal woman, Savitri and her dumb acolyte, Sarala whom she lectured about how to be a little woman and a good wife-mother. Here was a carefully template for an ideal Hindu woman whose morality, purity and chastity were to be the bedrock for the ideal Sanatan Hindu family, which in turn was deemed the building block of a truly Hindu Rashtra for the Hindu Right wing, that strongly opposed Gandhi and Ambedkar's vision of an egalitarian, secular India with caste and communal considerations gradually evaporating. Savitri's clearly enunciated views in the tract published by the Gita Press Gorakhpur firmly said that a liberal western education to girls posed a grave threat to the nation and must be opposed. As they matured, women's strong sexual urges posed a threat to all. So, to contain and channelize their strong sexuality before it created mayhem, girls must be married off before attaining puberty. It was only as mothers of sons that women became venerable and important as an ideal crucible for raising obedient and devoted citizens to serve the nation state.

With a template in place, the figure of the traditional Hindu Mother Goddess was soon invoked. And in 1936, from Bengal, the land of Durga worshippers, came Anand Math, a novel in Bengali by Bankim Chandra Chattopadhyay. It laid a solid foundation for a cult of Bharat Mata. In the preface to an English translation in 1992, the translator B K Roy declares that Bankim's "great achievement for India was that he made patriotism a religion and his writings have become a gospel of India's struggle for political independence." He goes on to describe how *Bande Mataram* (I bow to the Mother Nation), a song sung by a band of revolutionaries in the novel, became a nationalists' rallying call. The translator thanks Bankim richly for having created a lineage of revolutionaries that would always be kept alive by Bharat Mata's militant Hindu nationalist sons and daughters.

The above vision was evoked on a spectacular scale in 1983 by the Vishwa Hindu Parishad when it combined the traditional abstract concepts such as gender, religious identity and sought to give them a physical shape by weaving together legends about the Mother Goddess and national heroes and consecrating them through age old Vedic rituals. The tapestry thus created became the basis of a Hindu nation-state which in turn was based on a combination of European political concept of the nation-state, progress and order and patriotism by Veer Savarkar in 1922. But invented traditions are not static. They need to be reinvented in specific contexts to produce and challenge newer class, religion and gender-based identities. Post-1950s, justifying the Hindu patriarchy's differentiation of social space into private and public, required a new vision of the motherhood of Bharat Mata. None of the three major Hindu Goddesses: Maha Kali, Maha Lakshmi, and Maha Saraswati, are biological mothers. So, the state's apotheosis into a Mata goddess required that the image of the Mother Goddess be trimmed somewhat and she be presented primarily as a devoted, selfless and spiritually inclined mother of Hindu sons. She inspired her sons to shed blood of all those who resisted her aura, and be ready to lay down their lives, if need be, to save her honour and punish the infidels. The latter, we are being told repeatedly, are non-Bharat Mata worshippers who are unpatriotic seditionists and need to be taught a swift lesson by being beaten up and jailed. To inculcate this philosophy there has been a repeated insistence that all citizens, from cinema halls to the campuses, show unequivocal respect for Bharat Mata's symbols: the national anthem, Vande Mataram and the tri colour.

A temple to Bharat Mata had come up in the 1920s in Varanasi. In the mid 1980s, another Bharat Mata temple was established in the pilgrimage town of Haridwar. It was built by one Swami Satymitranand Giri, a VHP leader praised (in the handbooks available at the temple) for having raised substantial funds in India and abroad from non-resident children of Bharat Mata. The English guidebook, *Bharat Mata Mandir, A Candid Appraisal*, traces the Swami's decision to build a temple arose from a vision. "In all ancient cultures, the Divine mother is the cause off (sic) Creation," says the booklet. "It is hoped that the visit to this shrine...will inspire devotion and dedication to Motherland." (pp1-2). Six weeks after the area for the temple was consecrated, the VHP mounted an all-India Ekatmata *Yajna* or Sacrifice for National Unity, a carefully planned six-week event during which trucks dressed as Raths were used as mobile Bharat Mata temples. These transported images of Bharat Mata with pots of Gangajal all over India for mass rituals of public worship by all her deemed children (read Hindu nationalists). This made Bharat Mata or the concept of the nation as a militant goddess, a distinct all-India phenomena. Th cult of Bharat Mata, like the Ram temple in Ayodhya, would be used by the political arm of the Sangh Parivar for whipping up support for a Hindu Rashtra and consolidating the Hindu votes in its favour. "It is our resolve to uitilise all gifts and endowments received at the shrine towards service to our *Vanvasi* brethren...and Harijans ...a portion of this will be utilised for the education of Brahmin youth in proper Vedic rites, rituals and research."

The three floors above the Bharat Mata shrine contain shrines to *Shoor* (military heroes), *Sants* (Saints) and last but not the least, *Satis*, pious women who chose to burn themselves on a pyre after their husbands died. The floor dedicated to great spiritual teachers is dominated by statues of Ramakrishna and his disciple, Vivekanand. There is also a statue of Shri Aurobindo, but his French wife, the Mother of the Pondicherry Ashram, is missing. The only woman honoured with a statue is Sharada Ma, the wife and disciple of Ramakrishna.

The problem is, democracy, like capitalism is ultimately a numbers game. Today the heady mix of religion and politics is generating toxic side effects among the 69 per cent. population that did not vote Right. This troubles the BJP. In the aftermath of the JNU events we saw its hitherto cocky leadership betray a paranoid sense of embattlement, as first the intellectuals and then the students and Dalits raised their voices against the State. The lesser members of the Party immediately delivered hate speeches against the dissidents. They called for an all-out war against the seculars, the intellectuals the Left and all those suspected of being Left sympathisers. Soon it was hard to dismiss them as the lunatic fringe since responsible members of the Union cabinet and BJP MLAs began to articulate a deep hatred for the secular principles, gender justice and free speech.

Something other than a lapse of logic seemed to be at work here. First a Dalit student killed himself leaving behind a note that squarely blamed an anti-Dalit government that had cut off his meagre stipend on grounds of his being deemed a Left sympathizer. Soon a mob of *Jai Bharat Mata* chanting *Bhakts* (devotees) in black coats were seen thrashing students, dissident lawyers and media men and women within court premises, baying for the blood of those they called *Desh Drohi* (anti-national) Pakistan sympathisers (read Muslim). The TV Channels who supported these self-appointed children of Bharat Mata, whipped up this hysteria further with doctored tapes and called for action against those that did not support their theory of nationalism. Damage control failed. Dalit leaders, intellectuals and students refused to buy the argument first articulated by the Bharat Mata temple compendium, and later theatrically articulated by the Union Minister for HRD.

No political power on earth has been able to muffle public dissent forever. It emerges first within homes and hostels, tea *dhabas* and office canteens, then spills over in public places till university campuses erupt like volcanoes. Prescribed normality then turns into a myth. At a point like this one finds, the only way to stay calm is to take each day as it comes, and to use what we know from history. Let them all come: the Right, the Left, the Socialists, the Dalit Panthers and Tamil Tigers, feminists and LGBT activists. Let our histories mix, anything if they do not set about building a wall.

First published in *Scroll.in*

# Dragging India away from tradition of dissent

ASHOK VAJPEYI

2017

*Bow to him who is the word,*
*both occult and manifest,*
*his glory revealed by the power*
*of the independent mind.*

> -From Subhashitavali, an anthology of Sanskrit verses compiled in the 15th century by Vallabhadeva (translated by A.N.D. Haksar)

It can be reasonably argued that in India, from the beginning of its civilizational enterprise, nothing has remained singular for long; in fact, nothing has been, in a sense, allowed to be singular for long. Whether God or religion, philosophy or metaphysics, language or custom, cuisine or costume, every realm is marked by plurality. It is not accidental that in many Western languages the word India is plural - Indes', meaning 'Indias. It is impossible, therefore, to talk about the Indian tradition: there are multiple traditions, all authentically and robustly Indian. Even within a single major religion, Hinduism, there are four Vedas, millions of gods, eighteen Upanishads, six schools of classical philosophy, two epics (and numerous versions of both), four *purusharthas* or goals of life. India as a country—and, equally, as a civilization-is an unending celebration of human plurality. This is how it has survived through millennia.

Central to the plural tradition, or sensibility, is the notion that there are different ways of looking at and living in the world. Plurality accommodates differences; and differences, in their turn, embody and enact dissent. When the Vedic seer ordains, *'Aano Bhadrah Kratvo Yantu Vishwatah'* (Let noble thoughts come to us from all directions), what is being sanctified is the idea that there are different ideas and truths spread all over the world and they are all welcome. Another Vedic saying, *'Vasudhaiva Kutumbakam'* (The world is one family), embraces all humanity, and therefore every idea, emotion, lifestyle that exists. Such openness and acceptance, or accommodation, is the core of the Vedic cosmic vision. Through the millennia, many dilutions and distortions may have occurred in real life and practice, as would inevitably happen everywhere, but Indian tradition and civilization never lost this remarkable, largely inclusive vision.

Prof. Amartya Sen has pointed out in his book *The Argumentative Indian* that the *Nasadiya Sukta*, the *Hymn of Creation*, a major verse in the *Rig Veda*, ends with radical doubt:

Who really knows? Who will here proclaim it? Whence was it produced? Whence is this creation? The gods came afterwards, with the creation of this universe. Who then knows whence it has risen? Whence this creation has risen—perhaps it formed itself, or perhaps it did not —the one who looks down on it, in the highest heaven, only he knows— or perhaps he does not know.

This is evidently the beginning of Indian skepticism. Nothing, not even the creation of the universe, or the supremacy and omniscience of God, is taken for granted. It may be noted that the hymn is also clear that the gods came after creation-they are, in that sense, no different from fish or trees or human beings. Into a major *sukta* of perhaps the oldest and one of the most important texts of Hinduism, then, the Vedic seers inserted a deeply metaphysical note of dissent.

A similar note was struck by sage Kauntya, who declared that if what had been said in the Vedas could not be communicated in any other language or in any other way, the Vedas must be meaningless. This was pure blasphemy since the Vedas were held to be inviolable, *apourusheya*. But Yaska, an ancient grammarian and commentator on the Vedas, includes this view in *Nirukta*, his compilation of Vedic interpretations which became one of the central texts of Sanskrit scholarship. In these and other passages from the earliest texts of Hinduism, there is ample evidence that the Indian traditions begin with enquiry, doubt and challenge— the hallmarks of plurality.

These traditions continued and grew with the other major religions that arose in India-Buddhism, Jainism and, later, Sikhism. Their founders, Buddha, Mahavir and Nanak, dissented from the ritualistic and caste rigidities of orthodox Hinduism to discover new paths of spirituality, metaphysics, social organization and liberation. Here was religious plurality being created through religious dissent. Buddhism and Jainism were particularly radical faiths; they were not posited on the notion and existence of God, and they rejected completely the scriptures of Hinduism and many of its foundational concepts like the eternal soul and the four goals of life. The rejection was forceful, fearless and rooted in intellectual inquiry and debate. Buddha, the great challenger, was later included as one of the ten avatars of God —*Dashavatar*—in classical Hinduism, along with Rama and Krishna. Here, too, was proof of India's irrepressible plurality and genius for accommodation!

There was also a strong and multi-layered tradition of disagreement and debate in the fields of thought, conduct, knowledge and morality in pre-modern India. Two aspects are easily noticeable. First, no one could propose a new concept or insight or theory without first faithfully summarizing the existing body of reflection on it. This was *poorvapaksha*, and only then could there be *uttarpaksha* —the thinker or debater proposing that which he or she claimed to be different or new, delineating it in meticulous detail. This was the standard intellectual practice.

Secondly, any new or different idea, theory or insight had to be publicly debated and accepted before being given a place in the scheme of things. The institution of *shastrarth*-philosophical contests-was well entrenched and there are many examples of this. The most celebrated instance is of the great thinker Shankaracharya having to engage in a *shastrarth* with Mandan Mishra and his wife Ubhaya Bharati over several days. There are many examples of such discussions and debates between Shaivites and Vaishnavites, Hindus and Buddhists, Buddhists and Jains; between different schools of philosophical and ethical thought; between agnostics and believers. The interrogative and dialogical ethos also finds place in literature, and the epic Mahabharata is full of such dialogues and debates. Dr Amartya Sen called us "argumentative Indians". The age-old conventions of dissent, dialogue, debate and disagreement are ample evidence that India created a civilization which was marked by curiosity and quest, by questions and doubts, by accommodation and acceptance of contrary viewpoints.

It cannot be denied that India had a very restrictive, indefensible caste system and elements of a feudal structure. But simultaneously it also had a republic of the imagination in which ideas and wisdom had a democratic remit. God, gods, spiritual ideas and practices, metaphysical and philosophical concepts, notions of morality and political structures, all have been brought into the realm of debate and interrogation. In 1950 when we declared ourselves a democracy it was, in many ways, a culmination of some age-old ideas of the democratic spirit.

Whether in traditions of creative expression or in the repertoire of intellectual articulation, in India dissent from faith or from the State has always not only been acknowledged but has also been allowed to grow. The vital condition of plurality has often been strengthened and expanded through dissent. For instance, when the tyranny of classical Sanskrit was questioned and subverted, the many modern Indian languages we speak today came into being. The vernacular did not demolish the classical, or even aspire to occupy the hallowed space of the classical; instead, it became a dissenting parallel. Every modern Indian language embodies and sustains a worldview that deviates from the classical worldview of Sanskrit. The presence of nearly a thousand versions of the Ramayana in India, ranging from Santhali and other tribal versions to retellings from the Jain point of view, is evidence that the dominant narrative and the worldview it enacted and expressed was creatively challenged and transformed. A Kannada *Ramayana* or a Hindi *Ramcharitmanas* deviate quite substantially from the original in Sanskrit by Valmiki, and all of them had validity.

It is also interesting to note that Buddhism and Jainism, born as religious and radical dissent, also got divided into different sects over time. The Mahayana and Hinayana sects in Buddhism and the Shwetamber and Digamber sects in Jainism can, arguably, be seen as dissent within an overriding structure of faith.

In Sanskrit drama, a lot of which has been preoccupied with the ironies of life and fate and the celebration of gods and regal heroes, there was, too, the irrepressible *vidushak*, the fool, the court jester, who not only provided comic relief but also sarcastic comments on kings, gods, fate and so on. He spared no one and his utterances were never censored or objected to. This tradition seems to have continued in more earthy and robust ways in folk theatre across the country. In many of these popular forms, watched night after night by thousands of faithful viewers, sometimes it is the narrator who assumes the role of the vidushak, just as he or she also enacts the hero or other heroic or divine characters.

The easy morality of the pious was also challenged or ignored altogether. In the twelfth century, Jayadeva composed Geeta Govind, a bold erotic poem which depicts in vivid detail the love and lovemaking of Radha and Krishna. Apart from occupying a central place in the classical dance form Odissi, this masterpiece of the Bhakti movement is still sung daily in temples across India, from Kerala in the south to Manipur in the north-east. The Bhakti period, beginning in the sixth century, saw a great and golden flowering of poetry and many other arts. While making God or gods accessible to all, without the negotiating instruments of priesthood, mosque, temple or holy books, this poetry democratized religions and spirituality. Most of the poets belonged to the lower classes (for instance, Kabir, a weaver; Madara Chennaiah and Ravidas, both cobblers; Soyarabai, a Mahar; Namdev, a tailor) and their poetry liberated devotion and poetic expression from the stranglehold of the Brahminical class. This poetry, widespread and popular till today, has been the most eloquent and passionate articulation of dissent, subversion and interrogation.

It may be recalled that during the freedom struggle, important political leaders recalled the work of Bhakti and Sufi poets to evoke a spirit of freedom and forge a unity of purpose amongst the masses. This was done most crucially and effectively by Mahatma Gandhi. In the prayer meetings of the Mahatma in Sewagram and elsewhere, the devotional poetry of all the major religions of India and the rest of the world was sung. These prayer meetings became a unique forum of political dissent vis-à-vis the colonial power. We may also recall that the Mahatma was shot dead while going to a prayer meeting by a Hindu religious fanatic a few months after Independence: a blinkered, exclusivist vision had announced itself through murder almost at the very moment of the birth of free India.

As we come to modern, independent India, there is no doubt that while many towering figures played a role in shaping it, the central figure was Mahatma Gandhi. In many ways, he epitomized radical dissent in the twentieth century. He articulated and practised the concepts of civil disobedience, satyagraha and non-cooperation. While all over the world empires were demolished through armed revolution and wars, Gandhi, dissenting from them all, took to truth and non-violence. A deeply religious man, he maintained that all religions were true but that all of them were also imperfect, thereby suggesting that they needed to learn from each other. He went to the extent of proclaiming that if it was proved that the Vedas supported untouchability in India, a form of racial and caste apartheid, he would reject the Vedas. It was at Gandhi's behest that the brilliant iconoclast B.R. Ambedkar, who often opposed him bitterly, was included by Nehru in his cabinet and assigned the job of drafting the Constitution of India is yet another instance of the Mahatma's respect for dissent.

In 1950 India chose to become a democratic republic and adopted a constitution that guarantees every citizen, among other freedoms, the freedoms of life, faith and expression. This was entirely in keeping with the millennia-long Indian tradition of creativity, reflection and fearless articulation. The Constitution also prescribed that any infringement of these basic freedoms by the State or anybody else would be legally actionable and an independent judiciary would be charged with the task of protecting them. However, it has not been easy to ensure these freedoms, which are also organically related to the right to dissent. Unfortunately, the conduct of the State, our political parties and institutions has often been hypocritical, even cynical. While they zealously guard their own right to protest, they all endeavour to suppress dissent and interrogation by others.

In recent years these paradoxes have assumed violent and murderous dimensions. It began with the assassination of the Mahatma himself. Since then, self-styled 'armies' of upper-caste landlords have slaughtered the dispossessed who have dared to ask for what is rightfully theirs. The Naxalites have killed innocent civilians who did not follow or support their violent means. And in many parts of the country- Kashmir, West Bengal, Assam, Manipur, Bastar, to name a few-the State, insurgents and communally furious groups have taken to annihilating those who oppose them.

Democracy's one glaring failure in India has been that it gives the elected representatives of the people unbridled power and sanction to crush or curtail the people's right to question, differ and disagree with the government and official narratives. The Emergency, imposed by Indira Gandhi's regime in the mid-1970s, was the first clear evidence of the danger that democracy reduced to mere numbers in Parliament could pose to liberty and human rights. The judiciary, which should have acted to check the excesses of a government that had turned dictatorial, also failed in its duty.

Forty years after that dark period in Independent India's history, the spirit of democracy is being undermined and subverted again. A political party-the Hindu majoritarian Bharatiya Janata Party (BJP) - that was elected with less than 32 per cent of the total votes polled, has been in power since the summer of 2014. In just over three years in office, it has either directly suppressed dissent, especially on the university campus, by terming it anti-national, or has kept quiet when Dalits and minorities have been attacked, often brutally, by social outfits affiliated to it. There are open attempts to punish dissent by raising the bogey of beef-eating, religious conversion, 'love jihad', national security or 'hurt sentiments'.

All these actions are throwing India into social turmoil. If you disagree with or question the government, you are branded an enemy of the country. The distinction between the State and the nation is being blurred. A large majority of Indians — almost 68 per cent-did not vote for the BJP in the 2014 national elections. But that has not prevented the party from arrogating to itself the right to decide what Indian society should be, what we can hear, see, eat, wear, speak, read or think. The Modi regime has convinced itself that it has the democratic right to crush all dissent, disagreement and opposition, even independent thought.

A lot of this is sought to be justified on the grounds that Indian traditions are being wrongly interpreted, and that there's an urgent need to correct such distortions and prevent a civilizational collapse. In providing such a corrective, bypassing the rule of law is unavoidable, and violence is acceptable, even necessary. Also central to this enterprise is propaganda and distortion of history. A massive cultural amnesia is being spread through biased, unpardonably partisan cultural events, education and media. Majority Hindu communities are told repeatedly that they have been wronged, discriminated against and unjustly treated. Selective facts and figures and downright lies are being brazenly propagated by right-wing groups that have appropriated the right to speak for all Hindus, and the current Indian State is either complicit or provides tacit support to these divisive forces by its silence and inaction.

When three courageous intellectuals, namely, Narendra Dabholkar, Govind Pansare and M.M. Kalburgi, were killed for no ostensible reason except for the fact that they were rationalists and creative dissenters who questioned religious tradition, it brought the simmering intolerance against rationality, knowledge, reason and creativity into the open. The governments at the Centre and in the states reacted to these murders with callous disregard, and investigations into the killings were delayed for several months. Some of us writers, nearly fifty from various Indian languages, spontaneously decided to protest by returning our Sahitya Akademi awards and other state honours. A statement we issued in November 2015 summarized the situation and our concerns:

> "We are deeply disturbed at the growing trends of violence, intolerance, and undermining of the age-long plurality of faith, belief, values, viewpoints, etc., the almost daily assault on amity and mutual trust. We believe that at this juncture of our democratic existence and growth, there is, unfortunately, increasing evidence of the emergence of an ethos of bans and disruptions, physical assault on and suppression of dissent and difference. We strongly hold that Indian tradition, Indian democratic polity and indeed its complex social structure have been sustained and nourished by an innate and deeply rooted sense of multiplicity, mutual respect and trust amongst communities and values of cooperation, social amity and harmony. We are witnessing a socio-political climate in which minorities, whether of faith, belief, opinion or ideas, are feeling threatened. We see that voices of dissent and difference are being increasingly subjected to unethical attacks, character assassination, mudslinging, etc. We also watch that some of the most important national institutions of culture and education are being meddled with, their stature and vision being systematically diluted and devalued. We are forced to conclude

that the liberal space, both of thought and action, is fast shrinking. As members of the creative and reflective community of India we have decided to raise our voice in protest and in resistance.

We urge the people of India, our fellow-citizens, who are primarily and ultimately responsible for strengthening and sustaining both Indian democracy and Indian tradition, to pay heed and act in unison to ensure that the divisive forces fail and that both democracy and tradition continue to deepen and nurture our plurality. We call upon the political parties, the Central Government and the State Governments that they actively discourage such trends [and refrain from supporting or encouraging by deed or in action, by words or silence, institutions and groups which are undermining the cardinal republican values and which are working to spread an atmosphere of hatred, revenge, violence without fear of the law and in utter disregard of the constitutional spirit of India. We wish to remind them that they draw their legitimacy from the Constitution and, therefore, it is incumbent upon them not to bypass or subvert the basic principles and vision of the Indian Constitution. We wish to request our MPs that they should fully and responsibly use their right of free speech in the Parliament in public interest.

We appeal to our fellow writers, artists, intellectuals, academics, scientists and all thinking people across the country to be alive and alert to the threats and dangers that our pluralistic culture, creative and intellectual courage, dissent and difference are facing and offer the divisive forces moral, creative and intellectual resistance at all levels. We must not allow misinterpretations and vested misreading of our culture, our traditions, our religions and forms of spirituality, [and] of our intellectual, ethical and spiritual underpinnings, to go unchallenged and uncontested."

This protest was immediately joined by over 400 artists and art critics, more than 100 historians, social scientists and intellectuals and nearly 500 scientists and technocrats. The President of India, the then Governor of the Reserve Bank of India and a few prominent industrialists and film personalities also warned against growing intolerance. The protest had international resonance as well, and the International PEN passed a resolution condemning violence against the creative and reflective community in India. Even the then President of the USA, Barack Obama, at the end of his Indian visit, pointed to the growing religious intolerance in India.

Indian literature in the last seven decades or so, since Independence, has been written, historically for the first time, in a democracy. Equally remarkable, though hardly noticed by political parties or modern sociology, is the fact that this literature has been largely anti-establishment. It has been, both eloquently and subtly, adversarial towards controlling regimes and narratives. It has questioned the country's political setup and ideological muddle and the established norms of morality. It has lamented or raged against the continuing and growing injustices and inequities in our society. It has protested the tyranny of the market and big business, the shrinking conscience of the elite and middle classes, the imposing zeal of the global, the disappearance of the local and the displacement of the community by the market.

In a manner of speaking, some of the values that informed the freedom struggle, including constant questioning of the State, continue in post-Independence Indian literature. These values are also alive, and often centre stage, in the visual arts, theatre and other forms of creative expression. The nation-wide spread of these values must also be seen as an unbroken continuum of the vital, irrepressible millennia-old Indian tradition of difference, doubt, disagreement and resistance. Dabholkar, Pansare and Kalburgi, to name just three creative minds, spoke as Kabir or Akka Mahadevi did centuries earlier, or the anonymous sage poets who composed the *'Nasadiya Sukta'* of the *Rig Veda*. It is a comment on where we are as a society today that unlike the Rig Vedic poets, unlike Akka and Kabir, the three rationalists were killed for expressing themselves.

Despite the challenges and dangers that artists and thinkers have faced in recent times, Indian literature continues to celebrate and nurture plurality, dissent and difference, and remains open to new ideas and insights from all over the world. Three distinct movements can be mentioned in this context: Marxism, feminism and the Dalit movement. Each of these has been born in dissent from the dominant literary and cultural establishments and has brought within the geography of creative expression new experiences, new perceptions, new anxieties, new aesthetic strategies, thus enriching the spirit of plurality and democracy.

When Bheeshma, the sagacious elder in the *Mahabharata*, lying on a bed of arrows, close to death, was asked about raj dharma, or royal duty, he said that it was the duty of the king to respect the wise men who lived in his domain, not engage foolish and greedy persons in running the affairs of the state, and protect his subjects from all kinds of fears. In Tulsi's *Ramcharimanas*, an epic which in north India enjoys the status of a scripture, Rama, after being coronated as the King of Ayodhya, beseeches the citizens to intercede without any fear if they ever feel that he is acting unethically. In the winter of 2015 and later, some of us tried to remind the powers that be of these wise insights contained in our glorious literary tradition. They responded by orchestrating a campaign against us, indulging in character assassination and accusing us of 'manufactured politics'.

Commenting on the climate of intolerance, the *Economic and Political Weekly* writes, "While Dabholkar, Pansare and M.M. Kalburgi's murders as well as the harassment meted out to others like them are deplorable, what is even more despicable is the silence of large sections of the population and the continuing support of political interests to their tormentors. This lack of response is a clear indication that citizens feel they are not safe if they speak out against entrenched religious vested interests and that the State will not take their complaints seriously. A society that cannot tolerate dissenting views or keeps quiet in the face of a violent reaction to such views is staring at a cultural and intellectual abyss." Anticipating the difficult time that is upon us today, the great Hindi poet Gajanan Madhav Muktibodh wrote nearly half a century ago:

> *Litterateurs and poets*
> *thinkers and artists and dancers*
> *are all indifferent:*
> *It is all a rumour, they think.*
> *They are all parasites.*
> *of the bloodsucking classes.*
> *They are all impotent and self-indulgent.*
> *They are all Superficial,*
> *unaware of the way*
> *the oppressors run riot—*
> *a fire here, a firing there.*

We can derive some satisfaction that there are, in fact, writers, artists, intellectuals, teachers, students, and many nameless brave men and women who have refused to be silent. They have protested and continue to raise their voices against oppression, demagoguery and bigotry. They have stood by the glorious and unbroken tradition of plurality and dissent in India. May the spirit and tradition of dissent in India grow ever larger. Hopefully, many of us will continue the good fight — the fight, through creative and intellectual means, for the values of freedom, justice and equality enshrined both in our tradition and our Constitution. We owe it to the Indian heritage that we profess to be so proud of.

Introduction to *India Dissents* published by Speaking Tiger

# We or our nationhood re-defined

*Excerpts from the 2014 Rajendra Mathur Memorial Lecture organised by the Editors Guild of India*

ANAND PATWARDHAN

**World Leader:** Modi's ascent from a Sangh *Pracharak* to the PM and 'world leader' needs to be seen operating in two correlated ideologies. The one is related with the Sangh. The more recent one has emerged in the context of global environmental changes post 1985. Modi's "development" ideology is not an accident. Nor were Manmohan Singh, Ahluwalia and Chidambaram accidents. It is just that they could not quite keep pace with the ever-increasing demands of resource capturing corporates. So, if a Modi did not exist, he would have been invented. Handing over common resources by interlinking of rivers, mining projects and disinvestment corroborated by the stock market is not enough. The ideology must sink roots. The Gujarat State Standard VIII Social Science Textbook of 2013 in its 8th Chapter of 'Our Economy' is evidence of the pervasive ideas of Liberalisation, Privatisation and Globalisation as panacea for all the problems our country faces today. Modi's triumph as a *chaiwala's* boy becoming the PM fits the bill.

**The Makeover:** It is remarkable. Modi wears different cultural hats (though his upbringing made him rebel when offered a Muslim one), garlands the statue of Dr. Ambedkar, talks to children on TV, picks up a broom to clean India, a feat that will remain purely cosmetic until the caste system itself is destroyed. Modi even takes a photo-op with the Chinese premier while spinning Gandhi's charkha. This photo is breath-taking. Not only was Gandhi the man his mentors murdered, the spinning wheel was the symbol of Gandhi's challenge not just to the corporate world but to the industrial revolution itself. It anticipated peak oil, global warming and the ravages of mad consumerism. I don't suggest that we go back to the charkha literally, but the charkha clearly pointed to ideals of sustainability. The development model that Modi follows can only speed us along our way, over the edge.

**No Visa:** In 2005 U.S. officials denied Mr. Modi a visa just as he was preparing to travel to New York to address Indian Americans at a rally scheduled in Madison Square Garden. The State Department invoked a U.S. law passed in 1998 that makes foreign officials responsible for severe violations of religious, ineligible for visas. The lobby to get Modi's USA visa drew not so strange bedfellows. Congressman Joe Walsh of Illinois, one of the loudest Tea Party Republicans in Congress wrote a letter to Secretary of State Hillary Clinton asking that Modi be granted a visa. Walsh told local reporters that he felt comfortable with Modi as someone "kind of like a Tea Party free market guy in India, which I found very appealing."

With Modi unable to go to the USA, his place was filled by Sri Sri Ravi Shankar, founder of the Art of Living Foundation. During a long interactive session with nearly 4,000 delegates of the Asian American Hotel Owners Convention Sri Sri was asked his views on Modi. He said, "I don't comment on individuals because individuals are just part of one wholeness." Sri Sri, the darling of the international corporate glitterati who has addressed the United Nations and the World Economic Forum in Davos, added "Everybody is what you call a *nimitta* — an instrument of the divine; so, branding someone good or bad or right or wrong and boycotting them is meaningless, useless." Sri Sri then went on to talk of the unprecedented progress occurring in Gujarat under the Modi Government. He noted that more than 40,000 dams had been constructed in just one year. "The water level has come up in Gujarat so much. People are so happy". No one seems to have told him that dams do not create water, they just take it away from those who cannot pay and give it to those who can.

**Manufacturing Consent:** "People are so happy" is now the theme song of our corporate controlled media. Those who refuse to sing it or sing it out of tune occasionally are already getting the boot. I will not list the casualties. In 2002 Celia Dugger of the New York Times had interviewed Modi a couple of months after the riots. "I asked [Modi] if he had any regrets about what had happened in his state in that period: Women openly raped, hundreds of people killed. He told me his greatest regret was that he didn't manage the media very well." It is a mistake he would never repeat. No media from TV to radio, print to internet is now left out of the ambit. Paid advertising has been taken to new heights. For weeks before the elections right up to polling day full-blown Narendra Modi ads were on all the front pages. If the funds available seem inexhaustible so do the acolytes. And just in case some truths manage to rise to the surface, there is the triad of State censorship, extra-state censorship and self-censorship. Shubhradeep Chakravarty's documentary that exposed how the riots in Muzzaffarnagar were engineered, is banned by the State. Following threats, Wendy Doniger's book on Hinduism is voluntarily pulped by her publisher. And no mainstream paper deems it worthy to report that outside the Wankhede stadium even as an RSS man takes the Chief Minister's oath in a lavish ceremony, 50 people are arrested for protesting the killing of 3 Dalits. Sunil Jadhav and his parents were brutally hacked to death because he allegedly had a relationship with an upper caste girl whose family is connected to the BJP, Shiv Sena, NCP and Congress. No one has been arrested.

In 2009 Modi hired the American APCO company. Famous for doing public relations for dictatorships, APCO is a strong advocate of expanding armaments and the US military role in world affairs. Amongst its many notorious business clients is Monsanto. Its network and affiliates include conservative pro-Zionist lobbyists and consultancy groups including Henry Kissinger Associates, Heritage Foundation and the Jewish Policy Centre.

**The Gujarat Model:** In Modi's Gujarat, Hitler is a textbook hero. *The Times of India*, Ahmedabad, Sept 30, 2004: Gandhi is not so great, but Hitler is. Welcome to high school education in Narendra Modi's Gujarat, where authors of social studies textbooks published by the Gujarat State Board of School Textbooks have found faults with the freedom movement and glorified Fascism and Nazism. While a Class VIII student is taught 'negative aspects' of Gandhi's non-cooperation movement, the Class X social studies textbook has chapters on 'Hitler, the Supremo' and 'Internal Achievements of Nazism' presenting a frighteningly uncritical picture of Fascism and Nazism.

**Rehabilitation of the RSS:** For two decades after the Gandhi murder, the RSS remained abhorred by the mainstream. But away from scrutiny, it continued to organize local centres called *shakhas,* recruiting children from the ages of 6 to 18, getting them up at 4 am, imparting militaristic physical training and instilling in them loyalty, discipline and a brand of "patriotism" which included the inevitable dose of anti-minority hatred. One such child, recruited from the age of eight from a relatively poor family, is Prime Minister Modi. Another is Party Chief Amit Shah. Five Chief Ministers and 17 of the 23 Cabinet-level senior ministers are current or former RSS members. In March 2014, *The Guardian* reported that the RSS has at least 50,000 branches across the country with over 40 million members. It runs a network of 18,000 schools. Anyone who hopes that the current Prime Minister has distanced himself from his roots should read his eulogy to Golwalkar, *Shree Guruji: Ek Swayamsevak* published in 2010.

**Demonisation of the Muslim:** It is the very raison d'etre of Hindutva. Historic myths of their cruelty, of temple destruction and rape is a steady diet fed since childhood. The Muslim's allegiance to a foreign God and foreign holy shrine and the 'barbaric' practice of eating beef is a source of unmitigated rage in the hearts of the Hindutva votaries. Onto this tinderbox if you throw a match by starting a rumour that a Muslim male has abducted or raped a Hindu female, no one will wait to ascertain if the rumour is true. Deadly pogroms are that easy to ignite.

**International corroboration:** The fact and the myth of Islamic jihad are mixed up. Hence the popular saying, "Not all Muslims are terrorists, but all terrorists are Muslims." If you add the paranoia of the USA and Israel to the mindset of Hindutva you have the makings and justifications of the counter terrorist.

**Saffron terror disguised as Muslim terror:** In 2006 and 2008 Muslims in Malegaon were accused of bombing their own graveyard and mosque. After 7 years of blaming Pakistan and arresting and torturing Muslim suspects, in May 2013 the National Investigation Agency (NIA), India's leading anti-terror agency filed charges against 4 Hindu radicals, all former RSS workers. In jail an ageing and ailing Aseemanand was looked after by a young Muslim prisoner. Before making his confession, Aseemanand reportedly told the magistrate that he knew he could be sentenced to death but still wanted to make the confession because of the arrest of the boy Kaleem, wrongly it now transpires, for the Mecca Masjid blast. Kaleem's plight motivated Aseemanand to think of "atonement" so that innocents don't suffer." Aseemanand also linked Hindu radicals to the blast in Gujarat's minority dominated Modasa town. RSS pracharak Indresh, Aseemanand claimed, helped enlist members, including Sunil Joshi, for this plot.

From *The Times Of India*, Sept 17, 2014:

RSS activist Sunil Joshi, a suspect in the Samjhauta Express blast case, was shot dead in Dewas in Madhya Pradesh on December 29, 2007. NIA charged Sadhvi Pragya Singh Thakur and three others for the murder of Sunil Joshi. According to NIA chargesheet Pragya Singh Thakur, who is also a key accused in the 2008 Malegaon blast, got Joshi eliminated as she was wary of Joshi's sexual advances and scared that the plan for Malegaon blasts might leak. Mumbai Police deployed Anti-Terrorism Squad to assist the local investigating authorities in Malegaon. Police say that unsophisticated, crude bombs, identical to those that detonated in Delhi three days before, were used. The investigation was led by Mumbai Anti-Terrorism Squad chief Hemant Karkare, who was later killed in the 2008 Mumbai Attacks.

The arrests of ex-army personnel by the ATS, brought to light the workings of two groups, Rashtriya Jagran Manch and Abhinav Bharat. Abhinav Bharat derives its name from Savarkar's Abhinav Bharat created in 1905. The president of Abhinav Bharat is the niece of Nathuram Godse, married to Savarkar's nephew. Uma Bharti, currently the Union Minister for Water Resources, and the Shiv Sena, publicly defended the accused. BJP parliamentary leader L. K. Advani alleged that "It has become clear that the ATS is acting in a politically motivated and unprofessional manner. I demand a change in the present ATS team." When serving Lieutenant Colonel Prasad Shrikant Purohit was arrested in Pachmarhi, learning Arabic, call records between him and Major Upadhyaya around the time of the Malegaon blasts were said to be incriminating. It later emerged that he, along with the sadhvi, may be connected to the Samjhauta Express bombings. Facing reports of at least three more Army men under scrutiny, Purohit's counsel claimed that the ATS was acting in "utter haste" and alleging that Purohit could even be eliminated by the ATS. Late Hemant Karkare, then chief of ATS investigating the blasts came under severe attack from the Sangh Parivar. After Karkare fell to terrorist bullets in 2008 his wife, Kavita Karkare, refused to receive her portion of the Rs.1 crore reward announced by Gujarat Chief Minister Narendra Modi. The reason was stark. Modi along with other leaders of the BJP including prime ministerial candidate L. K. Advani and the Shiv Sena had been baying for Karkare's blood for his investigations into terrorist activities by the saffron brigade.

**Civil Rights eroded:** The current regime is in place to rapidly subsume all citizen's rights at a faster pace than what the UPA could manage. Assurances of rapid environmental clearances for mega projects, weakening safeguards in the Land Acquisition Act, withdrawal of the Gram Sabha's right to decide the fate of mega-projects by the Ministry of Environment and Forests, handing over large tracts of reserved forest land to corporates like Adani, amending the Coastal Regulation Zone to allow coastal lands to fall into the hands of builders, promoting the production of cars and expanding the o expensive highways and flyovers, increasing the Foreign Direct Investment in Defence and Retail, along with the withdrawal of free medicines in Maharashtra and the alarmingly high rate of malnutrition in Gujarat – these are a few symptoms of a phenomenon reminiscent of the embrace between Hitler's Germany and the mega-business of his day.

**Law&Order:** The "clean chit" for Modi's closest aide Amit Shah, is more astounding. He is accused of being a key player in the cold-blooded false encounter killings of Sohrabuddin, Kauser Bi and Tulsi Prajapati. The case is still going on even though Amit Shah has been strangely allowed to skip court on a regular basis. Despite the grave charges against him Modi chose him to be BJP's star campaign manager in Uttar Pradesh. Under Shah's watch there was a communal riot in Muzzaffarnagar and polarised voters gave BJP a landslide victory. Shah as elevated as the BJP President and he delivered victories in Haryana and Maharashtra.

# Modi's India: mustn't pretend you didn't know

ARUNDHATI ROY

*On the occasion of the publication of the French translation of her latest essay collection,* Azadi: Fascism, Fiction, and Freedom in the Time of the Virus, *the novelist and essayist was awarded the Swiss Charles Veillon Foundation's 45th European Essay Prize for lifetime achievement in 2023. "Arundhati Roy uses the essay as a form of combat, analysing fascism and the way it is being structured," the foundation said. Here is her acceptance speech for the prize.*

I thank the Charles Veillon Foundation for honouring me with the 2023 European Essay Award. It may not be immediately apparent how delighted I am to receive it. It's even possible that I am gloating. What makes me happiest is that it is a prize for literature. Not for peace. Not for culture or cultural freedom, but for literature. For writing. And for writing the kind of essays that I write and have written for the past 25 years. They have mapped, step by step, India's descent (although some see it as an ascent) first into majoritarianism and then full-blown fascism. Yes, we continue to have elections, and for that reason, to secure a reliable constituency, the ruling Bhartiya Janata Party's message of Hindu supremacism has relentlessly been disseminated to a population of 1.4 billion people. Consequently, elections are a season of murder, lynching, and dog-whistling—the most dangerous time for India's minorities, Muslims, and Christians in particular. It is no longer just our leaders we must fear, but a whole section of the population.

The banality of evil, the normalization of evil, is now manifest in our streets, in our classrooms, in very many public spaces. The mainstream press, the hundreds of 24-hour news channels, have been harnessed to the cause of fascist majoritarianism. India's constitution has been effectively set aside. The Indian Penal Code is being rewritten. If the current regime wins a majority in 2024, it is very likely that we will see a new constitution. It is very likely that the process of what is called "delimitation"—a reordering of constituencies—or gerrymandering as it is known in the US, will take place, giving more parliamentary seats to those Hindi-speaking states in North India where the BJP has a base. This will cause great resentment in the southern states and has the potential to balkanise India. Even in the unlikely event of an electoral defeat, the supremacist poison runs deep and has compromised every public institution that is meant to oversee checks and balances. Right now, there are virtually none, except a weakened and undermined Supreme Court.

Let me thank you once again for this very prestigious prize and for the recognition of my work—although I must tell you that a lifetime achievement award makes a person feel old. I'll have to stop pretending that I'm not. It's a great irony in some ways to receive a prize for 25 years of writing—warning about the direction in which we were headed—that was not heeded but instead often mocked and criticized by liberals and those who considered themselves "progressive" too. But now the time for warning is over. We are in a different phase of history. As a writer, I can only hope that my writing will bear witness to this very dark chapter that is unfolding in my country's life. And hopefully, if my work and the work of others like me lives on, it will be known that not all of us agreed with what was happening.

My life as an essay writer was not planned. It just happened. My first book was *The God of Small Things*, a novel published in 1997. That happened to be the 50th anniversary of India's independence from British colonialism. It had been eight years since the Cold War had ended and Soviet communism had been buried in the rubble of the Afghan–Soviet war. It was the beginning of the US-dominated unipolar world in which capitalism was the uncontested victor. India realigned herself with the United States and opened her markets to corporate capital. Privatization and structural adjustment were the anthem of the free market. India was taking her place at the high table.

Then, a BJP-led Hindu supremacist government came to power in 1998. The first thing it did was to conduct a series of nuclear tests. They were greeted by most people, including writers, artists, and journalists, in a language of virulent, chauvinistic nationalism. What was acceptable as public discourse suddenly changed. At the time, having just won the Booker Prize for my novel, I had inadvertently been cast as one of this aggressive New India's cultural ambassadors. I was on the cover of major magazines. I knew that if I didn't say something, it would be assumed that I agreed with all of this. I understood then that keeping quiet was as political as speaking out. I understood that speaking out would be the end of my career as the fairy princess of the literary world. More than that, I understood that if I didn't write what I believed regardless of the consequences, I would become my own worst enemy and would possibly never write again. So, I wrote, to save my writing self. My first essay, *"The End of Imagination,"* was published simultaneously in two major mass-circulation magazines, *Outlook,* and *Frontline.* I was immediately labelled a traitor and anti-national. I received those insults as laurels, no less prestigious than the Booker Prize. It set me off on a long writing journey, about dams, rivers, displacement, caste, mining, civil war—a journey that deepened my understanding and entwined my fiction and nonfiction in ways that can no longer be separated. One of the essays in my book *Azadi,* is about how these essays live in the world. It's called *"The Language of Literature"*.

When the essays were first published (first in mass-circulation magazines, then on the internet, and finally as books), they were viewed with baleful suspicion, at least in some quarters, often by those who didn't necessarily even disagree with the politics. The writing sat at an angle to what is conventionally thought of as literature. Balefulness was an understandable reaction, particularly among the taxonomy-inclined, because they couldn't decide exactly what this was—pamphlet or polemic, academic or journalistic writing, travelogue, or just plain literary adventurism? To some, it simply did not count as writing: "Oh, why have you stopped writing? We're waiting for your next book." Others imagined that I was just a pen for hire. All manner of offers came my way: "Darling, I loved that piece you wrote on the dams, could you do one for me on child abuse?" (This happened.) I was sternly lectured (mostly by upper-caste men) about how to write, the subjects I should write about, and the tone I should take.

But in other places—let's call them places off the highway—the essays were quickly translated into other Indian languages, printed as pamphlets, distributed for free in forests and river valleys, in villages that were under attack, on university campuses where students were fed up with being lied to. Because these readers, out there on the front lines, already being singed by the spreading fire, had an entirely different idea of what literature is or should be. I mention this because it taught me that the place for literature is built by writers and readers. It's a fragile place in some ways, but an indestructible one. When it's broken, we rebuild it. Because we need shelter. I very much like the idea of literature that is needed. Literature that provides shelter. Shelter of all kinds.

Today it is unthinkable that any mainstream media house in India, all of whom live on corporate advertisements, would publish essays like these. In the last 20 years, the free market and fascism and the so-called free press have waltzed together to bring India to a place where it can by no means be called a democracy.

In January of this year, two things happened that serve to illustrate this in a way that nothing else probably could. The BBC broadcast a two-part documentary called *India: The Modi Question*, and a few days later, a small US firm called Hindenburg Research, which specializes in what is known as activist short-selling, published what is now known as the Hindenburg Report, an exposé of shocking wrongdoing involving India's biggest corporation, the Adani Group.

The BBC–Hindenburg moment was portrayed by the Indian media as nothing short of an attack on India's twin towers—Prime Minister Narendra Modi and India's biggest industrialist, Gautam Adani, who was, until recently, the world's third-richest man. The charges laid against them aren't subtle. The BBC film implicates Modi in the abetting of mass murder. The Hindenburg Report accuses Adani of pulling "the largest con in corporate history." On August 30, *The Guardian* and the *Financial Times* published articles based on incriminating documents obtained by the Organized Crime and Corruption Reporting Project that further substantiate the Hindenburg Report. Indian investigation agencies and most of the Indian media are in no position to investigate or publish these stories. When the foreign media does, it's easy then, in the current atmosphere of pseudo-hyper nationalism, to portray it as an attack on Indian sovereignty.

Episode one of the BBC film *The Modi Question* is about the 2002 anti-Muslim pogrom that raged through the state of Gujarat after Muslims were held responsible for the burning of a railway coach in which 59 Hindu pilgrims were burned alive. Modi had been appointed—not elected—chief minister of the state only a few months before the massacre. The film is not just about the murders but also the 20-year journey that some victims made through India's labyrinthine legal system, keeping the faith, hoping for justice and political accountability. It has eyewitness testimonies, most poignantly from Imtiaz Pathan, who lost 10 members of his family in the "Gulbarg Society massacre" in which 60 people were murdered by a mob, including a former member of Parliament, Ehsan Jafri, who was dismembered and burned alive. He was a political rival of Modi's and had campaigned against him in a recent election. It was one of several similarly gruesome massacres that took place over those few days in Gujarat. One of the other massacres—not in the film—was the gang rape of 19-year-old Bilkis Bano and the murder of 14 members of her family including her three-year-old daughter. Last August, on Independence Day, while Modi addressed the nation about the importance of women's rights, his government, on the very same day, pardoned the rapist-murderers of Bilkis and her family who had been sentenced to life imprisonment. They had spent most of their jail time out on parole. Now they are free men. They were greeted with garlands outside prison and are now respected members of society and share the stage with BJP politicians in public programs. The BBC film revealed an internal report commissioned by the British Foreign Office in April 2002, so far unseen by the public. The fact-finding report estimated that "at least 2,000" people had been murdered. It called the massacre a pre-planned pogrom that bore "all the hallmarks of ethnic cleansing." It said reliable contacts had informed them that the police had been ordered to stand down. The report laid the blame squarely at Modi's door. After the Gujarat pogrom, the US denied him a visa. Modi won three consecutive state elections and remained Gujarat's chief minister until 2014. The visa ban was revoked after he became prime minister in 2014. The Modi government banned the BBC film. Every social media platform complied with the ban and took down all links and references to it. Within weeks of the film's release, the BBC's offices were surrounded by the police and raided by tax officials.

The Hindenburg Report accuses the Adani Group of engaging in a "brazen stock manipulation and accounting fraud scheme," which—using offshore shell entities—artificially overvalued its key listed companies and inflated the net worth of its chairman. According to the report, seven of Adani's listed companies are overvalued by more than 85 percent. Modi and Adani have known each other for decades. Their friendship was consolidated after the 2002 Gujarat pogrom. At the time, much of India, including corporate India, recoiled in horror at the open slaughter and mass rape of Muslims that was staged on the streets of Gujarat's towns and villages by vigilante Hindu mobs seeking "revenge." Gautam Adani stood by Modi. With a small group of Gujarati industrialists, he set up a new platform of businessmen. They denounced Modi's critics and supported him as he launched a new political career as *"Hindu Hriday Samrat,"* the Emperor of Hindu Hearts.

So was born the "Gujarat model of "development"": violent Hindu nationalism underwritten by serious corporate money. In 2014, after three terms as chief minister of Gujarat, Modi was elected prime minister of India. He flew to his swearing-in ceremony in Delhi in a private jet with Adani's name emblazoned across the body of the aircraft. In the nine years of Modi's tenure, Adani became the world's richest man. His wealth grew from $8 billion to $137 billion. In 2022 alone, he made $72 billion, which is more than the combined earnings of the world's next nine billionaires put together. The Adani Group now controls a dozen shipping ports that account for the movement of 30 percent of India's freight, seven airports that handle 23 percent of India's airline passengers, and warehouses that collectively hold 30 percent of India's grain. It owns and operates power plants that are the biggest generators of the country's private electricity.

Yes, Gautam Adani is one of the world's richest men, but if you look at their rollout during elections, the BJP is not just India's but perhaps even the world's richest political party. In 2016, the BJP introduced the scheme of electoral bonds to allow corporations to fund political parties without their identities being made public. It has become the party with by far the largest share of corporate funding. It looks very much as though the twin towers have a common basement. Just as Adani stood by Modi in his time of need, the Modi government has stood by Adani and has refused to answer a single question raised by members of the opposition in Parliament, going so far as to expunge their speeches from the parliamentary record.

While the BJP and Adani accumulated their fortunes, in a damning report Oxfam said that the top 10 percent of the Indian population holds 77 percent of the total national wealth; 73 percent of the wealth generated in 2017 went to the richest one percent, while 670 million Indians who comprise the poorest half of the population saw only a one percent increase in their wealth. While India is recognized as an economic power with a huge market, most of its population lives in crushing poverty. Millions live on subsistence rations delivered in packets with Modi's face printed on them. India is a very rich country with very poor people—one of the most unequal societies in the world. For its pains, Oxfam India has been raided too. And Amnesty International and a host of other troublesome NGOs in India have been harassed into shutting down.

None of this made any difference to the leaders of Western democracies. Within days of the Hindenburg–BBC moment, after "warm and productive" meetings, Prime Minister Modi, President Joe Biden, and President Emmanuel Macron announced that India would be buying 470 Boeing and Airbus aircraft. Biden said the deal would create over a million American jobs. The Airbus will be powered by Rolls-Royce engines. "For the UK's thriving aerospace sector," PM Rishi Sunak said, "the sky's the limit." In July, Modi travelled to the US on a state visit and to France as the chief guest on Bastille Day. Can you even begin to believe that? Macron and Biden fawned over him in the most embarrassing manner, knowing full well that this would be spun into pure campaign gold for the 2024 general elections in which Modi will stand for a third term. There is nothing they would not have known about the man they are embracing. They would have known about Modi's role in the Gujarat pogrom. They would have known about the sickening regularity with which Muslims are being publicly lynched, how some lynchers were met with garlands by a member of Modi's cabinet and the precipitous process of Muslim segregation and ghettoization. They would have known about the burning-down of hundreds of churches by Hindu vigilantes.

They would have known about the hounding of opposition politicians, students, human rights activists, lawyers, and journalists, some of whom have received long prison sentences; about the attacks on universities by police and suspected Hindu nationalists; the rewriting of history textbooks; the banning of films; the shutdown of Amnesty International India; the raid on the India offices of the BBC; the activists, journalists, and government critics placed on mysterious no-fly lists; and the pressure on academics, both Indian and foreign.

They would have known that India now ranks 161 out of 180 countries on the World Press Freedom Index, that many of the best Indian journalists have been hounded out of the mainstream media, and that journalists could soon be subjected to a censorious regulatory regime in which a government-appointed body will have the power to decide whether media reports and commentary about the government are fake or misleading. And the new IT law that is designed to shut down dissent on social media.

They would have known about the sword-wielding, violent Hindu vigilante mobs that regularly and openly call for the annihilation of Muslims and the rape of Muslim women.

They would have known about the situation in Kashmir, which, beginning in 2019, was subjected to a months-long  internet shutdown, the longest internet shutdown in a democracy, and whose journalists suffer harassment, arrest, and interrogation. Nobody in the 21st century should have to live as they do, with a boot on their throats.

They would have known about the Citizenship (Amendment) Act passed in 2019 that barefacedly discriminates against Muslims, the massive protests that it touched off, and how those protests only ended after dozens of Muslims were killed the following year by Hindu mobs in Delhi (which, incidentally, took place while President Donald Trump was in town on a state visit, and about which he uttered not a word). They would have known about how the Delhi police forced grievously injured young Muslim men who were lying on the street to sing the Indian National Anthem while they prodded and kicked them. One of them subsequently died.

They would have known that, at the same time they were feting Modi, Muslims were fleeing a small town in Uttarakhand in northern India after Hindu extremists affiliated with the BJP marked x's on their doors and told them to leave. There is open talk of a "Muslim-free" Uttarakhand. They would have known that, under Modi's watch, the state of Manipur in India's northeast has descended into a barbaric civil war. A form of ethnic cleansing has taken place. The Centre is complicit; the state government is partisan; the security forces are split between the police and others with no chain of command. The internet has been cut. News takes weeks to filter out.

Still, the world's powers choose to give Modi all the oxygen he needs to destroy the social fabric and burn India down. To me, this is a form of racism. They claim to be democrats, but they are racists. They don't believe their professed "values" should apply to non-white countries. It's an old story, of course. It doesn't matter. We will fight our own battle — and ultimately, we will win our country back. However, if they imagine that the dismantling of democracy in India is not going to affect the whole world, they must indeed be delusional.

For all those who believe India is still a democracy, these are a few of the events that have happened just over the last few months. This is what I meant when I said we have moved into a different phase. The time for warnings is over, and we must fear sections of the people as much as we fear our leaders. In Manipur, where a civil war rages, the police, who are entirely partisan, handed two women over to a mob to be paraded naked through a village and then gang-raped. One of them watched her young brother being murdered before her eyes. Women who belong to the same community as the rapists have stood by the rapists and have even incited their men to rape. In Maharashtra, an armed Railway Protection Force officer walked down the corridor of a train shooting Muslims and calling on people to vote for Modi.

A hugely popular Hindu vigilante, often photographed hobnobbing with top politicians and policemen, called on Hindus to participate in a religious march through a densely populated Muslim-majority settlement. He remained at large even though he was the prime accused in the murder of two young Muslims who were tied to a vehicle and burned alive in February. The town of Nuh abuts Gurgaon, where major international corporations have their offices. The Hindus in the march carried machine guns and swords. The Muslims defended themselves. Predictably, the march ended in violence. Six people were killed. A 19-year-old imam was butchered in his bed, his mosque vandalized and burned. The response of the state has been to bulldoze all the poorest Muslim settlements and cause hundreds of families to flee for their lives.

The Prime Minister has had nothing to say about any of this. It is election season. Next May, there will be a general election. It's all part of an election campaign. We are braced for more bloodshed, mass killing, false-flag attacks, pretend-wars, and anything to further polarize an already polarized population.

In a chilling little video filmed in a classroom of a small school, the teacher makes a Muslim child stand by her desk and asks the rest of the students, Hindu boys, to come up one by one and slap him. She admonishes those who haven't hit him hard enough. The action taken so far has been that the Hindus in the village and the police have pressured the Muslim family not to press charges. The Muslim boy's school fee has been refunded and he has been taken out of school. What's happening in India is not that loose variety of internet fascism. It's the real thing. We have become Nazis. Not just our leaders, not just our TV channels and newspapers, but vast sections of our population too. Large numbers among the Indian Hindu population who live in the US and Europe and South Africa support the fascists politically as well as materially. For the sake of our souls, and for those of our children and our children's children, we must stand up. It doesn't matter whether we fail or succeed. That responsibility is not on us in India alone. Soon, if Modi wins in 2024, all avenues of dissent will be shut down. You must not pretend you didn't know what was going on.

I will end by reading a section from my first essay, *The End of Imagination*. It's a conversation with a friend about failure—and my personal writer's manifesto: I said in any case hers was an external view of things, this assumption that the trajectory of a person's happiness, or let's say fulfilment, had peaked (and now must trough) because she had accidentally stumbled upon "success." It was premised on the unimaginative belief that wealth and fame were the mandatory stuff of everybody's dreams. You've lived too long in New York, I told her. There are other worlds. Other kinds of dreams. Dreams in which failure is feasible. Honourable. Sometimes even worth striving for. Worlds in which recognition is not the only barometer of human worth. There are plenty of warriors whom I know and love, people far more valuable than myself, who go to war each day, knowing that they will fail. True, they are less "successful" in the most vulgar sense of the word, but by no means less fulfilled. The only dream worth having, I told her, is to dream that you will live while you're alive and die only when you're dead. (Prescience? Perhaps.) "Which means exactly what?" (Arched eyebrows, a little annoyed.) I tried to explain. Sometimes I need to write to think. So, I wrote it down for her on a paper napkin: *To love. To be loved. To never forget your own insignificance. To never get used to the unspeakable violence and the vulgar disparity of life around you. To seek joy in the saddest places. To pursue beauty to its lair. To never simplify what is complicated or complicate what is simple. To respect strength, never power. Above all, to watch. To try and understand. To never look away. And never, never to forget.*

Let me thank you again for the honour of this award. I loved the part in the prize citation in which it says, "Arundhati Roy uses the essay as a form of combat." It would be presumptuous, arrogant, and even a little stupid of a writer to believe that she could change the world with her writing. But it would be pitiful if she didn't even try. Before I go ... I just want to say this: this prize comes with a lot of money; it will not stay with me. It will be shared with the very many impossibly courageous activists, journalists, lawyers, and filmmakers who continue to stand up to this regime with almost no resources. However grim the situation is, there is a tremendous fight back.

Thank you.

Courtesy: Swiss Charles Veillon Foundation

# One Man's Victory: Nation's Defeat

VINAY LAL

June 2019

I opened the newspapers on May 24th to a stupefying story that caught the world's attention. The incumbent Prime Minister, Narendra Modi, had not only retained his seat in Varanasi by a huge margin but had led his party to a decisive victory, scattering his opponents like atoms in the dust. *The Indian Express*'s chief political columnist, Pratap Bhanu Mehta, headlined Modi's achievement as, "Staggering Dominance". Some in the media spoke of his "landslide re-election", while others described the "unambiguous mandate" leading to Modi's second coming as the Prime Minister.

What is distinct about Modi is that he stands in singular and sinister isolation at the summit of Indian politics. The BJP had almost wiped out the Congress, and nearly all other opposition, in 2014; no one, barring perhaps the BJP, which in the voice of Modi has declared that it aims to win the votes of all 900 million Indian voters, thought that the 2019 election outcome would result in the further decimation of the opposition. With only 44 seats in 2014 the Congress did not qualify as the "opposition" in the Lok Sabha, which has a membership of 543. Having fallen short of the target of 55 seats by 3 seats in the 2019 elections, the Congress still does not qualify.

It may be comforting for Modi's critics to believe that those who rise so spectacularly to the top are likely to have a precipitous fall: that is not always the case. The greater concern, to invoke Lord Acton's maxim, is that "power corrupts, absolute power corrupts absolutely". If Modi and the BJP have captured all the institutions of state power, and bankrupted or emasculated those which are not so readily pliable to the will of the party, the circumstances for the longevity of Indian democracy in any meaningful sense of the term cannot be described as propitious. More than 70 years after independence, the political summit should have been crowded—with ideas, with the play of the imagination, with parties speaking in different tongues and articulating compelling narratives of social justice. Instead, what do we find? The Congress has become moribund, the Communists eviscerated. There is only one narrative now—call it Hindu pride or call it the Hindu nation-state, but it is more effectively captured by one word: Modi. "In New India," as one newspaper put it, "the Prime Minister towers above all parties, including his own." Modi in solitude controls the threads of the narrative of conquest—the of twitter and selfies of these times.

We don't know how many lives have been discarded on the ascendant path that Modi took and where it will stop. The contemporary scene itself causes grave anxiety to all, barring the ardent followers of Modi who have dreamt up a Hindu Nation in which the minorities will be turned into second-class citizens. The insertion of religion into politics led to the consolidation of Hindu votes and handed victory after victory to Modi. The stories coming out of India in recent years tell a tale that is chilling to the bones, a tale which leaves behind a stench that no amount of sloganeering about '*Swacch Bharat*' or even something more than a symbolic wielding of the broom can eradicate. If inclusiveness is the touchstone of a Republic, what is characteristic of India today is how increasingly large constituencies are being excluded from the nation. Muslims and Dalits have been hounded, garrotted, and lynched; the working class is being trampled upon; the Adivasi is nothing more than an obstacle for a mining company. None of this is news, some might argue; perhaps things have only become worse. Such a view is profoundly mistaken, because whatever India may have been in the past, it has never been, certainly not to the extent it is today, a Republic of Inhospitability and Fear.

We are already witnessing the dreadful consequences that include the distortion of the idea of India and of Hinduism. The country, as I have already hinted, though an example or two might be usefully illustrative of general trends, has been awash with news of "mob lynchings" over the last few years and another case has come to light of a Muslim man in Jharkhand who was tied up, beaten, and forced to chant Jai Shri Ram for 12 hours. Tabrez Ansari died. Horrific as this atrocity is, it is also part of an orchestrated chaos. Early in January 2018, an eight-year-old girl belonging to the Bakharwal community was abducted near Kathua, which lies a little short of 90 km. south of Jammu. The girl was sedated, taken to a Hindu family temple (*devasthan*), and repeatedly gang raped by several men for five days before being bludgeoned to death. A demonstration led by the *Hindu Ekta Manch* [Organization for Hindu Unity] was held in support of the racists and killers of the 8-year-old minor. One atrocity follows another; attention shifts from one 'event' to another, and we do not pause long enough to consider the moral implications of any atrocity. Whatever the economic and communal dimensions of the underlying animosities, nothing can explain the sheer scale of the precipitous moral decline into which the country has fallen.

This is the backdrop against which Narendra Modi achieved a victory of such calamitous proportions that its consequences will reverberate for decades to come. The BJP and its supporters are describing it as a magnificent achievement, a stupendous outcome—and stupendous it is, not merely on account of the evisceration of what one even hesitates to call "the opposition", but because the victory has been delivered by a massive and largely unsuspecting electorate rather than having been achieved by the barrel of the gun or just coercion. It is pointless at this juncture to argue whether some EVMs were tampered with, or the extraordinary resources that the BJP brought to this election, including vast sums of unaccounted money contributed by the crony capitalists who must be exulting yet again at the victory of their champion, a self-proclaimed ordinary *chai-wallah*. Most analyses of the election have focused on Narendra Modi's spectacular success in projecting himself as indispensable to the nation and as the only person capable of catapulting India on to the global stage as a supposed world power. One study after another has shown, or has attempted to establish, that many electors cast their vote for Modi, and Modi alone. If Donald Trump is now the Republican Party, Modi is the BJP. The BJP has a massive following, and many among the ranks have shown an ideological commitment. Amit Shah has since his rehabilitation within the BJP before the 2014 election, demonstrated a mastery of organizational details and a ravenous appetite for propaganda. Nevertheless, Modi stands at the summit of Indian politics.

The consequences of this election, however, cannot be reduced to questions about the personality of Modi or his style of governance. The battle lines are likely to harden between the Hindu extremists who have been emboldened by the victory and those terrified at the prospect of a Hindu Rashtra. The BJP's warriors may already be starting to prepare for the next battle. The rot has tragically already set in. The BJP spent the previous five years in decimating the institutions that are the bulwark of any democracy. The country's leading public universities, among them Delhi University and JNU, have been gutted; the Election Commission has been shorn of much of its credibility; and the army, which was long been distinguished from the army of neighbouring Pakistan as an institution that stayed outside the fray of politics, has increasingly been drawn into political scandals.

It is difficult to identify institutions of the state that have not been hollowed out. The BJP is utterly devoid of any imagination, and the party hacks and their devoted followers have nothing but absolute contempt for intellectuals. The Prime Minister has made the customary noises, following the election, about carrying everyone along with him and the need for "inclusive growth". There are the usual slogans about *sabka saath, sabka vikas,* and the call to the party to strive for *sabka vishwas:* all mindless chatter, the most predictable ploys to shore up the idea of the magnanimous victor.

The BJP has described this victory as total, as, so to speak, the war that ends all wars! I have described the electorate that delivered a victory to Modi and the BJP as "unsuspecting", and I do so with the full awareness that among those who voted for the incumbent many did so with the expectation that he will stand up for the Hindu, fill (as it is imagined) the much-maligned

Hindus with pride, make India Congress-free, and vindicate "the common man". But the electorate is unsuspecting because there is, in my view, little realisation that with this victory an entire generation of Indians is now lost to values of civility, decency, and moral probity. An entire generation will now have to pay the price for the obliteration of social goods that we hold in common and the values that are enshrined in the Constitution of India. It will take a generation, I suspect, to recover our humanity even partially from what has been wrought by "the hollow men" of our times.

Courtesy: Author's blog *Lal Salaam*, published as *Victory of Hollow Men*, with a few lines added.

# The remaking of Narendra Modi

SHIV VISVANATHAN

January 2013

Power fascinates and when self-obsessive, it is even more fascinating. Subject to continuous churning, a dynamic sense of power has a magic few other processes possess. Narendra Modi is not just a man obsessed with power, but one who sees himself as a basic medium for it. Here is a Frankenstein redoing himself, creating a new self in a new costume. The remaking of Modi must be understood because he stands as one of the major threats to the Indian polity. His projection of himself as a future prime minister has paid dividends. Here is an attempt to understand the remaking of Modi, the modernist as fascist.

Recently, *Time* magazine asked us to be realistic and adjust to him. The Brookings sees him as a necessary evil, more necessary than evil. The report of think tanks should serve as a warning that recognises that policy makers are already assuming the coming era of Modi. Yet, there is a paradox here. While Modi consolidates his image outside Gujarat, the state itself might be turning more lukewarm to him. The lack of enthusiasm emerges from three sources. First, elements within the BJP find him a hot potato and would be content to queer his pitch. A whole array of small movements, from the boat *yatras* to the battle against the Nirma plant, betray an unease with his development policies. Third, the shadow of the 2002 carnage still hangs over him and not all the perfumes of the SIT (Special Investigation Team) have been able to cleanse his little hands.

As opposed to this, the middle class who loves a winner sees in Modi a man who caters to their vulnerabilities and projects their fears in searching for solutions. The middle class sees in Modi a decisive, security oriented, and development centred, urban fixated politician who has voiced all their fears about Muslims, anarchy, security and transformed it into a huge vote bank. The future and Modi appear twinned in the middle-class mind. So how did a simple, lower middle class *pracharak*, already diagnosed as a fanatic and a fascist by psychologist Ashis Nandy, try to change his spots? It is this remaking of Modi that we must understand if we wish to unmake it.

A decade ago, he was a simple cadre functionary. As the *pracharak* became chief minister, he extended the *pracharak*'s lens on to his new world. Gujarat was seen a cadre to be transformed. Modi's world was simple but his idioms were powerful. Like most RSS organisers, he evoked a *swadeshi* cultural idiom which was ascetic, nationalist and nativist. What was good for Gujarat was good for Gujaratis, if Modi determined it. Here was a man uneasy with difference and sought to meet it either by erasing or denying it. He lived out a parallel history where Delhi was seen as an alien region controlled by foreigners. He enacted out the feelings of many Hindus who thought of electoral democracy as majoritarian tolerance that had gone too far, convinced that official history had been unfair to Gujarat which had produced both Sardar Patel and Mahatma Gandhi. Even worse, that Delhi acted as if Gujarat was a non-place. Rectifying history was Modi's and the RSS' favourite idea of justice. This process paralleled the rewriting of history by Stalinists. The Stalinists rewrote history to suppress dissent. Modi rectified history to construct and consolidate the mentalities that would sustain him in power. Both used production statistics to create legitimations. Stalin had Stakhanov, the legendary worker who always met unreal production quotas. Modi cited Gujarat as a continuous example of business booms and found the semiotic Stakhanov in himself. He worked overtime to project an image of Gujarat as if he alone was responsible for Gujarat's success. Continuous repetition creates its form of legitimation and loyalty. By repeatedly reciting the story of Gujarat's success, Modi created a sleight of hand. The propagandist of Gujarat's success was gradually seen as the creator and cause for it. It was an act of usurpation that was swift and complete.

The man who complained that history was unfair decided that fairness comes from rewriting it. Modi was sure that propaganda by creating self-fulfilling prophecies becomes true. He realised that he could not be a Gandhi or a Patel. They were ideals or icons he could not mimic. He also understood that the Gujarat of his time had no national figure. The textile strike and the collapse of the industry had created a *tabula rasa* in terms of models. With the death of textiles, the *mahajans* and *seths* who reinforced its orderly world lost their halo. Modi saw that the time was ripe for a new construct, an image constructed out of anxieties, fears, and even the traditions of achievement that have made Gujarat into an urban society.

Narendra Modi is a master of the language of populist politics. He understands the cultural idiom, both the dialects and the dialectics of resentment; his grasp over the cultural politics of relative deprivation convincing Gujaratis that their contribution to the nation, GNP and history was not recognised. By playing on this unconscious, he shaped it to suit his instrumental politics. Any complaint about Gujarat would immediately switch to these cultural tracks, creating the logic of insider/outsider politics. The insiders were patriots, the outsiders were illiterate, unfair and arrogant. The corollary was obvious. Any insider who criticised Gujarat and its synecdoche, Narendra Modi, was automatically classified as an outsider. This classificatory exile was the task of enthusiasts who found in English journalists and newspapers their targets. English was an alien language and represented the outside.

The imaginary house that Modi built had two sites, the Gujarat of his imagination and Delhi as his imaginary. Delhi was the last colony. It was the location where the imperial forces of the Congress ruled by the empress Sonia lived. Delhi embodied an extension of Mughal rule perpetuated by the Congress. Delhi was non-Gujarat, it embodied colonial history without a hearing aid, deaf to the complaints of its opponents. Delhi was soft on the Muslims creating an invidious politics which favoured bootleggers and smugglers. Modi was adept at taking partial ethnic truths and transforming them into political slurs.

Narendra Modi is a shrewd politician. In recognising the limits of Hindutva politics conducted in Hindutva idioms, he unconsciously realised that a rampant Hindutva might eventually threaten Hindus. In that sense, his co-religionists were a problem as they are soft on history, preferring a soft democracy more in tune with their syncretic mentality. Modi sensed, early on, that his role as the lumpen speaker gorging on the violence of the riots had to be a temporary phenomenon. He sensed that while such resentment could be a layer in the unconscious, what one needed was an image of a more positive politics, something that could exorcise the ghosts of 2002. More than exorcism, one needed a semiotic makeover to create a set of self-fulfilling prophecies around the new Modi to survive politically. Populist politicians can perpetuate their tyranny by letting the rumour and gossip of a new leader play itself out. As a wag put it, Narendra Modi became 'The Gentleman'. **M**odi is a cultural construct whose semiotic grammar we must understand. Semiotics as a theory of signs and symbols served to update Modi. Originally Modi appeared in the drabness of white kurtas, which conveyed a swadeshi asceticism. Khadi is the language for a certain colourlessness. Modi realised that ascetic white was an archaic language. His PROs forged a more colourful Modi, a Brand Modi more cheerful in blue and peach, more ethnic in gorgeous red turbans. His ethnic clothes serve as diacritical markers of respect. He plays the chief in full regalia. Having earned traditional respect, he needed a more formal attire – suits for Davos, a *bandhgala* for national forums. Hair transplants and Ayurvedic advice served to grow his hair. Photographs show him even trying a Texan hat. Hoarding after hoarding proclaims not only the same message and a diverse attire of designer garments. He must sustain himself as both icon and image of a different era.

Modi grasped that the core competence of a politician must be built around different cores or, to switch metaphors, he needed a set of second skins which people would see as natural. The Hindutva man in him had to be deconstructed and recomposed. Like Eliza

Dolittle, he had to project a new grammar. He (or I guess his PROs) disaggregated elements of his Hindutva to create a new image. Hindutva or the RSS training evoked the state as the God of society, organizational skill, asceticism, a cultural embedding of ideas, a sense of competence as machismo, a clear idea of history. Modi presented himself as the Vivekananda in politics.

The chameleon in him could transform Hindutva into a more neutral but aggressive technocratic idiom. Management became a form of masculinity and the idea of Hindutva conventionally seen as local or parochial now became globalized. Modi's Gujarat behaved like a city state, a combination of Singapore and Shanghai on a larger scale. What came to his aid was the language of the World Bank. Modi's expert handling of the earthquake was decisive. The World Bank transmuted its ideologies into methodologies of audit and standards, creating as it were a new kind of accountability. Modi was responsive to World Bank idioms and norms. The language suited him as he could preen himself with numbers.

The aura of accountability found its hyphen in the obsession with security. Security was the technocratic idiom of nationalists. Security was also the machismo that would fight terror. Gujarat's handling of terror was presented as exemplary. The brilliance of it was that security and accountability were positivist terms measured by tonnage or control. In Modi's thesaurus, they substituted for the ethics of responsibility. Responsibility is more encompassing in its philosophy, more inclusive in involving minorities. As a way of life, it involved dialogicity, an accommodating mentality, while security or accountability could be handled with forceps. They were distancing terms. If responsibility sounded soft, security was hard. It exuded power, control, and hierarchy. Gujarat was secure under Modi while Delhi was vulnerable to terror under an effete Congress. Technology needs cosmopolitanism which Modi's presence in Davos as the only Indian chief minister provided.

Sreekumar, the ex-Inspector General of Police who is an acute observer of Modi, is full of insightful nuggets into the craft and craftiness of the man. He said, 'For all his Hindutva, Modi has become a devotee to power. Power is his only idol. Power secularises Modi by instrumentalising him. Modi will have no problem attacking Hindus to retain control.' In fact, Sreekumar claimed that Modi's 'secularism' can be double-edged. Modi, he said, demolished 600 temples to clear road obstructions in Ahmedabad. The message was clear. It was not that he was secular but that he was in control. The act could also be used secondarily to show how Modi can control Hindus when they get out of line. Modi began playing the Lee Kwan Yew of Gujarat emphasizing that all problems could be dealt with at a single window – Modi.

The myth of efficiency epitomised as security and stability needed investments as a continuing barometer of success. Modi played the self-styled magnet for investments. In this new age of liberalisation, investments are manna, the gift, the grace all tyrants are looking for. Investments are more powerful than riots in silencing critics. Gujarat was soon to become the Camelot of investments and its centre was Sanand. Modi created a dreamland for the automobile industry, successfully inviting Ford, Tata, Maruti and contouring this hub with a stunning array of ancillary industries which could add to employment. Modi's message to the corporations was clear and Ratan Tata was among the first to sense it when he said, 'It would be stupid not to be in Gujarat at this stage.' Modi had become Gujarat's best political salesman and his clients were the corporations and the diaspora. He played or enacted his vision of shining Gujarat impressing diasporic Indians, starved and nostalgic for efficiency and decisiveness. For them, as for *Time* magazine later, here was an Indian who could stand up to the Chinese. This was a helpful aura to have especially with the US government. Modi's tactics were not taking place in a vacuum. The chief minister is a very tactical man and his initial tactics differentiated between opposition and dissent. The Congress, as the opposition, willingly or inadvertently had tied itself into knots, raising issues which it could not follow up. He sensed that the Congress was afraid of opposing him nationally, afraid to lose the Hindu vote. The Congress opposition in

Gujarat was reduced to sniping with little effect. Modi discovered that it was dissent, not opposition, that was devastating. Small pockets of activists created little colonies of resistance that was effective. For example, Teesta Setalvad and her team created a memorial for the survivors at Gulberg House, the housing colony where the Congress MP, Ehsaan Jaffri and 69 others, were brutally murdered. The event at Gulberg House was not organized or instigated by any party. A loose network of citizens put it together. The impact was stunning. Over 2500 people came and spent the day in a quiet act of solidarity. Shubha Mudgal sang powerfully, creating a circle of emotion, with the survivors in tears. Modi understood that it was this form of protest that most threatened him and as part of his new repertoire he chose to suppress dissent in the academe. A senior professor at DAIICT, Gandhinagar, was asked to resign. What one is now witnessing is Modi's effort to take control of key national institutions like CEPT and the Indian Institute of Management. The report by *Time* was publicised and translated into Gujarati to submerge such dissent. He has been successful, temporarily, in part because many academics see in the future Modi a career to be pursued. Modi is shrewd enough to anticipate that even if Gujarat becomes an intellectual corridor, dissent is one epidemic he cannot afford.

Modi's effort to mobilise film stars like Anupam Kher, Sunil Shetty, Ajay Devgan, and Amitabh Bachchan is an attempt to create a groundswell of cinematic support for the regime. The use of Visvanathan Anand to announce and inaugurate Gujarat as a major chess culture is another powerful example. To combat dissent, Modi has created a brains trust of advisors, including corporate dons like Narayana Murthy and Azim Premji, giving him legitimacy in entrepreneurial and managerial circles. IIM Ahmedabad's decision to invite him as CEO for the day is one more example of academic institutes falling in line. He nurtured a bureaucracy that is only a prosthetic extension of him.

The tactical brilliance of Modi lies in his ability to use law to thwart justice and employ democratic ideals to perpetrate his control. The politicians who tout the importance of democracy at the federal level are reluctant to allow democracy at the state level. Modi's contempt for his own partymen is projected as part of his honesty, his refusal to recognise party politics as a spoils system. In fact, distance becomes tactical. Initially, Modi was presented as a politician almost tactilely in touch with the masses. Now he is presented as a hoarding, a larger-than-life creature to be quoted, cited, his every act a policy event.

It is Modi's use of the law, however, that appears most cynical. The Nanavati Commission continues happily creating an archive that means little. The SIT, behaving technically and narrowly, gave him a clean chit. He seemed to enjoy all the moral luck till the

Ramachandran Report queered his pitch. But the pseudo trial by commission and committee sanitized a space around him, blurring basic ethical questions. What it conflated specifically was the difference between guilt and responsibility. Assume that the CM had no direct role in the riots, yet was he right in disowning responsibility for the victims of the riots? Gujarat was the first example of a state government in India which refused responsibility for the aftermath of the riots, disowning any connection with the refugee camps that mushroomed after the carnage. The argument was that to accept responsibility for the camps was to signal a guilt about the riots. With one bad syllogism, a huge sector of victims were declared less than citizens and forced into subhuman lives in transit camps. Ten years after the riots, transit camps have acquired an air of permanence while everything within is ramshackle. Yet, Modi denies the camps exist or claims that they have shut down. Their very names, Ekta Nagar and Citizen Nagar, provide an ironic note to the ethical presence of the regime.

Yet viewed objectively there is a shrewdness to this tactic. Modi has injected the idea of development as a credo deep into the middle class. For them and him, development is a process that cannot wait, that has an inevitability to it, that is Darwinian in that the fittest survive. The Modi credo then suggests that those who act tangential to or are recalcitrant about development are reluctant citizens. The idea of development creates a double demand on ethnics, marginals, minorities. It throws them two specific challenges. First, it asks them to de-ghettoise and de-ethnicise themselves and erase, if necessary, identity and memory. It asks them to forget the riots, plainly stating why wait for justice when we are offering you development. It argues that development can be more distributive than justice can. The catch is that they must become citizens and citizenship is defined as joining the mainstream. Here Modi's discourse also suggests that minorities have hidden behind their ethnicity and behave like reluctant citizens. He claims that his is the 'true' secular option. He seems to suggest that the majoritarian electoral democracy of Congress plays to religious sentiments, while the BJP's offer of development is an invitation to secular citizenship. With this, Modi acts as if he has claimed the higher moral ground.

Many Muslims find this suggestion tempting. They realise that they need to join the mainstream but they also sense the craftiness of the Modi option. He is asking them to abandon memory and justice, to forget, erase and accept entry into development, yet realizing that development too might be a zero-sum game. They sense that the new urbanisation in the aftermath of the riots may disempower them further. Many Muslim women had an answer for Modi. They (in a composite sense) said, 'We want to go on but this society won't let us. We do not want our children to carry the burden of violence. We want to forget the past; they want us to erase it. Yet, they will not let us return to our livelihoods.' The politics of memory has become a millstone around the Modi neck and the many commissions have not sanitised him completely.

Politicians are word splitters and consequently world splitters. Muslims like J. S. Bandukwala, a civil rights activist and retired professor of physics from Baroda, talked of apology and forgiveness as rituals of healing. For Modi, power which apologises is no longer power. He lacks the wisdom and empathy of a Willy Brandt who knelt and asked for forgiveness of the victims of the Holocaust. Brandt rose in stature after the act but a Modi, afraid of the label of guilt, is unable to imitate him. But politicians can create parallel worlds which mimic the authenticity of the real. Modi lacks the courage to ask for forgiveness. He feels no empathy for Muslims. They remain a problem to be solved. Instead of forgiveness, Modi chose magnanimity. Magnanimity is imperial; it evokes the height and distance of power. Modi's *Sadbhavana Yatra* was an act of piety. Inaugurated on his birthday, where he received a *Ramcharit Manas* from his mother, the rituals felt like a *darbar.* The signal to the outside world was that Modi was a changed man. Yet, the message inside Gujarat was different. Minority groups came like subjects to swear fealty to a lord. Attendance was a performance to be noted. There was no sense of community; the entire drama spoke of power speaking to vulnerability. What betrayed Modi was his body language. When a Muslim cleric offered his cap, Modi shrugged. There was a sense that he was not speaking from his heart. One could sense a politician waiting to be prime minister.

The viewer by now realises that Modi was on a double stage, a CM fighting to be elected and waiting to be proclaimed a prime-ministerial candidate. Such was Modi's confidence that even Lal Krishna Advani, Nitin Gadkari and Sanjay Joshi, stalwarts from the RSS, surrendered the stage to him. Modi's autocracy, however, created an interesting shift in messages. Earlier, as a pracharak and a chief minister, the BJP was the text of his messages. Given his distance from internal party democracy, the party began appearing as a context for politics slowly withering to a pretext.

Yet, evil for all its flaws is more inventive. Modi, like the devil in *Paradise Lost*, still has the best lines. More critically, Modi is consolidating power beyond electoral rhetoric. His unease with his party and with his communal image nudges him towards a new discourse, one which make one want to reread the past. Modi seems to have rewritten the scripts of modernization. His modernization no longer seeks the scapegoat in the Muslim; it sees its power in the collective force of the city. Now riots appear to be a clearing house of a project called the city. The fascist as modernizer has found a new symbolic project, the city.

Gujarat has always been the most urbanised part of India with at least 57 major towns. Modi is building on it a new wave of urbanization. Modi articulates the fact that urbanization is both process and a promise. As a process, there is logic to its demands which necessitates certain decisions. Instant cities unlike instant coffee are complex entities. Yet, Modi grasps the fact that cities are a coalition of opportunities. The city caters to a middle class, to corporations hungry for land, to a network of fixers who create opportunities around a city. Each act of Modi invokes a corporation and urbanises Gujarat. Modi has allied himself with a newly emerging entrepreneurs like Adani and Mittal, with the pharmaceutical industries, and with Nirma, while tying up with the Tatas. He has offered the Japanese, always hungry for land abroad, two cities for development. He has hypothecated the coastline to the corporations like the Adanis, whose control of pipelines and ports make them a formidable force. Corporations desperate for land find him amenable.

The middle class seeing in investment the prospect of employment is content. Modi has become the new urban hero. Yet, one senses an unease about these new cities. One wonders if they are a kind of enclosure movement, a new way to displace nomadic and pastoral populations as ways of life. Gujarat has long been the home of these great nomadic and pastoral civilizations. The speed of Modi's policies of urbanisation makes one wonder whether marginals and minorities are doomed in this feat of citizenship we call the city. The *swadeshi pracharak* has transformed himself into a development hero with the city as his script. Modi as a development statesman now projects messages at three levels. Locally he is a BJP CM; nationally, he is a future hopeful for the prime ministership; globally, he is a player articulating the rhetoric of climate change. His idiom and his style are now completely different.

There is also a struggle for a symbolic domain, some claim to a myth or legend of India. In some ways the idea of class now lacks the appeal and Naxalbari, the romance of revolution. The Congress also realises that its narratives of Nehruism and nation-building ring hollow. As a symbolic entrepreneur, Modi senses it. He realises that he cannot cite Savarkar or Hedgewar. They make for poor mnemonics, lacking any real appeal for the new generation. Modi needs a floating signifier, something all India can claim and he can claim in a particular way. The choice of Vivekananda appears immaculate. Unlike Ramakrishna, he is not the mystic. He is an outward looking, organisation centred religious monk who built an institution. By juxtaposing himself to Vivekananda, Modi becomes a cultural innovator, seeking to revitalise society to face the next wave of modernity. His is not a spiritual pulpit; he is at heart a propagandist. He unleashes thousands of plastic balls with Vivekananda quotes to bounce around a society's mind.

What does Modi's performance teach one about electoral democracy in India. Modi embodies a paradigm of violence forged out of resentment with history. His *swadeshism*, tinged with the folklore of a Bhagat Singh, sees the state as a masculine trope and the administrator as a decisive person. It is a denial of softness as a part of duty and a summons to violence as a part of patriarchal responsibility. Like many in the Hindu majority, he senses an effeteness about politics and democracy, a minoritarian bias that vitiates power. In seeking to create a strong India, it emphasises efficiency, security and decisiveness.

The emphasis is more on duty. Minorities in this discourse have a duty to join the mainstream and respect majority sentiments. Violence or a threat of violence becomes an administrative tactic to keep them in line, to create order. Such a sense of order is uneasy with difference and is often punitive about imagined disorder. The body language is patriarchal, more used to dictates than discussions. The dream is of the motherland, but as fathers see it. A strong state, preferably nuclear because the nuclear commands respect; a strong leader because leadership is the leitmotif of democracy; a strong people, often cadre-like in action, who will help constitute a different India. Such a notion of order sees minorities, dissent, difference as sources of disorder. A minority that is reluctant needs to be disciplined in this model. A minority that emphasizes rights over duties is not ready for citizenship and is thus open to majoritarian violence as a pedagogical punitive exercise. In such a conception, minorities should episodically be taught a lesson to keep them in line. Such a notion sees the majority as a victim of democratic normativeness.

To many Modi represents a public policy hero, a Hindu Bismarck as a technocrat. Modi has consistently been ranked as the most able chief minister by *India Today*. As an administrator, he shows an impressive set of skills; as a politician he is adept at survival. Gujarat scores high in terms of electricity, investment, quality of roads. He is a cultural dream for Hindus tired of softness and gentleness who welcome his technocratic machismo.

The diaspora sees in him an almost American competence, a quickness and a decisiveness rarely witnessed in Indian politicians. But Modi is a Rorschach for these people. They project on to him the qualities they wish to have – economy, decisiveness, a patriarchal brusqueness, a modernity rooted in tradition but without succumbing to it. He is a creation emerging out of a subculture's deepest fears, hybridized with its sense of the correct response to these fears. If fear and resentment were the mother of invention, Modi as a cultural figure would be one product of such anxieties. A Vivekananda spouting manager, he seems an invention from some B grade commentary on the *Bhagvad Gita* speaking of security, nationalism and efficiency. He is a bully dressed up in managerial values and projected as the problem solver, an Indian answer to Chinese planning.

Modi realises that there is an economy to the waiting game. He does not have to do much. He can laugh at the antics of his opponents, create an occasional spectacle, to grab the front page. By simulating a PM in waiting, he is convincing people that he is going to be one. He is creating a self-fulfilling prophecy around himself. The press falls for it. *India Today* keeps saluting his powers of governance; *Outlook* creates the outlines of an unequal battle between him and Rahul Gandhi. This is pre-emptive politics and Modi plays it beautifully. As a politician he knows that he thrives on other people's and other party's mediocrity. It is not that he has an eloquent vision or an idea of India. He, however, guesses that an India without ideas is sure to vote him into power. Democracy, in this age of political mediocrity, will always pick the caricature of the lowest common denominator. Modi combines the worst of our anxieties with the most authoritarian of solutions. Authoritarianism like technocracy is a particular approach to problem solving. The charisma that fascism needs mixes with the pragmatism of technocracy to create a frame of thought as a way of life. Once a society accepts Modi as a mentality, a mode of thought, it might well have to live out its consequences over the next few decades. A friendly fascism can be a lethal mode of governance.

Finally, one must recognise the moral luck of the man. *Time* and Brookings go out of their way to give him good conduct certificates for governance. Corporations feel he is the flavour of the year. The one thing that rankled was the refusal of the British and US governments to give him a visa. In October 2012, the British government withdrew its objections, contending that the laws of the land had given Modi a clean chit. Britain, like other countries, realised that Modi was heaven-sent in terms of business investment and the prospect of investment silences conscience. The British, like many others, felt that here was a politician whose time has come. The ensuing hysteria made one wonder whether he had received an OBE. This luck is something we need to acknowledge. Demagogues love signs and the signs are that Modi is a politician ready for a bigger stage. The modernist as fascist breathes a legitimacy that electoral pundits love.

Courtesy: *Seminar*

# Emerging India ruled by fear

AMIT CHAUDHURI

October 2019

Four months have passed since Narendra Modi and the BJP came back to power in India, and more seems to have happened there than in the last 40 years. The sense of severance that many experience today, of being divorced from the workings of the nation, exceeds even the helplessness felt during the suspension of civil liberties in the emergency of 1975 to 1977 and the political traumas that followed. This is because – without the matter being explicitly articulated – citizen has been set against citizen: not just Muslim against Hindu or, say, Kashmiris against the rest of India, but those who subscribe to the BJP's new conception of the nation against those who do not, leaving one without trust in the other. Indian parties are only democrats when in opposition. But no government has been as punitive towards dissent as this.

How to judge these past four months? A series of disruptions has dwarfed the now distant seeming upset of Modi's economically disastrous demonetisation programme of 2016. In August there was the abrogation of article 370 of the Indian constitution, which granted "special status" to Kashmir in acknowledgment of its contested history. This was followed immediately by the "house arrest" of elected Kashmiri leaders and the imprisonment of thousands of others. What we saw was the attempt to take a difficult and divisive issue and place it to one side by an act of will, so that it requires no further discussion. There is the impression that not just the Kashmiris' but all our fates are now being decided for us. Home Minister, Amit Shah, would have us believe that the "restrictions'" in Kashmir are all in the mind. I asked a Kashmiri how she interpreted this. She speculated that what was being implied was that the lack of protest in Kashmir was equal to normalcy. But a lack of protest in a democratic country is strange, and a sustained lack of protest alarming. Is this the normalcy that Indians wish to be bestowed on them by their government?

Then there is spectacle of a different sort: of the Government borrowing an unprecedented sum of money from the Reserve Bank of India; of it failing to pay the Central Reserve Police Force; of the economy tanking, of Modi pronouncing that India is in the ascendant. We live simultaneously in disparate realities: a "normal" Kashmir, an abnormal country; a bankrupt economy; a rising India – competing scripts, none of which acknowledge the existence of the other, as distant as countryman has grown to countryman. If asked what this government's one great recent achievement is, some people might draw attention to the number of toilets built in a country with poor sanitation. Others, whose experience of the new India is different, would say that its greatest success has been in creating a climate of fear. Therefore, dissent has a purer form now. It's no longer, as it was once, preaching to the converted. It's not even the pointing out of unpleasant facts. It's simply a demonstration that dissent continues to be possible.

India has not, outside of Indira Gandhi's declaration of emergency, been in this place before, and certainly not with the degree of popular support we see now, which can only be characterised as a form of inebriation. The judiciary, the police and other law enforcement agencies are all seen, rightly or wrongly, to "belong" to the government, and many high-profile lawbreakers seem to be those who, coincidentally, disagree with the BJP. The number of cases of "sedition", a charge left over from colonial India, has risen dramatically. Of course, the erosion of institutional independence didn't happen overnight. Over the last 30 years all governments in India, state and central, have had limited respect for civil liberties and democracy: Indian parties are only fervent democrats when they're in opposition. But no government has been as openly and robustly punitive towards dissent as this one.

Could this ferocious and successful discouragement of dissent herald the *achhe din* ("good times") Modi has advertised to Indian voters at his rallies? A dissent-free country is a "normal" country; a dissent-free political environment constitutes a "good time" for its rulers. I have first-hand experience of this. I signed a letter of protest addressed to the prime minister, drawing attention to increased religious violence. My co-signatories were 48 of India's most eminent film-makers, academics, activists, artists and writers. In response to a petition in Muzaffarpur, Bihar, a court has now asked the police to open a case against us.

Then there's the National Register of Citizens (NRC), a central government-backed project in the state of Assam aimed at uncovering and expelling "foreigners" (that is, Muslim refugees from Bangladesh who don't have the relevant documents, though the reality has turned out to be far messier, and the majority of those now deemed "foreigners" have turned out to be Hindus). Many are threatened with being uprooted, and others in the region are being asked to help uproot their neighbours. These extraordinary developments got me thinking about ethnicity and citizenship. About the trajectory of Indians in the 20th century: of Gandhi's relocation to England and then to South Africa, where, made conscious of his race and colour, he first moved towards politics; of Sikhs settling *en masse* in Canada after murderous violence against them in 1984; of Bengalis departing a declining Kolkata in the 70s. Indians are a many-sided people: entrepreneurial, curious, cultured, open-minded, adventurous. They have great writers, scientists, businessmen; they have Gandhi. They're also great migrants: they've gone to and worked and settled in every part of the world. They know the pain of discrimination and upheaval intimately. In this context, the fraught rhetoric surrounding the NRC, where "illegal migrant" is time and again conflated with "Muslim", and "Muslim" with "foreigner", shows a disconnect between what Indians have historically known, felt and achieved as migrants, despite hostility and opposition, and how, at home, they perceive those they suddenly decide are the "other".

It's odd that our past hasn't given us a more immediate sense of the value and inevitability of plurality, of accommodating difference. Instead, many of us have refashioned ourselves as north Indian Brahmin manqués, wanting Hindi as the official national language, wanting to be what we're not, wanting our nation to be what it can't be. Only a determined abstention from self-inquiry could have got us here. Rather than accepting an India where lack of dissent is expected, it is time to look inward: to recollect the journeys we've made and assess whether we've ended up where we wanted to be.

Courtesy: The Guardian

# A Community Besieged

RAM PUNIYANI

A more comprehensive plan could not have been drawn up for a multi-pronged attack on a community. Muslims are targeted by the state with new laws used as weapons. They are victimised by a biased police and bureaucracy and by a section of the judiciary. They are attacked by the Hindutva warriors. Social media is suffused with hate speech against them. Their homes. shops and places of worship can be endangered anytime. Calls are given for their economic boycott. And generally, every section of the Muslim community faces suspicion, hate and antipathy because the Hindu psyche has been *en masse* starved of the oxygen of reason by the toxic communal atmosphere. Observe the array of weapons massed against one community by individuals, institutions and the State. This article gives just three examples -- the passage of a Bill to regulate the Waqf properties of Muslims, falsification of history and the use of hate speech to demonise the community and target its places of worship. One hears the anguished mutter from an average helpless Muslim, "What to do?"

The Modi Government, amid much controversy and protests by some opposition leaders and the Muslim community, got the Waqf amendment bill passed.

Rahul Gandhi, Leader of Opposition, stated that after this the religious properties of other communities will be targeted. He was on the dot as immediately after the passage of the Bill, the RSS mouthpiece *Organiser* published an article about the property of the Catholic Church. Though it immediately withdrew the article, the message was loud and clear.

One Jharkhand minister expressed her anguish that in a similar way the RSS-BJP will target the Adivasi properties. During the debate on the bill the non-BJP NDA allies like Nitish Kumar, Chandrababu Naidu, Chirag Paswan and Jayant Chowdhary also fell in line with the BJP and betrayed the Muslim community. Had they any principles of pluralism they could very well stopped the bill from passing? As Pastor Martin Noemollers classic anguish shows the methods of Fascists is to target one group at a time with the help of others and then by and by crush other communities. The Catholic Bishops enthusiastically supported the Waqf Amendment Bill, and they may be the next target. They are infested by Islamophobia and so in a short-sighted manner support communalism.

Waqf is a property donated by Muslims (even others can donate) for religious purposes. India has vast property which comes under this provision. While claims are that Waqf is the third largest property owner in the country but as such, Hindu trusts and temples have much more property. The amendments in the Waqf bill are totally dictated by the Hindu nationalist agenda to diminish the control of Muslims in the Waqf Board. The control of Hindu temples and trusts are exclusively in the hands of Hindus. Now Waqf, in contrast, will have non-Muslims on the Board and the district collector will be the main authority in issues related to ownership of the property. The contrast between the ownership of Hindu trusts and Waqf is partisan and the Government is determined to undermine the authority of Muslims in these matters.

The minority minister Kiran Rijuju said the bill is aimed at improving the condition of poor Muslims. Waqf as such is for religious and social purposes. Poverty alleviation is the job of the Government but its policies serve the corporate interests. And if his logic is correct why not begin with the majority Hindu community? Our Hindu temples and trusts have astronomical wealth which can nurture many educational institutions, health facilities and support employment generation. Why is this Government, guided by RSS agenda of Hindu nation, not undertaking the task of ensuring that temple trust properties are used to help poor farmers, unemployed youth, and other marginalized sections of society?

Thousands of Muslims organizations registered their opposition to this Amendment which the BJP imposed on the country to reduce the power of Muslim community. Muslims have been the worst victims of BJP Government. They are beaten for offering Namaz on roads, targeted for eating beef, boycotted on the pretext of Corona Jihad, or spitting jihad among others. Despite instructions by the Supreme Court the states are using bulldozers against Muslim properties. The Waqf Amendment Bill totally violates the Indian Constitution in letter and spirit.

This was direct action by the State which has been intimidating Muslims and regulating their affairs in different ways by taking recourse to several indirect methods. At its bidding, history is distorted to demolish mosques and demonise Muslim. Films were the medium through which inter-faith harmony was promoted and progressive messages were conveyed to the public. Now sponsored films have become a major medium for spreading communal hatred. *Kerala Story* and *Kashmir files* succeeded in this mission. There have been other not so successful films like *Swatantraveer Savarkar, 72 Hurain, Samrat Prithviraj,* to name a few. Now a film called *Chhava*, is running to packed houses, especially in Maharashtra. This is not a historical film. It is based on the novel *Chhava* by Shivaji Samant. Already the filmmakers had to apologise for inaccuracies in the film. It selectively picks up a few incidents from Chhatrapati Sambhaji Maharaj's life and projects the cruel and anti-Hindu nature of Aurangzeb. In the 126-minute film; good 40 minutes are devoted to the torture of Sambahji Maharaj. The filmmaker may have taken lot of liberties in this part. The narrative presents noble Hindu Kings versus the evil Muslim kings. Sambhaji Maharaj was the eldest son of Chhatrapati Shivaji Maharaj. As

Shivaji set up his kingdom, he had his officers who were Muslims also. Maulana Haider Ali was his confidential secretary and there were 12 Generals in his army who were Muslims, Siddi Sambal, Ibrahim Gardi, and Daulat Khan to name the few. When he confronted Afzal Khan, he was advised to carry iron claws, which were given to him by his subordinate Rutom-e-Jamaan. After killing Afzal Khan, the latter's secretary Krishnanji Bhaskar Kulkarni tried to attack Shivaji. From Aurangzeb's side Raja Jaisingh led the army to attack Shivaji. Shivaji was made to appear in Aurangzeb's Court and later imprisoned. The person who helped him escape was a Muslim Prince, Madari Mehtar. The Hindutva progenitors Savarkar and Golwalkar, raise questions about Sambhaji's character, wine and women. For this he was imprisoned by Shivaji in Panhala Forte. Later Sambhaji did ally with Aurangzeb in his battle against Shivaji. Sambhaji also allied with Aurangzeb in his battle against Adilshah of Bijapur. In the battle of succession after Shivaji, Sambhaji's stepbrother Rajaram (son of Shivaji's another wife Soyrabai) tried to poison him. As the conspiracy was unearthed Sambhaji got many Hindu officers killed. In the battle against Sambhaji, Aurangzeb had sent his general Rathod to fight against him. Once Sambhaji was captured he was humiliated and subjected to torture, which has been presented in a blown-up version.

Aurangzeb is shown to be very cruel. It is ignored that many Kings inflicted cruelty on enemies with gay abandon. Historian Ruchika Sharma tells us that when Chola Kings defeated Chalukya's army, they beheaded Chalukya's General Samudraraj and cut the nose of his beautiful daughter. Ashok's Kalinga battle is known for the worst type of brutalities. The ways of Kings against their enemies was atrocious and cannot be judged by today's standards. As such what will we say when bulldozers raze to ground the houses of those who happen to be Muslims for the crimes not tried in Court of law? What will we say that one Hindu king had a fort on the top of a hill, where those conspiring against the King were thrown deep down into the valley with his feet and hands tied? Bal Samant in his book describes the atrocities done by Shivaji's army while plundering Surat. Army and atrocities were closely associated; cruelty against enemies is condemnable but was not unusual. When Sambhaji's Marathas attacked Goa, a Portuguese account (cited by historian Jadunath Sarkar) says, "up to now nowhere else in India has such barbarity been seen..." While such atrocity narratives must be treated carefully, what it shows is that violence was pervasive, even if its degrees varied.

Was Aurangzeb anti-Hindu? One can say that Aurangzeb was neither Akbar nor Dara Shikoh. He was orthodox and did not welcome Hindus and non-Sunni sects of Islam at one level. At another level, he was the master of alliances and had a number Hindu officers in his administration. As Prof. Athar Ali points out, Aurangzeb had the highest number of officers in his administration (33 per cent.). He destroyed some temples but he also gave donations to many temples, including Kamakhya Devi (Guwahati) Mahakaleshar (Ujjain) Chitrkut Balaji and Lord Krishna in Vrindavan. Even Shivaji used to give donations to a Sufi dargah of Hazrat baba Bahut Thorwale. To humiliate the enemy, the victorious king used to destroy the particular place of worship associated with that king --Richard Eaton (*Frontline* December-January 1996). The communal historians selectively pick up temple destruction by Muslim kings, hiding the donations given for Hindu temples by the Muslim kings. Aurangzeb did impose Jazia after 22 years of his rule; but Brahmins, disabled and women were exempted. It was not a means of conversion as it was a property like tax and was 1.25% while Zakat which was paid by Muslims was 2.5%. The torture of the Sikh Gurus was wrong, but the underlying reason was the power struggle between the Sikh Gurus and Mughal Administration.

The communal historians pick up the incidents without referring to the overall context of the period of the kingdoms. Kings used religion to inspire their armies to fight the enemy. Hindu Rajas used *Dharmayuddh* and Muslim kings used Jihad. These right-wing historians' communal narrative sees kings in the light of their religion and not as kings seeking power and wealth. Religion was incidental in their goal of expansion of their kingdoms.

Demonisation of a minority has become the favourite activity of the RSS-BJP and its affiliates. Despite legal provisions, no one is punished for hate speech. In the past decade, with a communal party in power, negative perception of religious minorities has grown. As reflected in the community WhatsApp groups and social attitudes, hating minorities has become a sort of normal discourse among large sections of society. Sectarianism and the politics of religious identity are playing havoc. What is aggressively propagated is not true. The truth is lost in the din of hysteria created by politics in the name of religion.

Perceptions like Mughal kings were outsiders and wrought injustices to Hindus, they were temple destroyers, they imposed Islam by force have rapidly been added on to slogans like, '*Hum Do Hamare do, who Panch unke Pacchis*', (We [Hindus] are two, and they [Muslims] are 25). The refugee camps housing victimized Muslims were called 'child production factories'. They are killers of our Holy mother - the cow, they are luring our women through 'love jihad'. Now there is a 'jihad' series, the latest being 'land jihad' and 'vote jihad'. There was even 'corona jihad'. A Hindu Baba who runs a mega business in consumer products, condemns a rival product manufactured by a company run by a Muslim organisation. He calls it syrup jihad and warns people against consuming that syrup. The dog whistle politics has increased divisiveness. Prime Minister Modi said in a speech that some people can be recognised by their clothes. As per the Human Rights Watch, Modi made 110 hate speeches during the 2024 poll campaign. The report says, "Modi made Islamophobic remarks intended to undermine the political opposition, which he said promoted Muslim rights, and to foster fear among the majority Hindu community through disinformation." The BJP leaders incited discrimination, hostility, and violence against marginalized groups during his campaign to win his third consecutive term of office. Several BJP state governments demolished Muslims' homes, businesses, and places of worship without due process and carried out other unlawful practices, which have continued since the election. These demolitions are often carried out as apparent collective punishment against the Muslim community for communal clashes or dissent, and BJP officials dub them "bulldozer justice", the report said.

Following the outbreak of the Covid-19 pandemic in 2020, Indian authorities contributed to a surge in anti-Muslim hate speech and violence. They announced that many coronavirus cases were found among the Muslims who had attended a mass religious congregation in Delhi. Some BJP leaders called the meeting a 'Talibani crime' and 'Corona terrorism', and some used the term 'Corona jihad', with the hashtag going viral on social media. Soon, social media and WhatsApp groups were flooded by calls for social and economic boycott of Muslims. There were numerous physical attacks on Muslims, including volunteers distributing relief material. They were accused of spreading the virus deliberately, the Human Rights Watch noted.

The reservation for Muslims is called "appeasement". Prime Minister Modi said it is a part of despicable attempts to Islamise India and to push it towards divisions. He blamed the UPA Government. The Justice Verma committee report and the Sachar Committee report were called attempts by the Congress to loot the reservation of OBCs, SCs and STs. The Assembly elections in Jharkhand and Maharashtra saw the peak of such a mischievous campaign. In Jharkhand, Assam Chief Minister Himanta Biswas Sarma of the BJP focused on "Muslim infiltrators" in the state. The BJP issued a demeaning advertisement, showing a large Muslim family invading a Hindu household and taking it over. For a change, the Election Commission got the advertisement pulled down. It was said that Muslims marry the Adivasi women and take over the Adivasi land. The slogan given was that the Muslim infiltrators were taking away your *'Roti, Beti, Mati'* (Livelihood, Daughter, Land). This statement came from the Prime Minister of the country! The core slogan came from Uttar Pradesh Chief Minister Yogi Adityanath of BJP. *'Batenge to Katenge'*... (If we are divided, we will be butchered). He called for Hindu unity. Backing him up, Dattatray

Hosabale of the RSS said when Hindus are united, it will be beneficial for all.

Modifying on Yogi's *'Batenge to Katenge'* slogan, Modi came up with *'Ek hain to safe hain'* (If Hindus are united, they will be safe) putting forward that the Hindu unity will keep them safe from apparently the minorities, because of whom *'Hindu khatre mein hai'* (Hindus are in danger). The impact of this was visible not only on polarisation and thereby the voting pattern, but also on social perceptions, as reflected in thousands of WhatsApp groups and drawing room chats in the Hindu households. Christophe Jaffrelot, the scholar focusing on the rise of Hindu nationalism, quotes from a study conducted by CSDS (Centre for Study of Developing Societies) from March 28 to April 2024 showing negative perceptions in society. The spiral of hate is worsening by the day. It is leading to ghettoisation and pushing the Muslim community toward 'second class citizenship'. Two recent books chart the intensity and increase in communal violence and hatred since 2014, particularly during religious yatras. The communal historiography, looking at history through the prism of religion of the ruler, introduced by the British, led to the emergence of narratives forming the base for various communal streams, Muslim, and Hindu. These streams devised their own mechanisms to create a 'social common sense' and instigate religious violence in the communities. Now one needs to study the newer ways to communalise the majority community and initiating violence. A dogged journalist, Kunal Purohit, in a path-breaking book, *H-Pop- Inside the Secretive World of Hindutva Popstars,* brings to our notice how popular culture is being shaped by songs that are spreading hatred against the heroes of the national movement, such as Gandhi, Nehru and against Muslims. He warns us that Hindutva pop stars are adding intense hatred, particularly in north India.

Another important book is *Weaponization of Hindu Festivals,* by Irfan Engineer and Neha Dabhade. In the wake of the violence being orchestrated during Hindu festivals, particularly Ram Navami, the authors focus on how festival celebrations have been made aggressive towards Muslim. Hindu festivals used to be celebrated not only in the Mughal courts but were jointly celebrated with Muslims. Here is an in-depth inquiry into the violence instigated by religious during festivals, Ram Navami in 2022-2023. The violence covered in the book relates to Howrah and Hooghly (2023), Sambahji Nagar (2023), Vadodara (2023), Biharsharif and Sasaram 2023, Khargone (2022), Himmat Nagar and Khambat (2022) and Lohardagga (2022). Irfan Engineer, in the introduction, points out, "Even a small Group of Hindu nationalists could insist on passing through minority inhabited area and provoke some youth using political and abusive slogans and playing violent songs and music, hoping that a stone would be thrown at them. The state would do the rest by arresting many members of the minority and demolishing their homes and properties without any judicial procedure." The well-armed processions deliberately pass through the Muslim majority areas. It has become a pattern that someone will climb over the mosque, replace the green flag with a saffron flag and the crowds down below will dance and applaud. The Khargone incident is revealing. A minster of the Madhya Pradesh Government said stones were thrown on the procession from Muslim households, so these households are to be turned into stones. These hooligans feel that 'it is their Government' as the popular phrase says, "*Sainya Bhaye Kotwal to dar kahe ka*" (If your husband is chief police officer, why be afraid of anything). Religious processions, *Ganga Aarti,* (prayer for river Ganges), *satsangs* (religious meetings) and other religious programmes are being started with similar goals. The *Kanwad Yatra* (the holy pilgrimage to collect Ganges water and to be offered to Lord Shiva) participants always become aggressive. The U.P. and Uttarakhand governments (both BJP-ruled) issued orders that all stalls and eateries on the path of the *Kanwad Yatra* should display the name of the owner so that the *Kanwadiyas* (participants in the pilgrimage) can avoid those owned by Muslims. Fortunately, the Supreme Court put a stay on the orders.

False history is used to instil sectarian hate. The Supreme Court declared the demolition of the Babri mosque was a crime. It acknowledged that there was no evidence of a temple below the mosque. An article in *Sabrang* says, "A top-notch archaeologist, Prof. Supriya Varma, who served as an observer during the excavation of the Babri Masjid site in early 2000s along with another archaeologist, Jaya Menon, stated that not only was there "no temple under the Babri Masjid," if one goes "beyond" the 12th century to 4th to 6th century, i.e., the Gupta period, "there seems to be a Buddhist stupa." Numerous reasons have been given for destroying temples, plundering wealth, and humiliating rival kings being the chief of them. If we go a bit back in history, the primary cause of the destruction of Buddhist Viharas was religion. Swami Vivekananda said, "The temple of Jagannath is an old Buddhist temple. We took this and others over and re-Hinduised them...". Swami Dayanand Saraswati, while describing the contribution of Shankaracharya in his tome, *Satyarth Prakash* wrote: "For ten years he toured all over the country, refuted Jainism and advocated the Vedic religion. All the broken images that are now-a-days dug out of the earth were broken in the time of Shankar, whilst those that are found whole here and there under the ground had been buried by the Jains for fear of their being broken."

According to the Buddhist narrative of ancient Indian history, the last of the Maurya dynasty's Buddhist king (Ashoka being one), Brihadratha, was assassinated by Pushyamitra Shunga, a Brahmin, in 184 BCE, thus ending the rule of a renowned Buddhist dynasty and establishing the rule of Shunga dynasty. D N Jha, an outstanding ancient Indian historian, referred to Divyavadana, a Buddhist Sanskrit work describing how Buddhist and Jain religious places were destroyed by Pushyamitra Shunga. "He is said to have marched with an army, destroying stupas, burning monasteries and killing monks as far as Sakala, now known as Sialkot, where he announced a prize of 100 dinars for every head of a Shramana (opposed to Vedas)." Jha says Mathura, a flourishing town in western Uttar Pradesh during the Kushana period, had some present-day Brahminical temples, such as Bhuteshwar and Gokarneshwar, which were Buddhist sites in the ancient period. The British policy of 'divide and rule,' promoted communal historiography. The kings are presented as representatives of their religion. The focus is mainly on the medieval period when many Muslim kings ruled. During this period, many temples were plundered, and many others were demolished to humiliate the defeated kings. Raja Harshdev appointed an officer (Devottapatan Nayak) to plunder the wealth of temples (Kalhan's *Rajtarangini*). Maratha kings destroyed a temple in Seringapatam. Religion had very little role to play, unlike in the post-Mauryan Period when Buddhist Viharas were targeted with an aim to root out Buddhism.

At the time of the demolition of the Babri mosque, the mob shouted, *Yeh to kewal jhanki hai, Kashi Mathura baaki hai* (This is just the beginning; Kashi and Mathura will be next). Sambhal Mosque! Ajmer Dargah! How far back can we go? A couple of years ago, the issue of Kashi and Mathura was brought to the fore for surveying despite the Places of Religious Worship Act 1991 being in place. Justice Chandrachud opened the floodgates by saying that the Act does not cover surveys and that Hindus have the right to know the ancestry of the place. This gave a big boost to the Hindutva activists. Currently, over 12 cases of surveys are pending in courts. Other issues like Kamaal Maula Mosque, Baba Budan Giri Dargah, Haji Malang Dargah and many more mosques are being pursued by Hindus. The Sambhal Jama Masjid and the centuries-old Ajmer Dargah are also being claimed by the Hindutva leaders.

Indian judiciary have opened the Pandora's Box, deepening religious divides in society. What is the need of the hour? To search for temples underneath every mosque? Or to build "Temples of Modern India," as Pandit Jawaharlal Nehru defined them as he flagged off the construction of the Bhakra Nangal Dam? The direction that India chooses will define its destiny.

# Letter to the Prime Minister calls for end to politics of hate

*Sensing the danger to the nation, some retired bureaucrats, diplomats and police officers formed the Constitutional Conduct Group. They have been writing open letters to express their anxiety about the growing sectarian hatred, break-down of law and order and erosion of civil liberties. Here is one of their letters:*

26 April 2022

Dear Prime Minister,

We are witnessing a frenzy of hate filled destruction in the country where at the sacrificial altar are not just Muslims and members of the other minority communities but the Constitution itself. As former civil servants, it is not normally our wont to express ourselves in such extreme terms, but the relentless pace at which the constitutional edifice created by our founding fathers is being destroyed compels us to speak out and express our anger and anguish.

The escalation of hate violence against the minority communities, particularly Muslims, in the last few years and months across several States – Assam, Delhi, Gujarat, Haryana, Karnataka, Madhya Pradesh, Uttar Pradesh and Uttarakhand, all states in which the Bharatiya Janata Party (BJP) is in power, barring Delhi (where the union government controls the police) – has acquired a frightening new dimension. It is no longer just the politics of an assertive Hindutva identity, nor the attempt to keep the communal cauldron on the boil – all that has been going for decades and in the last few years had become a part of the new normal. What is alarming now is the subordination of the fundamental principles of our Constitution and of the rule of law to the forces of majoritarianism, in which the state appears to be fully complicit.

The hate and malevolence directed against Muslims seems to have embedded itself deep in the recesses of the structures, institutions and processes of governance in the States in which the BJP is in power. The administration of law, instead of being an instrument for maintaining peace and harmony, has become how the minorities can be kept in a state of perpetual fear. Their constitutional right to practice their own faith, follow their own customs, dress code and personal laws and exercise their own food choices, is threatened not merely by letting vigilante mobs inflict violence on them with impunity but, by twisting the law itself, to circumscribe their freedom of choice and make it convenient for a prejudiced, communal executive to make colourable use of state power. State power is thus used not only to facilitate vigilante violence targeted against a community but to make ostensibly legal means available to the administration (anti-conversion laws, laws proscribing consumption of beef, encroachment removal, prescription of uniform codes in educational institutions) to strike fear in the community, deprive them of their livelihoods and make it evident to them that they have to accept their status as inferior citizens who have to subordinate themselves to majoritarian political power and majoritarian social and cultural norms. The likelihood of our becoming a country that systematically makes sections of its own citizens – minorities, Dalits, the poor and the marginalized – targets of hate and knowingly deprives them of their fundamental rights is now, more than ever, frighteningly real.

While we are not aware if the current spurt in communal frenzy is coordinated and directed by the political leadership, it is evident that the administration at the state and local levels provides a facilitating environment for mischievous lumpen groups to operate without fear. Such facilitation and support is not limited to that offered by the local police and other administrative officials; it appears to have the tacit approval of the highest political levels in the state and central governments, which provide the enabling policy and institutional environment for local level tyranny. While the actual commission of violence may be outsourced to fringe groups, there is little doubt as to how the ground for their operations is made fertile, how each of them follows a master script and shares a common 'tool kit' and how the propaganda machinery of a party as well as the state is made available to them to defend their actions. What distinguishes the incidents that are taking place now from earlier communal conflagrations is not merely that a master design is being unveiled to prepare the grounds for a Hindu Rashtra, but that the constitutional and legal framework designed to prevent such a development from taking place is itself being twisted and perverted to make it an instrument of majoritarian tyranny. No wonder then that the bulldozer has now become the new metaphor for the exercise of political and administrative power, literally and figuratively. The edifice built around the ideas of 'due process' and 'rule of law' stands demolished. As the Jahangirpuri incident shows, even the orders of the highest court of the land are treated with scant respect by the executive.

Prime Minister, we, the members of the Constitutional Conduct Group – all of us are former civil servants who have spent decades in the service of the Constitution – believe that the threat we are facing is unprecedented and at stake is not just constitutional morality and conduct; it is that the unique syncretic social fabric, which is our greatest civilizational inheritance and which our Constitution is so meticulously designed to conserve, is likely to be torn apart. Your silence, in the face of this enormous societal threat, is deafening.

We appeal to your conscience, taking heart from your promise of *Sabka Saath, Sabka Vikas, Sabka Vishwas.* It is our hope that in this year of '*Azadi Ka Amrit Mahotsav*', rising above partisan considerations,

you will call for an end to the politics of hate that governments under your party's control are so assiduously practising. The idea of India that our founding fathers had envisioned and fought for needs a climate of fraternity and communal harmony to thrive. Hate will engender hate, rendering the environment too noxious for the idea to survive.
SATYAMEVA JAYATE

Yours sincerely,

**Constitutional Conduct Group**
(108 signatories)

# Mock murder of Gandhi
# vivifies Godse

RAM PUNIYANI

The campaign to diminish Mahatma Gandhi's stature has been intensified during the last few years. On October 2nd, 2021, Mahatma Gandhi's birthday was "celebrated" by flooding social media with tweets, "*Nathuram Godse Amar Rahen*" (Long live Nathuram Godse), Nathuram Godse Zindabad (Hail Godse). It was the top twitter trend for the day. Twitter storms glorified a killer. Poonam Prasun Pandey enacted the "shooting" of Gandhi's effigy, with fake blood dripping from it. It shocked many. This trend was beyond the wildest imagination of the most. Now the communal right-wing projects Gandhi's flaws and diminishes his contribution to freedom. At times, one sees the drama of hating Gandhi and loving Godse.

Eric Hobswam famously stated that history is as important to nationalism (sectarianism) as poppy is to an opium addict. The right-wing ideologues are reconstructing history to suit their political agenda of glorification of their past and exclusion of the other. India's medieval history is mauled by showing that it was an era of Islamic imperialism and by projecting the

Muslim Kings in a bad light to direct hate against today's Muslims.

Even ancient Indian history, a golden period for them, is manipulated to show the Aryans, their ancestors, were the indigenous people of this land. Coming to the freedom movement, they targeted Nehru, the colossus who articulated and practiced secularism in India. He was aware that practicing secularism in India is not easy as large sections of Indian society are in the grip of blind religiosity. He was the one to see the threat of majoritarian (Hindu) communalism and equated it to fascism. He said minority communalism was at worst separatist. His mentor Gandhi, murdered by the one who was trained by RSS and was working for the Hindu Mahasabha, could not be demonised easily. Gandhi had a stature in the global arena and a place in the people's hearts.

This 30th January 2025, as the nation was paying tributes to the father of the nation, many portals were relaying videos to propagate that Gandhi's efforts had only a marginal effect on the British leaving India. National mourning on 30th January used to be observed by sounding a siren at 11 AM for two-minute silence. The siren has been muted. This year the Maharashtra state circular on two-minute silence at 11 AM, did not mention even the name of Gandhi. As we observed the Martyrdom Day, these irritants flashed before our eyes. Gandhi was given the honorific Mahatma by Guru Rabindranath Tagore. It is propagated that Gandhi-Congress ignored Netaji Subhash Chandra Bose. Bose and Congress had some differences on strategy but the core agenda of freedom from British rule was shared. It was Netaji who addressed Gandhi as the 'father of the Nation'. He named one of his battalions of Azad Hind Fauz (Free India Army) as Gandhi Battalion. It was Gandhi's Congress that fought the cases of prisoners of Fauz by forming a committee with top lawyers including Bhulabhai Desai, Kailashnath Katju and Jawaharlal Nehru.

Also, it is being propagated that Gandhi did not do anything to save Bhagat Singh's hanging. It was Gandhi who wrote to Lord Irwin to cancel Bhagat Singh's hanging. Irwin showed his inability to accept this request as all British officers in Punjab had threatened to resign if Gandhi's request was accepted. Most interestingly, Bhagat Singh requests his father Kishan Singh to support the 'General' of the Freedom movement (Gandhi), which his father did by working for the Congress.

The attempt to undermine Gandhi comes in the form of nit-picking the three major movements which Gandhi launched. The non-cooperation movement of 1920 which was the first real attempt to involve the average people in the struggle against the British. The critics say it was ineffective as it was withdrawn due to the Chauri Chaura incident, where the crowd had burnt the police station, killing many policemen. Also, they allege that Gandhi's support for Khilafat was demoralising, as it related to supporting the restoration of the Ottoman Empire in Turkey. It was this move which brought in Muslims in large numbers into the vortex of popular anti-British struggle. Also, Mappila (Moplah) rebellion is supposed to have been an aggressive move by Muslims against Hindus. This rebellion was a rebellion of poor Muslim farmers against the Janmis (Landlords, who were mostly Hindus), whose interests were protected by the British authorities.

As to the Civil disobedience of 1930, they say it just led to Gandhi–Irwin Pact. This pact was a major step in furtherance of the pressure by Indian freedom struggle. Then there is the accusation that the Salt March did not lead to the abolition of the salt tax which it had aimed at. The fact is people could produce salt after this and its illegality was lifted. As far as the 1942 'Do or Die' and 'British Quit India', it is true that as Gandhi and the major leaders of Congress were arrested; the movement did take a violent turn. But it created a huge awareness about getting freedom from the British, it came as a culmination of the long process of creating mass consciousness which began increasing after the 1920s Non-Cooperation Movement.

There is no denying that the revolutionaries, Bhagat Singh and his likes, Subhash Bose's Azad Hind Fauz, and revolt of Naval ratings, were valuable add-ons to the whole process of rising consciousness among the people towards longing for freedom. Gandhi's contribution is monumental as it created the fraternity, Indian-ness among the people. Surendranath Bannerjee very aptly described it as "India: Nation in the making".

The freedom movement had twin aspects. One was to struggle against the British and two to 'build a Nation: India' through this. Gandhi understood that bringing people together is the core of the process of getting freedom. The Right-wing communalists totally ignore the process of the masses waking up and constituting India as a nation. This was the greatest endeavour for which Gandhi is called the 'Father of the Nation'.

To keep the praise of Godse under wraps has been the tactic of the sectarian nationalists. The RSS, the supra political organization, steering the politics of Hindu nationalism can speak in many languages at the same time. With Modi coming to power in 2014, the Hindutva nationalists did not need to hide their celebration of Godse's act.

In the aftermath of Gandhi's murder, Sardar Patel, the then Home minster and the most ardent follower of Gandhi, in a letter wrote, "as regards the RSS and the Hindu Mahasabha... our reports do confirm that, as a result of the activities of these two bodies, particularly the former (RSS) an atmosphere was created in the country in which such a ghastly tragedy became possible."– Sardar Vallabhbhai Patel, India's first home minister, on the assassination of Gandhi, in a letter dated July 18, 1948 to Shyama Prasad Mukherjee. (Sardar Patel Correspondence, Volume 6, edited by Durga Das) The RSS claimed that Nathuram had left the RSS, while Nathuram's brother Gopal Godse in his book writes that all three brothers had practically grown up in the RSS and Nathuram never left the RSS. Sardar Patel did blame the extreme wing of Hindu Mahasabha. Later the Jeevanlal Kapoor Commission confirmed the complicity of Vinyak Savarkar in the gruesome act.

Sardar Patel also writes that the RSS celebrated this assassination by distributing sweets. They also this as Gandhi *Vadh*. '*Vadh*' is used for killing a demon. The RSS Chief Golwalkar declared a 13-day mourning. These two acts at the same time, distributing sweets and then declaring mourning shows this organization's double-speak. The RSS regarded the Gandhi-led anti-British movement as a mere reactionary movement not leading to a Hindu nation, so it did not participate in it and did not unfurl the tricolour for decades over its office.

Gandhi touched the heart and minds of most Indians irrespective of their religion, region, language, or region. He was in a way embodiment of the Indian-ness and very much in continuation of the tradition of saints. The World leaders could see the import of the Gandhian principles. The UN declared his birthday as the Peace Day. Many outstanding global personalities like Nelson Mandela and Martin Luther King (Jr.) drew inspiration from Gandhian teachings and acknowledged his debt for their own struggles for equality, peace, and justice.

It is for this reason the top leadership of RSS-BJP make the show of paying respect to Gandhi on his birthday. Many junior leaders openly articulate their real view, the ideology that drove Godse to murder Gandhi and for which they praise and worship him. One RSS chief Rajendra Singh did state that "Godse's intention was good". A large section of these leaders has started openly praising Godse's violent act. Temples and statues of Godse have been coming up in various places in (including one in Gwalior) north India. Similarly, a library was set up in Gwalior, where the assassination was plotted. It had to be closed in couple of days due to severe opposition.

BJP MP Sakshi Maharaj called Godse a patriot and nationalist. It's another matter that he had to retract it later. Pragya Thakur, the accused in Malegaon blast, did state that Nathuram Godse was a nationalist; is a nationalist and will be a nationalist. She was asked to withdraw this comment and was dropped from Parliamentary Defence committee. BJP's Anil Kumar Saumitra called Gandhi 'Father of the Nation, but of Pakistan'. He was expelled from the party but later appointed as head of a prestigious institute in Madhya Pradesh.

In Maharashtra, the Marathi play '*Mee Nathuram Boltoy*', (I am Nathuram Speaking) drew packed houses in Maharashtra. On other side, by word-of-mouth Gandhi is presented as anti-National, anti-Hindu and pro-Muslim. One book has come out with the title 'Gandhi was anti-national'! Anant Kumar Hedge ex-Union Minster of BJP stated that there is no need to feel apologetic about Godse. He did withdraw his comments after he was reprimanded by the party. Noted actor Kamal Haasan was trolled when in May 2019 he said the independent India's first terrorist was a Hindu named Nathuram Godse.

As part of the 'Hate Gandhi' camaign, the makers of biopic on Modi have declared the launch of biopic on Godse. The statements coming from the RSS stable show the real face of their ideology. Godse was no freak; he was ideologically motivated by Hindu Rashtra, Akhand Bharat. The ideology of Hindu Rasthra has been propagated not only though the Shakhas and Shishu Mandirs but also through the large sections of corporate-controlled mainstream media and social media. The twitter storm in praise of Godse indicates that the ideology which caused the murder of Gandhi, is now coming out in the open. The glorification of Godse reveals the deep roots of Hindu nationalism in India.

Courtesy: countercurrents.org

# Religious hatred is on autopilot

AVAY SHUKLA

June 2022

So, the BJP national spokespersons, Nupur Sharma and Naveen Jindal have been served the first serving of their just desserts. But anyone who thinks that this represents a course correction for the party must have the brain of a guinea fowl. The BJP is doing nothing of the kind, it is simply firefighting the backlash in the gulf countries which provide employment to millions of Indians who repatriate US$ 42 billion every year to our coffers, are a major market for Indian goods, and supply 60% of our petroleum products. The BJP's response was dictated not by any change of heart but by the potential damage to the business prospects of its sponsors. Because for a whole week it did nothing, even as protests erupted across the country and violence broke out in Kanpur.

Even more breath-taking was our Government's statement in response to the demarches issued by Kuwait, Qatar, Iran, Oman, Saudi Arabia and the OIC (Organisation of Islamic Countries): it is nothing but a treatise in duplicity, dissembling and double-speak. It accuses these countries of divisiveness and a communal agenda. It speaks glowingly of the protection of minorities in India, their constitutional guarantees, our secular credentials- even as their persecution has become almost a state policy now. The most bizarre claim was that these inflammatory statements were made by "fringe elements" and not by anyone associated with the ruling dispensation! Which begs the question - how can the Ministers, MPs, MLAs, national spokespersons, who churn out this venom every single day, be considered as fringe elements? In how many countries are "fringe elements" followed on Twitter by the Prime Minister, senior Union Ministers, and a whole host of party functionaries? As someone said, this is a new concept in physics -- when the fringe becomes the core. Not surprisingly, this crap did not cut any ice with the Gulf states (to mix a metaphor) who are demanding an apology and punishment for the two spokespersons.

Some 18 countries and the U N spokesperson protested. Given the escalation in Muslim bashing that has become the new normal, the remarks against the Prophet were just a matter of time. The litany of Muslim persecution - bans on beef, halal meat shops, offering namaz, shops near Hindu temples, the hijab; bulldozer justice, love jihad, conversion, judicial applications to dig up mosques, challenges to the Places of Worship Act, one sided state action whenever communal violence broke out, *Dharm Sansads* calling for genocide- had become so persistent and its practitioners so emboldened, that it had to reach its apogee soon. Nupur Sharma was a disaster waiting to happen, that the statement came from her was just a happenstance, for it could have been anyone from a long list of arachnids encouraged by the party and the Government - Sambit Patra, Gaurav Bhatia, Prem Shukla, or anyone else of their ilk. This apogee has also, unfortunately for the BJP, become the tipping point for many countries.

The suspension of Nupur Sharma and expulsion of Naveen Jindal is too little, too late. Dozens of people, including journalists and intellectuals, have been thrown in jail for far lesser "offences"; these two should be criminally prosecuted. As should the anchors of the TV shows in which they were allowed to make such statements. Navika Kumar of *Times Now* who was the anchor when Nupur Sharma made the despicable statement, did not intervene to stop her from spewing venom - she neither stopped the BJP spokesperson, nor muted her, nor took her off the air. At the very least she should have asked her to apologise and should have tendered an apology herself. She did none of this; instead, she later claimed that as this was a live show, she could have done nothing! It is also disappointing, but not surprising, that none of the media self-regulators - except for the Editors' Guild which issued a strong statement deploring the role of TV channels and their anchors in subverting our Constitutional values of secularism and comparing them to Radio Rwanda - censured Kumar for her irresponsible conduct. The physical threats to Nupur Sharma on social media are reprehensible and should be dealt with an iron hand. But I find it ironical that Nupur Sharma should now claim that her life is under threat - did she not put the lives of countless others at risk by her provocative remarks whose sole purpose was to incite hatred against the Muslims? This daily baiting and demonising of minorities on evening prime time shows has gone on for far too long. If the government means business, it should use its powers to shut down these Spanish Inquisition type programmes immediately. Even this will not detoxify the poison that has been injected into our society and system over the last eight years. For the hatred, bigotry and religious intolerance has now gone into autonomous mode and can no longer be controlled by one central authority and the centrifugal forces that have been generated cannot be easily stopped. To understand this phenomenon, one needs to refer to the theory of Cumulative Radicalisation propounded by the British historian Sir Ian Kirkshaw. His theory was based on his study of developments in Nazi Germany in the 1940s. He postulated that this radicalisation begins with a Supreme Leader and quickly percolates down through the political executive, bureaucracy, judiciary, and the media. The tipping point is reached when the ideology of hate, intolerance and majoritarianism infects the society at large. This becomes a kind of chaotic authoritarianism, as opposed to a Stalin kind of programmatic authoritarianism. At this point the vigilantes, social media trolls and non-state actors take over. Society is carved out into two parts- the Believers and the Silent Acceptors. The former now do the job of the ruling dispensation, thus providing the government a deniability to ward off any criticism. This process is faithfully mirrored in the present imbroglio and explains the current situation in the country. The BJP and its govt. at the centre have carefully promoted and nurtured an eco-system of hate in our polity and society and are now no longer fully in control of what its followers and savants do. The hatred is no longer a command performance but has gone into autonomous mode, with every party functionary or group doing what he or they think the Supreme Leader wants or the party ideology demands.

This is demonstrated by the backlash to Nupur Sharma's suspension, from the cadres and supporters of the BJP itself. They resent the action taken against her, with Modi being called out on social media for his "pusillanimity." Mohan Bhagwat's placatory statement that Hindus should not look for a *shivling* under every mosque, has angered the Hindutva fanatics, with one prominent seer even commenting sarcastically that age is making Bhagwat incoherent and confused.

The BJP should realise that it has gone too far with its ideology of Islamophobia. It is in danger of losing control of its own poisonous narrative, its deniability is eroding, and the reputation of the country is suffering notwithstanding Jaishankar's Alamo-type heroics. India has the largest immigrant population in the world - 32 million, of whom about 12 million live and work in Islamic nations. It would be a folly to denigrate Islam at home and expect our citizens to prosper in Islamic countries, or to expect these countries to be our trading partners and quietly ignore what is happening to their co-religionists here. In an increasingly globalised world, we must be sensitive to global concerns even if we treat our own citizens with contempt. It's time to call off the Rottweilers and return to sensible and equitable governance, before the dogs turn on their masters.

The government would do well to relearn a basic postulate of governance - that in a globally integrated world, one cannot separate domestic policy from foreign policy. Hubert Humphrey had put it very well when he stated that "foreign policy is really domestic policy with its hat on." Wise words, but it's difficult to put on your hat when you have both hands on the controls of a bulldozer or are caught with your pants down.

Courtesy: *View from [Greater] Kailash*

# Land of Blood and Fear

RAKHSHANDA JALIL

I am 60 years old and confess to a crushing fear, one that weighs my chest with an inexorable weight and makes it difficult to breathe sometimes. Yes, with all my privileges – of education, of class, of having friends in 'high places' – I feel scared, more scared than I have ever been in my entire life. I must also confess to an almost persistent depression, like a low-grade fever, over the past many months, that doesn't quite halt the daily rhythm of life; it just slows you down by its continuous, relentless presence in your life making you feel sad and somehow empty

I suspect I am not alone in this. I feel this fear and depression among a great many Muslims in urban India. I hear it in their silences. I sense it in their steadfast refusal to get drawn into political debates. I notice it in their stoicism in the face of virulent hate swirling about in school and college WhatsApp groups as well as RWA/housing society group chats. I spot it in the hastily withdrawn social media posts drawing attention to some recent communal outrage or atrocity. I recognize it in their zeal to distance themselves from instances of any sort of violence, be it a Muslim man killing his Hindu girlfriend and chopping her into pieces or a Muslim man killing his non-Muslim partner in a business dispute.

If my own fear and despair and that of others like me, is so palpable and pronounced, what of those Muslims who are doubly marginalized by their poverty and illiteracy? Or vulnerable because they don't have the safeguards and barriers, however flimsy, that 'people like us' have in our gated communities and cushioned lives? What of those who live on the edge of survival because they must perforce go out into the real world every single day to eke out a living? What of the plumbers, electricians, painters, carpenters, maids and sundry service providers who don't give their real, Muslim-sounding names for fear they will not be hired? Or the vegetable vendors who festoon their carts with saffron flags after every call to boycott small Muslim businesses? Or the biryani vendors, kabab sellers, quilt makers, car mechanics who have traditionally plied these trades for generations but now fear for their lives? What of the meat sellers whose makeshift stalls happen to be along the routes taken by the *kawariyas* during every monsoon? What of the imams and naib imams, often from the poorest of families, who are hired by Wakf boards to serve as custodians of small, isolated mosques surrounded by hostile neighbours?

I don't 'look' like a Muslim so, to an extent, I am safe. Unless called out to chant 'Jai Shree Ram' to profess my Indianness, I am largely safe. But what of my name? How can I camouflage that on a railway booking chart? Or hide it when asked to provide proof of identity? While my first name can afford some benefit of doubt for it might pass as a Parsi's, my surname is a dead give-away.

When push comes to shove in the New India that is Bharat, not even speaking English will give me an exit pass if a mob baying for Muslim blood were to gherao me. All my so-called privileges can be brought to naught by a crowd of lumpens. The realization is chilling.

And if I were a man? Imagine, over 75 years after partition and after reading all the gory stories penned by Saadat Hasan Manto and other chroniclers of communal violence, having your pants pulled down to check whether you are a '*katua*' or not? But what if I did 'look' like a Muslim?

What if I chose to offer namaz perfectly peacefully and quietly while sitting on my berth in a train? Worse still, what if I had a beard, wore a topi or a hijab and indeed 'looked' like a Muslim? What if I worked as an imam in a mosque? So, what if I had just assured my family that all was well, that I was safe given the police presence all around me? What, then?

What if I, as an Indian, have been conditioned to believe that the tattered fabric of secularism will be held up no matter what? The violence in Gurgaon in July-August 2023 proved that these are no longer hypothetical scenarios. This is a lived reality for countless Indian Muslims.

*'Jab mulle kaate jaainge*
*Ram Ram chillainge'*
When the Mullahs are slaughtered
They will shout: Ram! Ram!
Or:
*'Hindustan mein rehna hoga*
*Jai Shri Ram kehna hoga'*
If you want to stay in Hindustan
You'll have to chant jai Shri Ram

And *'Goli maro saalon ko…'* (Shoot the buggers…) by someone who is now a union minister are no longer isolated instances of random, unrelated, personal biases and prejudices. They are dog whistles. They are a clarion call to a large, restive majority that is being brain-washed to believe they are second-class, nay "seventh class" citizens, in their own land. They are part of a larger narrative, a grand design.

Since we have clearly turned into a nation of 'whatabouters', each of these hate-filled, terror-inducing slogans will be instantly and viciously countered with those raised by the PFI or other fringe minority outfits. When questions about rapes, murders, corruptions, scams and scandals are thwarted in Parliament by elected representatives of the people by instances of whatabouts, how can these rising incidents of bigotry and hate be not similarly countered? It's easier to come back with counter accusations, to point fingers, to obfuscate, to fling more filth, to parry hate with hate than it is to understand fear, to acknowledge militant, muscular majoritarianism, to call out the elephant in the room.

As we spiral inexorably downwards, as every fresh instance of bigotry is outstripped and outdone by even bigger, bolder, more blatant, more bare-faced occurrences, we don't seem to pause to think of the consequences. This rampant whataboutery – both at the political and the individual level – is exhausting, predictable and eventually empty. It will derail the India we have known and loved – probably forever.

Excerpted from the Introduction to
*Love in the Time of Hate*

# Muslims are not alone

R K MISRA

In the current atmosphere of religious polarisation and intolerance, Hindu psyche gets hurt every other week. The self-made leaders of the majority community are always looking out for the alleged misdeeds of "the other" designed to insult Hinduism. Muslims face sustained violence. Social scientists studying the new divisive trends in society warn that the list of "the Other" will go on expanding. It is no longer limited to Muslims. Many Hindus have "hurt" the psyche of the Hindutva warriors and political Hindus. Christians face hostility and worse. A majoritarian state needs many minorities! Some recall the famous post-war confessional statement by a German Lutheran pastor: "First they came for the socialists, and I did not speak out – because I was not a socialist...Then they... Then they... Then they came for me – and there was no one to speak for me."

Recently, in Sagar town of Madhya Pradesh, a confrontation between Hindus and Jains took place over an attack on an old Hindu temple. A clash between any two communities is always possible since Sikhs can be called Khalistanis, Dalits are beaten up for no fault of theirs, and Christians are attacked for allegedly "converting" Hindus to their faith.

At a private school in Ahmedabad, a demonstration of how Muslims pray on Eid was publicised as "the Hindu students being forced to offer *namaz*". The right-wing activists stormed the school the next day, thrashed a teacher, extracting an apology from the school principal.

The minister of state for primary, secondary, and adult education Praful Pansheriya was quick to wade into the controversy. "It seems some people want to disturb the peaceful atmosphere of the state by organizing such programmes in schools. This is not at all acceptable", the minister was quoted as saying. He ordered an investigation to "find out the mentality and intention behind organizing such a programme and then take appropriate action". The inquiry commenced the next day. Ironically, it was a clip of the programme on the Facebook page of the school (subsequently removed) which was the first point of information for the protesters. The Principal said "we wholeheartedly celebrate all Indian festivals including Ganeshotsav, Navratri, Eid, Christmas, Paryushan, Navroz, Guru Purab. One of our students depicted how Namaz is performed while three students stood by the depiction. No student was forced to perform *namaz*, the students who participated had taken consent from their parents", she told media persons. Civil society organisations demanded an FIR against the forced violence including assault on a hapless school staff.

A controversy erupted in Gujarat among Hindus when sadhus owing allegiance to the *'sanatani'* traditions came out against those of the Swaminarayan sect. A mural installed at the Sarangpur temple depicted Lord Hanuman seeking the blessings of a Swaminarayan saint. This temple is located about 150 kms from Ahmedabad at Gadhada in the Botad district of Saurashtra region in Gujarat and comes under the Vadtal Swaminarayan sect. When a video clip went viral, the *sanatani* saints were incensed. They perceived subordination of a presiding deity of the faith to sect leader. They served an ultimatum seeking the removal of the mural. The issue snowballed as numerous religious heads waded into the controversy, arguing that Lord Hanuman existed thousands of years ago whereas Swaminarayan was born a couple of centuries ago. Shankaracharya Swami Sadanand Saraswati of Dwarka's Sharda Peeth said that "Swaminarayan sect is just 250-year-old, whereas *Skand Purana* is thousands of years old. There is no mention of Swaminarayan in the *Skanda Purana*, no one knows, if someone has added at a later stage to suit a sect."

The tremors with political implications set alarm bells ringing from Delhi to Gandhinagar and the politico-religious machinery moved in to douse the flames. A hectic round of behind-the-scenes parleys which involved saints and intermediaries and the RSS and VHP, created the platform for the overt intervention of chief minister Bhupendrabhai Patel. After another round of arduous efforts, a compromise was worked out and the murals removed from the temple.

Swaminarayan Sect leaders assured that their saints would be careful while making statements on Sanatani gods and goddesses. The Vishva Hindu Parishad (VHP) issued a statement claiming that Swaminarayan sect's Vadtal head Rakeshdasji has clarified that, "the Swaminarayan sect is part and parcel of Sanatan Dharma, it respects and follows the rituals of Vedic Sanatan religion, as the sect is part of Sanatan religion, it has no intention to hurt sentiments of Sanatan religion and its believers.". The three persons arrested for attempting to deface the murals, after the controversy ignited, were bailed out.

The ruling BJP could not have afforded to let this controversy simmer or take an uglier turn. The Swaminarayan sect enjoys great power in Gujarat as well as among Gujaratis worldwide. The Sanatanis countrywide form a critical source of BJP's popularity. The BJP cannot afford to alienate any of the two.

However, if the BJP leaders countrywide maintained a stoic silence about the 'saintly' controversy in Gujarat, they came out guns blazing on the DMK leader and Tamil Nadu sports and youth welfare minister Udhaynidhi Stalin's remarks on 'sanatana dharma'. He was speaking at a conference titled 'Sanatana Ozhippu Maanaadu' (Sanatana abolition conclave) organised by the Tamil Nadu Progressive Writers and Artists Association. Speaking at the conclave the minister is reported to have called for the eradication of Sanatana dharma instead of opposing it. Sensing a political opening for electorally taking up cudgels against I.N.D.I.A. of which TN-ruling DMK is a part, the BJP went into action. It's IT cell chief Amit Malviya was quick to interpret it as a call for the 'genocide' of the sanatanis who according to him make -up 80 percent of the population of Bharat. Union Home Minister Amit Shah pounced on the DMK leader's remark to pummel the Opposition alliance at an election rally in Rajasthan. Prime Minister Narendra Modi wanted a befitting response to it as well. Of course, Tamil Nadu chief minister M. K. Stalin gave his response by crushing the BJP in the parliamentary elections.

One expects more theological battles among Hindus and Hindutva warriors' attacks on liberal Hindus and atheists. "Hindus are in danger" has become a familiar slogan raised during every election campaign.

While the Hindutva warriors feel empowered to attack and destroy at will, the BJP state governments seem to have taken a new responsibility of protecting Hindus from minorities, passing new laws against religious conversion and inter-faith marriages. Under the combined might of official and nonofficial operators, law and order has collapsed in some states. It has affected journalists, artistes, students, farmers, eminent citizens, retired senior government officials, not necessarily Muslim. Much has been written about activists who wait for bail, remaining in jail for years.

To take just one example, a Dalit mechanic in U.P. spent 15 months fighting a false 'Conversion' FIR before he won. *The Wire* reported in January 2025 that after being attacked by the members of the VHP and Bajrang Dal, Sonu Saraf and his family were subjected to yet another attack – from the U.P. Police who misused the state's controversial anti-conversion law. The mob had accused Saroj of holding unauthorised prayer meetings to convert Hindus to Christianity.

*The Wire* is running a series of reports on such cases. It says there are at least 2,700 people implicated in 835 criminal cases under the anti-conversion law in the state, as per the official figures available till July 2024. Rights activists and lawyers have accused the government of lodging false cases under the law to harass those who deviate from it philosophy of Brahminical Hindutva. A wag says India is no country for minorities, women, Dalits and even non-Hindutva Hindus! Of course, the police is yet to turn their radar on the homes of the sections of elite Hindus who hold private meetings to worship as per religions other than Hinduism!

The vigilante's prime victims are Muslims, but they do not discriminate against Hindus while enforcing purification and making someone shout *Jai Shri Ram*. They rough up girls in beer bars without asking their names or looking at their clothes. They catch Hindu men buying St. Valentine's Day card. In Ahmedabad, two persons dressed as Santa Clause who were beaten up, may not have been Christians. Carol singers have been beaten up. Carol singing has been stopped in Rashtrapati Bhavan. Bajrang Dal warned Hindus against attending Christmas parties.

Courtesy: *Wordsmiths & Newsplumbers.blogspot.com*

# A Kashmiri Pandit hounded

NITASHA KAUL

June 2024

Narendra Modi won a third term as Indian prime minister after his BJP was returned to power, albeit as part of a minority government leading the National Democratic Alliance (NDA) coalition. Having expected to win another majority from which to pursue his Hindu nationalist – or Hindutva – agenda, Modi will have to operate within the constraints of a considerably reduced mandate. His government – dubbed "Modi 3.0" in India – has plenty to do including completing its programme of reforms and reworking foreign investment policy. Yet barely had the new government been sworn in, then the BJP's lieutenant governor of New Delhi was given the go-ahead for the prosecution of the noted author and public intellectual, Arundhati Roy, for remarks she made as far back as 2010 about the disputed territory of Kashmir. Roy and Sheikh Showkat Hussain, formerly professor at the Central University of Kashmir, have been charged under the Unlawful Activities Prevention Act (UAPA) – an anti-terrorism measure. The charges relate to "provocative" speeches they made at a seminar in October 2010, which apparently "propagated the separation of Kashmir from India".

But all this was 14 years ago, before the BJP took power nationally in 2014. So why is the Modi government risking international opprobrium by persecuting such an internationally famous figure about what she said years in the past? The answer is that picking a fight over Kashmir is an easy win for Modi's style of Hindu nationalism. Anyone who insists on raising the myriad problems of militarisation, mismanagement, human rights abuses and repression in Kashmir tends to be accused of being anti-national, seditious, pro-Pakistani or terrorist.

Modi's BJP has been in power for a decade and has introduced major constitutional changes in the Jammu & Kashmir region. But the government has addressed neither militancy in the region, nor India's loss of territory to China along the line of actual control. The BJP opted not to field any candidates in Muslim majority Kashmir in the 2024 election (it had two candidates in neighbouring Hindu majority Jammu). But voters shunned candidates from Kashmir's mainstream pro-India parties, preferring local independents who had opposed the Modi government's decision to revoke Jammu and Kashmir's special status. One of the candidates elected has been in prison in Delhi since shortly after the decision was taken in 2019.As a result, the BJP is clearly ultra-sensitive about

Kashmir. Targeting a globally prominent figure such as Roy in such a vindictive manner is part of a multi-pronged political strategy aimed at baiting and discrediting opponents of Modi's Hindu nationalist ambitions.

The BJP's wants to use the persecution of Roy – and other progressives and Kashmiris – as leverage over its main political rival, the Congress Party-led Indian National Developmental Inclusive Alliance, which outperformed expectations in the recent election. If it speaks out over stunts like this, it risks being delegitimised as "anti-national". If it stays silent, it risks alienating its own progressive supporters. Any discussion of Kashmir, meanwhile, is something of a dog whistle for right-wing Hindu nationalists. They tend to see any reference to human rights and freedoms in Kashmir as a sign of seditious tendencies. So, the prosecution of Roy and Sheikh Showkat Hussain for speaking out on the issue is also intended to galvanise the BJP's own support base. And it's a message to other Modi critics: if someone with Roy's profile can be targeted, so can you.

It is indicative of a wider pattern in Indian politics under Modi. This sort of targeting is particularly pronounced for those who defend democratic values and critique Modi's authoritarianism – but who have also spoken in support of Kashmiri people's rights or aspirations at any time in the past. I know this from bitter experience. I am an academic and author of Kashmiri origin focusing on democracy and human rights in India and beyond. In 2019, I provided testimony at a US congressional hearing on Kashmir, that pro-Modi government news agencies sought to suppress. In February 2024, I was invited by the Congress-run state of Karnataka to a constitutional convention. But when I arrived in India, I was denied entry by immigration, despite holding all the valid papers. "Orders from Delhi", was all I was told. I was detained under armed guard and deported. Several weeks later, I was sent a notice of intent to revoke my overseas citizenship of India (OCI). All the while I was subjected to coordinated and vicious attacks on social media from prominent right-wing individuals and Modi-supporting accounts. The chorus of online hate focused on a 2010 tweet of mine relating to Kashmir, which was cited as proof of my anti-national views. When Congress leaders spoke in my support, the Karnataka BJP referred to me as a "Pakistani sympathiser who wants India's break up" and criticised "Anti-national Congress" for having invited me. I have travelled to India numerous times since 2010.

The issue wasn't my 2010 tweet – which I explained in some detail. It was my more recent work on problems such as the increasing authoritarianism under Modi, the use of anonymous political funding instruments called electoral bonds, and the treatment of dissent by the BJP government. Though I grew up in, and work on, India, I cannot know when I will see my only living parent again – an elderly and ailing mother unable to travel to me. Various other authors, journalists, academics and activists have been similarly targeted. Many who have spoken up from Srinagar or from Delhi have been imprisoned. Roy's persecution is part of this wider pattern which attempts to delegitimise any criticism of Modi and his government and clamp down on freedom of speech, while trying to trap the opposition into being called anti-national. Roy and Showkat's persecution must be seen for what it is: a chess move that is part of a strategy designed to continue the undermining of democracy in India.

*Courtesy:*

**THE CONVERSATION**

# Dance and despair in memory of murdered Gauri Lankesh

Teesta Setalvad's birthday letter *to a colleague and comrade explores the hatreds poisoning India and the hope and joy that Gauri Lankesh, journalist and activist, had brought to counter them. She was shot dead in her garden on September 5, 2017. These pages carry Sagari Chhabra's poem on Gauri Lankesh.*

27 January 2022

Dear Gauri,

Two days from today you turn 60. What would we have done to celebrate this key milestone? There would surely have been anger and tears with the joys and spirits of celebration. We would have argued and bickered about how to be together in the third surge of the pandemic: you, me, Kavitha, Esha and your mother. But together we would have been. Together, though painfully separated, we are still. On the night of September 5, 2017, seven hate-filled bullets snatched you away from us, even as you walked through the lovely tree- and plant-laden garden of your home. The home where we sat and shared, always charting new paths of challenge to the hate that was poisonously eating away around us.

Our precious moments of such plotting and sharing happened both in your home and spread over the length and breadth of Karnataka, the state of southern

India that your profound activism spanned, from Chikmagalur to Udupi, from Mangalore to Tumkur. We deliberated and danced to the tunes and songs of protest and struggle. It is these moments that are barrenly absent now. The past four and a half years, since your laughter, chuckle, smile and fiery resolve were snatched away, has seen the transformation of this hate that took your vibrant life into an insidious state project. State power is abused to allow hate offenders to not just spew poison but incite to snatch dignity and kill. The collaborators of 'brown shirts', organised and oiled with funds, have found newer and sicker ways of hate dispensation. Unjust laws, passed by parliament and state legislative assemblies, have weaponised majoritarianism, making a mockery of the equality principles so fundamental to India, to us, to our constitution.

Though a birthday is time for rosy thoughts, I know that with you I would be speaking and ranting about the way in which our Muslim sisters have been brutalised and objectified on social media platforms. On Twitter, on Instagram, on Facebook, on Github, on Clubhouse. Technology is now the arena of evil hatred. That bands of men and women can indulge in this manner of targeting women and girls, from teenagers to grandmothers, reveals a dehumanising, supremacist political project that has rendered large sections of the influential majority silent. This project is seeking to transform India into a theocratic state.

You and I would have spoken and acted, as I am doing with our friends and comrades now, to break this silence. To become outspoken allies of minorities, to listen, to acknowledge, to grieve, to protest, to heal, to ensure justice and to bring lust-filled perpetrators to justice. The fight must go on.

Gauri, you faced in life and your bloody death the hazards of independent journalism. Today, after 38 years as a journalist, I see that honest and independent colleagues are a threatened breed. India was among the five most dangerous countries in terms of journalists killed across the world in 2021, according to media watchdog Reporters Without Borders. You were the outspoken editor of an independent liberal Kannada weekly, struggling to make it survive. Today, close to five years after your assassination, arrests and further assassinations, techniques mastered by the extreme Right, have made India one of the most dangerous places for journalists taking on the establishment.

For the journalist who is also a Muslim and a Kashmiri, the targeting is manifold. On 15 January, the government that dismembered the state of Jammu and Kashmir through the abrogation of Article 370 of our constitution killed the Kashmir Press Club in its infancy. Gauri, the tectonic events around this have barely drawn meaningful media debate here. But they have turned the spotlight, yet again, on to the dire state of media freedom in Kashmir. First, a group of journalists, reportedly close to the administration, barged into the premises of the press club accompanied by armed personnel (apparently assigned to protect some of these senior journalists) and literally took it over. Then, following an outcry by other journalists, including the elected committee that managed the club, the administration decided that it had become a battleground between 'warring' groups and hence must be abolished altogether. On 17 January it cancelled the lease to the premises and reverted it to the government. Most non-journalists have little idea what function a press club serves. They are hubs where journalists exchange information and views, and where they rest between hectic deadlines while they wait for the next interview, the next press briefing. They are places to get an affordable meal and a drink and to socialise with colleagues. They are invaluable. Now, in Kashmir, a state bitterly divided, the divisions have percolated down to journalists. They suffer arbitrary arrests anyway, as you knew and protested, Gauri: these detentions and interrogations continue unabated. On 5 January, Sajad Gul, a trainee journalist with *The Kashmir Walla*, was arrested for fomenting anti-government feelings. Last year, Salman Shah and Suhail Dar were arrested for 'breach of peace'. Journalist Aasif Sultan has been in jail since 2018 and is still awaiting trial. This level of government interference in the running of a journalists' club bodes ill for the future. What has happened in 'J & K' and India's north-east, regions at our country's margins where human rights and dignity have been eroded over decades, is now happening in 'mainland' India, Gauri.

Gauri, what we are witnessing first-hand all over India – and your beloved home state, Karnataka, is no exception – is a sense of fear and dread among our most vulnerable as laws and wings of the state are weaponised against its own people. Only three days ago, we reported how 19-year-old Sameer was killed and 21-year-old Shamseer is in a critical condition after they were attacked in Gadag district, allegedly soon after a Bajrang Dal event where anti-Muslim hate was instigated. This is only one of a series of incidents in your home state where Muslims and Christians have become brute targets, Gauri. Love between the young, intermingling, non- vegetarianism, different forms of dress, freedom of faith, the very diversity that is the joy and core of India is under attack.

Your life epitomised a wondrous intersectionality. Whether it was India's Indigenous women (Adivasis), the homeless, Dalits, other minorities or survivors and victims of targeted violence, you, in espousing so effectively their cause, became the living embodiment of hope and resistance. No wonder then that a group of Adivasi bonded labourers wept in uncontrolled sorrow at the mass protest following your killing on 12 September 2017. You are to them all and us both a hope and a connection. You among all of us realised the urgent need for this alliance-building among the most targeted to evolve a lasting political challenge. No wonder then, Gauri, that in a spontaneous outburst of outrage the slogan that arose was: "Those who killed Gandhi, killed Gauri." It reflects a deep understanding of the forces who felled you. Let's never forget that your murder was celebrated on Twitter by several Hindu right-wing handles followed by the Indian Prime Minister. Gandhi's assassination – three bullets shot at close range from the front on 30 January 1948, seven and a half months after independence – was the first threat and warning from Hindutva supremacists that they did not accept India's sagacious choice to remain a secular, pluralist, democratic republic, even after a bitter partition and violence. Of how far they would go. The fact that these assassins from the same ideology are so emboldened today is testimony not just to the pervasive impunity, but also a warning. Of how India is teetering on the brink.

Gauri, through much of the onset of this misery and pain, you continued to have fun with us, eat good food and drink, dress up, bicker, argue, apply a bright maroon or red lipstick and smile that gentle reaching-out smile that now encompasses us as tears brim over when we miss you. So much of the time. All the time. We know and feel you watching, smiling. Gauri, the past five years have brought me Kavitha. She, your sister and soulmate, has faced your loss with grace, courage and fortitude. Through sleepless nights, shivers of loss and fear, nightmares, Kavitha's feelings poured out in the poems she wrote to you in that first year. Every other morning, after a difficult night, I would find one of these poems in my mailbox. *'The Last Ten Seconds', 'The Tiffin Box', 'My Soul Mate', 'Akka'.* As a present and meaningful tribute, we gifted her a printed booklet with all these that first year. And Esha, your sister's daughter, yours too, your bright shining star? Though so difficult and painful, she stands with us at protests and gatherings. She says: "I hope I too stand for peace and unity as my Awwa [mum] did."

So much is embodied in your life and in your death, Gauri. Brute repression and boundless resistance. Bye, my fearless tigress kitten of a sister, from your almost-to-be-60-too friend.

Teesta Setalvad

Courtesy: OpenDemocracy

# An ardent Hindu speaks up

SURANYA AIYAR went on a three-day fast to protest the circumstances associated with the Ram Temple consecration in Ayodhya on January 22, 2024. She read out this statement on Facebook, explaining her going on fast to reaffirm her faith in true Hinduism and India's syncretic culture. *"Times are terrible, and I could not let things pass without making a stand, however small. It is also an opportunity to reflect on things and reiterate the values that one believes in for India."*

Dear friends and fellow travellers,
With the forthcoming event in Ayodhya on January 22, 2024, the atmosphere here in Delhi, already famous for being polluted in a material sense, has thickened to a spiritually poisonous and unbreathable concentrate of Hindu chauvinism, malice and bullying. I am deeply anguished by all this as an Indian and as a Hindu. And after thinking hard about what I can do, I have decided to go on fast starting January 20 and ending a day after the January 22 production at Ayodhya.

I am doing this first and foremost as an expression of my love and sorrow to my Muslim fellow citizens of India. I cannot let this moment pass without saying as loud as I can to my Muslim brothers and sisters that I love you and that I condemn and repudiate what is being done in the name of Hinduism and nationalism in Ayodhya.

I am also doing this as an expression of my love for my Mughal heritage. This is not only about feeling protective towards someone else. It is about my culture and my ethos. I love *dhrupad* and *khayal* music. I love *kathak*. I love the Mughal and Sultanate buildings in my city of Delhi – I cannot imagine Delhi without the Qutub Minar or Humayun's Tomb, or the Sabz Burj. Not to mention the Taj Mahal next door in Agra. I revere the magnificent culture spawned by the court of Awadh under Nawab Wajid Ali Shah. I see the Delhi Sultanate as <u>also</u> having given something precious to India, as it was with them that the Sufis and Amir Khusroe's father came here. In North India we owe so much of our language and culture to Hazrat Amir Khusroe. He adopted Hindavi into a language of poetry which later spawned the grand languages of Hindi and Urdu. He made innovations in music that laid the foundation of *Shastriya Sangeet* – the classical music of North India - of which we are all so proud. The list is endless.

There is no part of our high classical culture in North India which does not bear the stamp of the Sultanate, the Mughals, the nawabs and the nizams. This is not to say that any of these traditions were the sole product of these rulers, or that it was Muslims that enlightened us. On the contrary, this culture is the result of the mingling of the native arts, traditions and languages with those that were brought by the Sultans and the Mughals. A mingling which only happened because of the embrace by them of the existing culture. Can we speak of Amir Khusroe's music without speaking of Gopal Naik, the famous Hindu court musician from whom Khusroe learnt so much? Can we speak of Hindustani Classical music or Kathak without speaking of the Dhruvapadas or the Rasas of the *Natya Shastra*? Can we speak of Tansen without speaking of Pandit Haridas? Can we have Kathak without the traditions of the *raasleela*, and the performance of the Ramayana and the Mahabharat in India from times immemorial? Can we have Dhrupad without the worship of Lord Shiva? Can we have *Dhamar* without Holi? Read the writings of Abul Fazl, the court biographer of Akbar. See how he sings praises of Hindu beliefs, practices, sciences and philosophies. Do you know that Akbar commissioned a Persian translation of the Mahabharata to showcase what a great culture the Hindus had? And he was such an admirer of the Mahabharata, that when the translation was read to him, he scoffed and said that it was not good enough. Look up the work that Nawab Wajid Ali Shah did with *kathak* compositions, dance dramas and *kavits* (poems) – they were all inspired by the traditional celebration of Radha-Krishna by his Hindu subjects.

This is not meant to be a lecture in history so I will stop here, but the examples go on and on. And I have given them to explain that when I say that I love my Mughal heritage, I am saying that I love the composite culture that grew out of the Hindu and Muslim traditions of this land. A culture in which you cannot pick out what is Muslim and what is Hindu anymore; or what was native and what was foreign. It has been a millennium of intermingling, and of reciprocal inspiration and admiration. Influences are from everywhere. This is not an imposition of foreign things, it is how a culture develops in conversation with other languages, aesthetic traditions, faiths and philosophies. The dramatic form that is described in the *Natya Shastra* emerged from a culture that branched out of the encounter of the subcontinent with the Greeks. If you keep throwing things out by calling them foreign or non-Hindu, then what will we be left with? The culture that grew under the Mughal empire was not imposed, it was not developed anywhere else, it grew here, from this soil and is unique to this land.

And let me tell you that I do not consider my only heritage to be Mughal. I come from a mixed background of Tamil Brahmin and Punjabi Sikh – and I love and cherish all those parts of my heritage too. My husband has mixed Rajasthani Jat and Jath Sikh heritage with a family history in the military and I have been delighted to adopt his legacy, with all his tales of valour and chivalry as my own. In the work that I do helping Indian families abroad whose children have been snatched by cruel foreign child services agencies, I inevitably end up learning about the culture and religion they come from, and I found that they would seep into me. From my Bengali families I was introduced to Maa Durga whom I now celebrate with as much joy as my Bengali friends. From a recent case involving a Jain family, I have been intrigued enough to start studying some Jain scriptures. And this life history is not unique to me. It is repeated in countless Indians of all ethnic and religious backgrounds all over the country for centuries.

Hindutvavadis insist that you need one religion and one culture and one language to develop a coherent identity. It is simply not true. You can equally develop a cosmopolitan and porous identity. It is not a question of what you exclude or include, but of values and conviction. And this is not some new, modern idea. India has always been a land of diversity and these question of identity, community, authenticity and social division have always been there. And we have always been faced with a choice to be open or to be closed. This is a conversation going back millennia. Emperor Ashoka in the 3<sup>rd</sup> century BC said पियदसी राजा सर्वता इचति सवे पासंडा वसेयु, सवे ते सयामाम च भाव- सुधिम् च इचति । Meaning: It is always my wish for persons of all faiths live on my lands. For they all essentially believe in good thinking and good conduct. पूजेतया तृ एव पर-पासंडा तेन-तेन प्रकारणेना । Find numerous ways of honouring those of other beliefs. एवम् हि देवानंपियस इच्छा किंति सव - पासंडा बहु - स्रुता च असू कलाणागमा च असू । Be broad of knowledge and seek to understand others' beliefs. Cultivate an attitude of friendliness and openness to all.

Two millennia later in the 16<sup>th</sup> century, Emperor Akbar is saying the same thing: "He is a man who makes Justice his guide on the path of inquiry and takes from every belief what is consonant with reason. Perhaps in this way the lock, whose key has been lost, may be opened." Notwithstanding that at all periods of time, Hindustan has never been lacking in prudent men with excellent resolutions and well-intentioned designs, there are misunderstandings and quarrels between its different religions. Through the apathy of princes each sect is bigoted to its own creed and dissensions have waxed high. Each one, regarding his own persuasion as alone true, has set himself to the persecution of other worshippers of God. Were the eyes of the mind possessed of true vision, everyone would withdraw from this indiscriminating turmoil and attend rather to his own solicitudes, than interfere in the concerns of others so that dissensions within and without can be turned to peace and the thorn brake of strife bloom into a garden of concord. Five hundred years later Gandhiji said "The essence of true religious teaching is that one should serve and befriend all. I learnt this in my mother's lap. You may refuse to call me a Hindu. I know no defence except to quote a line from Iqbal's famous song: मज़हब नहीं सीखता आपस में बैर रखना, meaning, religion does not teach us to bear ill-will towards one another.

I have found no difficulty in embracing diverse ideas and practices while all the time thinking of myself as a Hindu. In my personal practice, for wedding or functions in my family I have rituals conducted in the manner of my paternal grandmother – as the *homam* is done among Tamils because, personally, I prefer the way Sanskrit is pronounced by the Tamil purohits and the way the *puja* is done. But that is because that is how I grew up seeing *pujas*. This does not stop me from feeling *shraddha, aastha* and comfort in any place of worship – whether Nizamuddin Dargah or the Vatican or Jama Masjid or the Ganeshji Mandir built by my grandfather here in Delhi on Baba Kharag Singh Marg or my favourite temple – the magnificent Brihadeshwara temple built by Rajarajachola in Tanjore which is a few minutes' drive from my ancestral village in Tamil Nadu.

I am not an orthodox Hindu; I do not know all the mantras or observe the fasts or dietary taboos or pray every morning or regularly go to any temple. But I don't see the votaries of Hindutvavad as being very orthodox either. All our saffron twitter influencers, actors and news personalities live very modern lives – and are not living the traditional orthodox Hindu way, whether in marriage, food habits, clothes or lifestyle. Even the January 22 function is not following the Hindu orthodox way - the Shankaracharyas are complaining that it is not being done according to the strict traditions. For me this is not an issue. Hinduism is not a hidebound faith. For every *shastric* way of conducting some prayer there is also an *upay* around it. This is the openness of Hinduism and its constant reminder to remain focussed on the spirit of things and not the material side, even in conducting prayers.

For me Hinduism is all the stories of our gods and goddesses which somehow define my very existence. It is like they are always present with their epic stories and great wars and loves and philosophical dialogues like an unseen but very real drama that is always going on around me and filling my inner world with colour, counsel and comfort. Everything comes alive with them and becomes an offering to them. When I bow to my harmonium or the stage (as my Muslim Ustads have taught me to) Devi Saraswati comes before my eyes. When I was exhausted and frustrated as a young mother with my naughty toddlers, it was the tales of Yashodha driven to distraction by the mischievous Krishna that gave me comfort and understanding. Feminists will start groaning when I say this, but when I gave up work to become a full-time mother, and everyone looked at me as though I was an alien, I found a wellspring of strength and self-assurance in the feminine Hindu ideal of *seva* – of devotion, sacrifice and service – in which you forget yourself and give everything – *tan, man, dhan* – to serving those, whom it is your duty to serve. So, I am sincere when I say that I think of myself as a Hindu. This is what Hinduism is to me. And if I am not a Hindu or if this is not Hinduism then you have to say that to my face.

Again and again, we are reminded by the Hindutvavadis that the Mughals invaded us. Yes, the first Mughal came here as a conqueror. But he did not take Delhi from any Hindu ruler. Whom did Babar fight in Panipat? It was Ibrahim Lodhi. Before that he defeated Daulat Khan in Punjab. Let us be clear, the Mughals entered India with the conquest of a Muslim by a Muslim. In fact, it was the conquest by a Muslim of several Muslims. Before defeating Lodhi, Babar had conquered the Afghans in Kabul. Some historians say that there might have even been proposals of an alliance between Babur and Rana Sanga, the Rajput king, to fight Ibrahim Lodi. That alliance did not happen, but when Ibrahim Lodi was defeated, his brother joined forces with Rana Sanga to try and defeat Babur. So, Babar's was not by any means a simple story of a Muslim conquest of India.

I am not going to say that Babur's victory here was not without its pathos. Conquest is terrible in its violence and destruction. No doubt each conquest is the end of something, the death of something. I can imagine that there would have been an adjustment that Hindus would have had to make, especially in the initial years, being ruled by non-Hindus. But Mughal rule in India was never particularly focussed on Islam. Though that would have already taken place under the earlier

Muslim rulers who had started coming here since the 9th century. That was the time of kings and conquests. It was the age of imperialism. And it was precisely to end imperialism, blood feuds and war that people turned to ideas of democracy, pluralism and secularism. Ideas that we in India are recklessly rejecting in the name of invasions from 1000 and 500 years ago. Is it not possible to say: can't we just move on from all this?

The Mughals were also not enemies of the Rajputs for all the 500 hundred years that they ruled here. They entered marriage alliance with Rajputs. Some of their senior-most generals and officials were Rajputs. Their clothes, architecture and culture took so much from the Rajputs. Get into your car and drive out of Delhi; within minutes you are in Rajput territory, with their forts, palaces and temples all around. Were they erased? Were they taken over by the Mughals? No. They were right there, a stone's throw from the Mughal capital.

This is why the Ram Janmabhoomi agitation was such a lie when it claimed to be fighting 500 years of Hindu *ghulami* (slavery). Mughal rule was nothing like that. It was about the ambitions of kings and conquerors; and neither Hinduism nor Islam played any other than an ancillary role in all this. Except for Aurangzeb, none of the Mughals were very observant. They drank wine, consumed opium, preferred the Sufis over the Ullema,

Akbar was even accused of being un-Islamic, his Din-e-Ilahi was seen as a direct challenge to the Muslim orthodoxy, his very name, Akbar, was seen as an irreverent appropriation of Allahu Akbar. Whatever you say about the pain of Mughal invasion, it did not give birth to centuries of Hindu repression or enslavement. It gave birth to a beautiful culture that took nothing away from Hindu religion or culture.

And now we come to the vexed question of conversions and breaking of temples by invaders. From today's point of view, both are wrong. But let us be clear, first and foremost, about the limits of the claimed historical wrong. We are not talking about hundreds of years of repression of Hinduism, or a state policy of conversion to Islam or of mass building-over of temples with mosques. While such things did occur both before, during and after the Mughals, it was not the policy of the Mughals to convert Hindus or break temples in India. In fact, they built temples, patronised native arts and many of them, like Akbar, made huge efforts in stopping religious prejudice, persecution and maintaining communal harmony here. So, at most we are talking of a handful of mosques, built hundreds of years ago on the one hand in a context and society that does not exist today, and causing hurt, mistrust, instability and division in the fabric of our society, along the length and breadth of our country, on the other. Look at what has happened in Manipur where old antagonisms have been provoked.

There is no justification for stoking such deep and lasting social turmoil for the sake of destroying a few mosques. It never ends. You heard what the Karnartaka BJP MP said about wanting to demolish mosques in Karnataka. Why can't we simply say that we have better things to do than to endlessly fight over mosques and build temples? The worst thing about these temple agitations is the ugly feelings they provoke; feelings that take us as far away as it is possible to go from religion. I was about fifteen years old when the Ram Janmabhoomi agitation started, with LK Advani's Rath Yatra. My entire school was for it. There is no ugly statement about Muslims that is made today, that I did not hear from my fellow students in school. I will never forget the malice in their eyes, the spite dripping from their lips. I will never forget the glee with which they would wave the tapes of Sadhvi Ritambra's speeches, which they would play in their cars on the way to school. But I never ever, before, then or after, heard them talk about Lord Ram, or any other god. It was the same with BJP supporters when I went to college. That was when the Babri Masjid fell. The saffronites were never short of snarky comments about Muslims but I never saw them express or demonstrate any devotion to any god, or any eagerness to go to any temple. And there was nothing particularly *dharmic* or Indic about these people and their families either. They lived a life which was no different to any secular, liberal family, save in their abusing Muslims. It was never about devotion to

Lord Ram. It was all always only and only about Hindu chauvinism and insulting Muslims.

How can anyone celebrate a temple built on the back of such lies, violence, spite and vengefulness? How can this be squared with the teachings of Hinduism? If there was cause for revenge in building this temple then how is such a motivation of revenge and anger justified in Hinduism? Take the Bhagavad Gita? Do those rejoicing at the building of the Ram Mandir consider the *Bhagavad Gita* to be a Hindu text? Well, what does the *Gita* say about morality in action? It says that your acts can be moral only if you perform them selflessly, in the spirit of duty, as an offering to god, not to fulfil your own desires and wishes. According to the Bhagvad Gita no act of revenge or anger or with an eye to the fruits of action is a moral act. *Karmenyev aadhikarastey, maa phaleshu kadachana.* This is what the Gita says about acting in anger:

क्रोधाद्भवति सम्मोहः, सम्मोहात्स्मृतिविभ्रमः। स्मृतिभ्रंशाद् बुद्धिनाशो, बुद्धिनाशात्प्रणश्यति ॥ Anger plunges you into Delusion, Delusion erases Knowledge. With loss of Knowledge, is Reason lost, With Reason lost, you Fall. The Gita starts with Arjun saying to Krishna that he does not want to fight. And Krishna's first response is तस्माद् युध्यस्व भारत. Get up you are a warrior; you must fight or you will be reviled by the world. This is the 18th shloka in the 2nd chapter of the Gita. So, if that is the message of the Gita then why does it continue to 18 chapters? What was more there left to say that the Gita carried on for 16 chapters more?

Does Krishna repeat his sayings about the duty of the warrior not to run from the battlefield? No. The dialogue goes on because there is so much more to the question of what moral action is; what a Dharma Yuddh is. Even when we breathe, we kill so many tiny beings, so how can we humans ever speak of moral action? All the chapters that follow the initial exchange between Arjun and Krishna are a deep reflection on this question. And the answer that emerges is that you can never truly renounce action; you can never be free of karma. Simply in living and by existing you perform karma. But equally, you must always be ethical in your actions. How can you do this? How can you keep your moral purity while engaging in any action, whether eating and breathing; or killing your brothers and uncles in war? And the answer is what we call *'nishkaama karma'*. Acting without desire, without greed, without anger, without any selfish interest. Does the slogan *'Mandir vahi banega'* strike you as anything but angry and vengeful?

What does Hinduism say about how to fight wrong? अक्रोधेन जयेत् क्रोधम्, असाधुं साधुना जयेत् । जयेत् कदर्यम दानेन, जयेत् सत्येन चानृतम ॥ The Mahabharata says: Defeat anger with calm, bad conduct with good; Win over meanness with generosity, and falsehood with truth.

And we all know *"Ahimsa Parmo Dharma"* which Gandhiji was so fond of quoting.

The *Manu Smriti* – there is a tendency these days to mock the *Manu Smriti* because of its description of the caste system. But all Hindu scriptures and epics have caste. If that is a reason then everything must go – the Gita, the Valmiki Ramayana - everything. What I say is follow the *Manu Smriti* but follow all of it. See what it says about the 10 principles of Dharama: धृति: क्षमा दमोऽस्तेयं शौचमिन्द्रियनिग्रह: । धीर्विद्या सत्यमक्रोधो दशकं धर्मलक्षणम् ।। Patience, forgiveness, self-restraint, not to take that which another's, purity, abstention, righteous action, pursuit of knowledge, truth, renouncing anger.

So, for all these reasons I call what is happening in Ayodhya on January 22nd a lie, a celebration of wickedness, a desecration of Hinduism, and an affront to our civilisational heritage. I am fasting as an act of protest and sorrow. I will take liquids and some sugar and salt to keep my health in balance. I will do readings from Tagore, Gandhi, Martin Luther King and other great people who came from this land or were inspired by the people of this land, in the hope that it will give us all some *margdarshan* (guidance) in these dark and hopeless times.

Jai Hind.
**Suranya Aiyar**

# Fellow Hindus threaten Suranya

After three weeks of hate mail in the name of the majority community, I don't feel safe from any stranger with a majority community name anymore. I don't feel safe inviting a *puFohit* to conduct prayers which I liked to do for my kids around *Vasant Panchami*. I don't feel safe inviting a *mehendi wali* to my house, I don't feel safe accepting friend requests, I don't feel safe walking into a shopping centre festooned with orange flags, I am even wondering whether if I went to a temple, I would be hounded out. I have a cousin uncle down South who is a Modi *Bhakt* and he did not approve of my fast. So, I sent him my explanation and a sample of the hate mail that I got and he had nothing to say about it. It showed me how blinded people are. My own uncle, who knew me from a babe-in-arms is unaffected by the gross threats to me, his own niece? Strangers have called to express their solidarity, but no call from my aunt, who is also a great saffronite. I haven't called her as I don't want the heart-breaking confirmation that she endorses what is going on.

Actually, no one taught me to be a Hindu. I came from a modern family where religion was left entirely up to us to adopt or not. We got exposure to all religions as we had a diverse circle of friends and family. Everyone in our family was of an artistic and philosophical bent of mind, so I learnt about many, many religions growing up. I could have chosen to be anything, including atheist. But right from the start Hinduism captivated me. I embraced Hinduism completely voluntarily because I found it to be enchanting, magnificent and profound.

Only once in my life after suffering a personal disappointment, suddenly I felt like the gods had gone silent and all the joy and counsel I would get from them just melted away. It was the most disorienting and awful experience. Like being lost in outer space. Utterly alone in the infinite vastness and the relentless mawing silence. Slowly it came back...I don't quite know how. Hand of God. Anyway, I don't believe in raising my children without god. I am fine if they embrace any other religion, but they must have faith that existence is more than what we see, and that there is magic in the world.

I don't understand atheism. I don't reject it on moral but on epistemological grounds. I simply can't understand a language of existence that does not have some form of Knowing Unknown behind it. I often feel that my sensibility about this is the converse of the athiest's - they do not see God anywhere, while I see god everywhere! So, I taught my children about all the gods, about taking blessings from Ganeshji before any exam or competition, about praying to Devi Saraswati for intelligence, about all the different forms of Lakshmi so that they don't see wealth only in riches, about our family deity, the mighty Shiva. I took my children in 2016, to my ancestral village in Tanjore and proudly showed them the Brihadeshwara temple. Now I hear that the temples down South have signs saying non-Hindus are to keep out. So, what does this mean for the possibility of my ever going there again, since I have been called a non-Hindu by the new age Hindus? Will I not be allowed in there? I don't even want to test the position by calling the priests of the temple that my grandfather built here in Delhi. How much more hurt shall I invite on myself? Lots I guess, before the madness dissipates, but certainly not going to test things at the temple just yet, at least not before Vasant Panchami. Half a century ago those priests of our family temple had refused to marry my parents as my mother was a Sikh. But these things are not cast in stone. Over the decades they softened and never again excluded my mother. But now that the bugle of rigidity has been sounded, God knows how they would react to me.

I remember my ancestral home and nearby small temple where we once had a homam (*hawan*) that my husband, kids and mother and father attended, along with my other family members who live there. This place is a few minutes' walk from the temple where Tyagaraja attained samadhi and which hosts the famous annual Tyagaraja festival that I had hoped to attend one day, but now? Half an hour's drive away is the Brihadeswara temple. I went there last April .... now God knows if I will be able to go there again. But no matter, there is a beautiful Bharatnatyam dance composition describing the splendour of the Brihadeshwara temple. I will watch that and it will be good enough. A temple is not everything. And God is everywhere.

# Non-Resident Indian cries
# for the land of her fathers

RASHMEE ROSHAN LALL

August 2020

Now that Indian Prime Minister Narendra Modi has laid the foundation stone of a Hindu temple in Ayodhya, I couldn't help but think of the chapter I contributed to the book *Making Sense of India* published in 2016, two years after Modi's first magnificent national election victory. This collection of essays by writers from academia, journalism, and politics sets out to answer a key question: "Where is India headed under Modi?" Today, we see the direction of travel clearer than ever before. India is fulfilling the destiny long promised by Modi's party, the BJP, as well as of the RSS, the fount of its ideology. India is becoming a theocracy, a Hindu-*desh* (Hindu country).

I titled my chapter "An *aam* (ordinary) NRI's view of the new India" and sub-titled it *The dharma of disenfranchisement*, accepting that most of my fellow Indians at home would not regard an NRI as an authentic voice. They would see the NRI as unentitled to critique the motherland. I acknowledged this as follows: "By that token, I have almost no right to cast a critical eye or god forbid find fault with the land of my fathers. I haven't lived there for any substantial length of time for 20 years, except for a brief, finite period (2008-11). So, I have no rights, I said, "but surely I can claim civic responsibility"? Surely I can claim "some sense of good citizenship of the world, of which 2.4 per cent of the land is occupied by India and in which one in every seven people is Indian"?

So, what do I see when Modi lays a symbolic silver brick at the site of the demolished mediaeval mosque and declares it to be "liberated". What are we seeing here? What should the world know about Modi's India? As I wrote in the chapter, "It is rare to be able to set a date for the transformation of a whole country and its mindset. But as a then-resident Indian journalist, I believe it really did kick off on September 25, 1990, when L. K. Advani, then leader of Modi's BJP, began his Ram *rath yatra* to the northern city of Ayodhya to build support for the movement to reclaim the disputed Babri mosque for Hindus. The goal was to erect a temple dedicated to the infant Lord Ram, Ramlala, at the site that the cultural nationalists believed to be his place of birth. A mosque, built in the 1520s on the orders of Babur, India's first Mughal emperor, stood on the site when Advani set off from Somnath on the western coast, in a Toyota cannily redesigned as a *rath*, a traditional chariot."

Five years before this yatra, the BJP's website had the following explanation of the symbolism of Advani's point of departure and the significance of the journey: "It was at Somnath that the assault on Hindu temples and shrines, the living symbols of an ancient nation, by Islamic invaders began – in 1026 the Somnath shrine was ransacked and its riches plundered by Mahmud Ghaznavi."

The BJP website also had the following promise about Advani's 1990 *rath yatra*: "The pilgrimage will be over the day Ram Lalla finds his rightful place in a temple commemorating the sacred site of his birth." (Interestingly, the same language doesn't seem to be on the website anymore. Perhaps the BJP feels it no longer needs it; the "pilgrimage" is over, after all, with the mosque having been razed and the foundation of the new temple laid.)

We are seeing Modi's India being built on the rubble of a violently destroyed place of worship. It is a troubling foundation. I weep for the land of my fathers.

# Give back my Old India, Mr Modi
# I do not want your New India

Farzana Behram Contractor

2019

I don't know anymore, what to make of what. All I know is, without exception, everyone seems to be afraid. Afraid of the outcome of the ongoing elections. Fear and uncertainty seem to be the general emotion everywhere. What will happen to our lives if the BJP comes back to power, majority or coalition, it doesn't matter. Twice as bad? Fact remains that we put our hopes in this party and they let us down. Lies, deceit, pretence ... they misled, mistreated, caused confusion, twisted and re-twisted facts, they really did make a mockery of our intelligence.

Governance ... did that really happen? Especially in the last three years. The government just seemed to be on a campaign trail, preparing for the elections. All they were doing is planning and plotting, playing all the time. Defending themselves, strategizing. PR machinery and IT department in full control, constantly in damage control mode. That is, when they were not churning out fake news, whipping up Nationalistic fervour, running the opposition down.

No stone was to be left unturned. By hook or by crook, they had to win these elections. Never mind what the world thought or believed. They believe they are the best.

I have two yardsticks with which I judge myself. One, when I sleep at night, do I sleep? Or toss and turn, let the demons of my mind take over. Feel awful about something. And two, when I wake up and go brush my teeth, first thing in the morning, can I look myself in the eye and smile at myself. If I can't, I try and be honest with myself, face things squarely. If I must apologise to someone, I do. Forgiving someone or even oneself is a cleanser. And 'sorry', simply is a promise that you will not repeat the offensive deed again.

But am I being naïve? Am I expecting something so evolved from a government that really has sown seeds of hatred all around? That turned a blind eye to lynching and a deaf ear to cries of pain and torture. How subtly it was done at first and, so blatantly later. So, emboldened they got, so brazen. Nothing mattered, absolute power and self-importance paved their bloody path. But you know what – naivete aside, I do believe like most of you, that what goes around, comes around. And heaven and hell are right here, on earth. So, let us stop for a moment and see what we have.

Hindus being led, urged to believe Muslims are bad, they must be done away with. Hurt them, hit them, kill them, wipe them off from the face of the earth. At least let's throw them out of India. Really! Pray, why? What gives you the right? Are we talking about living beings here or some robots? NRC: Assam, Bengal ... Get ready for bloodshed. If you are Hindus, Sikhs or Buddhists, we accept you. We will issue you citizenship even if you don't have the necessary papers. The rest can go to hell. Christians included!

And what's with the Christians. They are such peace-loving, fun-loving people, involved in their own small world, happy-going and what not, what have they done to raise your shackles? And the Dalits ... makes me want to cry, the treatment meted out to them. What have they done to deserve the inhuman atrocities inflicted on them. In this day and age, you differentiate human beings on caste.

Please pause for a moment and reflect on this very sobering thought. You or I, any of us, could have been born a Dalit. Taking birth in a hut or a palace, in a Muslim or Hindu home, is simply a matter of chance. Just think about it. Shouldn't we embrace them and all human beings in our fold? Love and respect and cherish one another ... like we did as children, when our friends were from every community. We were so much the richer for that. Christmas, Diwali, Eid, summer holidays, school tours, we looked forward to all this. We shared life and we shared laughter, and we were so happy. We never thought about religion, our parents never veered our thinking in that direction. Why can't it be so, again?

New India? I don't want it. Please give me back my old India. It was loving and secure, so comfy, so carefree. So unfettered. First it was Bombay that went down, it changed its colour and character, no thanks to the riots in the aftermath of the fall of the Babri Masjid, and then bit by bit the North of India. I shudder to think about women and young girls and the rampant rape cases:

Not so stray anymore, let me address the elephant in the room directly. Mr Modi, why did you allow our nation to come to such a pass? I trusted you. I believed you when you made all those promises. Yes, I am a Muslim and I voted for you the last time around. You let me down. You lied. You did not take care of our country. You caused immense human suffering. You were given the opportunity, you failed. Yes, you represented us well abroad and I used to feel proud at first. And then I was disillusioned; there wasn't any strong foreign policy in place, no real agenda. How was India gaining? It just seemed like personal growth, new friendships for you. Hobnobbing at the highest level must have been rather pleasure inducing.

Mr Modi, why did you look the other way when poor human beings were being killed, beaten with sticks, with bare hands, lynched to death. For what? Transporting cattle? Suspicion and charges of eating its meat? That's a crime, you must die! Does it matter that overnight livelihoods were callously snatched? That there were starving families, children dying at home? So, what if farmers are crying? So, what if they can't afford to feed their old and ailing cattle? So, what if they just let them loose to run amuck and destroy fields with whatever little they are managing to grow? Mr Modi, read what senior journalist Akbar Patel has to say. It's an eye opener. I want to give up milk, all dairy in fact, after reading what I did. I respect all animals, cows included.

And why did it take you eight days to come out and tell the nation, don't hurt the Kashmiri students? This was a tepid and lukewarm response to the unfolding tragedy in the wake of the Pulwama attack on our soldiers. Thousands of students, young and frightened, were left to fend for themselves, trying to find ways of going home back to Kashmir, trying to find ways of not getting raped, beaten and killed. It's horrific. The only way to understand this emotion is put yourself in that situation. Or imagine if your child, just 15 or 16 years old, was in that precarious position. What would you feel?

I would like our Prime Minister to know, I don't particularly care about development, economic glory, jobs – not in the face of what I am talking about. All I want is a sense of security, of peace and freedom. To know that if I have been wronged justice will be done. I want a sense of togetherness and, dare I say, I want to feel loved in my country, by my colleagues, my fellow beings. I want respect as a citizen. I don't want to feel threatened and scared, worried to speak my mind. To call a spade a damn spade. I don't want to feel alienated. I don't want to look over my shoulder all the time, speak in whispers or worry if I will be labelled unpatriotic, and anti-national.

I don't have to wear my nationalistic heart on my sleeve, do I? I never did in the past. Yet I know, then as now, I would defend my country's name in any manner, in any situation. That I am really, truly proud to be an Indian, the 'old' Indian, not the new one who looks at another in distrust and judges people solely based on caste and creed.

And yes, I don't have to be a Paki-basher to prove my credentials. They are our neighbours and that is all. Let them lead their lives and us, ours. Spewing hatred on them, bringing them onto the centre-stage, is giving a non-issue importance. And let's refrain from saying things like, "We are not saving our nuclear bombs for Diwali." That's very irresponsible of you Mr Modi. A war is easy to start but difficult to control. It charts its own course. Look at Afghanistan ... and how can we forget Hiroshima and Nagasaki? Escalated warfare in modern times – and the aftermath is unimaginable.

Not only will India and Pakistan perish, but so will our neighbours too. Let's keep their safety in mind and perhaps learn from Bhutan and its peaceful ways. Gross National Happiness is the philosophy which guides that little country. It includes an index which is used to measure the collective happiness and well-being of their population. And it is incorporated in their Constitution.

Humanity or the lack of it, is my biggest concern. Safeguarding the Constitution of India for me is foremost. It includes safeguarding all our institutions. How can we reduce our Judiciary? If that highest office is compromised, what is left? Supreme Court, the police force, CIA, RAW, Income Tax departments, Reserve Bank, leave them be. Let them be! We have fantastic people in India who, when left to do their jobs, will perform in exemplary fashion. And our Army! I, along with every Indian salute them. The army is ours, it's an emotion and the soldiers are our heartbeats. Let's not call them 'Modi Sena' for then we belittle them. Incidentally, this is a very touchy subject for me. I was too little to understand it when we were at war with Pakistan, but I saw my mother die a new death every day, when her first born was at the border. My eldest brother left college to go fight for India. He was commissioned into the Maratha Light Infantry and went on to become a Captain and an ace paratrooper. Also, I am proud to say my husband's cousin, my most favourite family member, was the late Khushru Rustamji. He was Founder Director General of the Border Security Force (BSF). There is much I learned from him. Yes, I am proud of our Army.

So, my friends, think. What do you want as a citizen of India? What are your priorities? What legacy do you want to leave for the children of today? Ask yourself, is it hate or love that wins hearts? If you say money and jobs, I say that will automatically happen ... but first there must be an atmosphere of peace, love, trust, safety and security. Indians are very resilient. We can deal with poverty and hunger, but not with hate and distrust with a life that is lived in constant fear. Let's love and look after one another.

# Academia and Bollywood
# Two major casualties

ZOYA HASAN

The present regime is more intolerant of criticism and dissent than the ones earlier even though it is more powerful than those. Despite the popular mandate in consecutive elections, it's thought control 'is not complete'. So, it is determined to 'control every person who thinks', observes Gyan Prakash. 'If you show signs of thinking, being able to change your mind' having ideas and a vision different from the ruling party's leaders, you will be throttled and proscribed. Democracy is diminished because dissent is the bedrock of democracy. This has affected individual freedom as well as the functioning of the executive, judiciary, Bollywood, media and the academia.

Academic freedom is closely linked with the right to dissent. It refers to the freedom of scholars to conduct critical enquiry, for teachers and students to engage with society in the way they want, to collectively deliberate on any idea without fear of sanction, censure or illegitimate interference. Universities and other higher education institutions are supposed to provide critical understanding through the promotion of reason, tolerance and democratic debate. Instead, we are witnessing a clouding of reason, and an obfuscation of facts and truth, which can be sustained only through unreason and prejudice. The most serious threat to such freedom comes from the prevailing 'anti-intellectualism' that finds the very idea of thought and thinking problematic. This approach has been strengthened through a variety of methods and propaganda tools. The concepts of fact and truth and expertise in academics has no place in the current scheme of things.

This regime seeks to conquer and impose its ideas and interpretations on the academy. The fear of independent thinking leads to an eagerness to control academic teaching, research, publication and promotions in universities. Academics are perceived as a threat because they raise questions that the regime wants to avoid, if not silence altogether. There's limited space for liberal thinking and values in universities, colleges or institutions as they are expected to defer to the sensibilities of the state. This requires controlling educational institutions, training institutes, and recruiting agencies like the Union Public Service Commission (UPSC) by pushing changes in their programmes and priorities, and by making key appointments of personnel who will execute such changes.

The urge to control premier institutes had begun early in the term of this party's regime. This trend can be traced to the Jawaharlal Nehru University (JNU) agitation of February 2016 and the protests against Rohith Vemula's suicide at the University of Hyderabad. The conquest of JNU was an important goal of this project. Hence, a concerted attempt to control JNU, one of the world's leading universities for the humanities and social sciences, and one which combines teaching and research which are to a great degree, institutionally separated in India. The idea of a public university that fuses research and teaching gained real momentum in universities like JNU. What is under attack is the idea of a public university, inclusive education, and the right to dissent and the study and research in the social sciences and humanities.

The standoff in JNU in 2016 after some students organized a meeting to discuss instances of capital punishment illustrates this regime's approach to academic activity. This involved the arrest of the president of the student union Kanhaiya Kumar on charges of sedition, and the battering of students, faculty and the media by a mob of lawyers, some with professed sympathies for the Hindu right, in the Patiala House court, with the Delhi Police refusing to intervene. Six JNU students were charged with sedition for alleged 'anti-national' slogans. Ever since, a troll army regularly labels JNU students as anti-national and urban Naxals. The idea is to stigmatise

JNU as an anti-national site and to pronounce protests in the university as illegitimate and illicit.

State interference in educational institutions is not new but the interference that we see now had never happened on this scale. Political parties have tended to interfere with education, but that had not prevented the flourishing of a vibrant academic atmosphere. The pervasive political control of universities is reflected in the sharp downward decline in India's position in an Academic Freedom Index, developed by the V-Dem Institute of the University of Gothenburg 2021. In their 2023 update to this Index, V-Dem Institute noted that India is among 22 countries out of 179 in the world, where institutions and scholars enjoy 'significantly less freedom today than 10 years ago'. The report notes that India's decline in academic freedom started from a comparatively high-level during India's democratic period and it is now associated with 'rapidly accelerating autocratisation'. India 'demonstrates the pernicious relationship between populist governments, autocratisation, and constraints on academic freedom', the 2023 update on the report says. This was the time that India dropped on the electoral democracy scale too and was labelled by V-Dem as 'an electoral autocracy'. The undermining of institutional autonomy aligns with the assessment that 'centralisation, bureaucratisation, and politicisation have historically weakened university autonomy in India. There is considerable pressure on academic freedom – institutional autonomy and campus integrity – and constraints on academic freedom. An Indian Report on Academic Freedom in India published in 2020 (prepared as part of a status report in response to a call for submissions on academic freedom by the UN Special Rapporteur on the protection and promotion of the right to freedom of opinion and expression) documented the diminishing scope for academic freedom, noting that since 2014, India has seen an 'unprecedented assault on academic freedom as well as academics'. The report identified the following areas of concern: Censorship of books and interference with university syllabi, denial of permission, disruption of seminars, meetings, events on campus, arrest of faculty members or criminal charges against them and arrest of students, attacks on faculty and students, termination, suspension, 'resignation' of faculty, and suspension of students, denial of research visas/restrictions on academic exchanges. Dissent, criticism and independent opinion are penalised by suspension, expulsion, withdrawal of scholarships or, in the case of teachers, stalling promotion and retirement benefits.

Deference to authority is rewarded which has affected the selection of vice chancellors, faculty, framing of courses, and several other aspects of the functioning and administration of universities. Their appointment and even that of the faculty is often done under political influence. People with RSS links have been appointed as administrators at several universities who allegedly favour research topics espoused by the Hindu nationalists. The heads of different institutions tend to be people showing ideological proximity to the regime in power. Important academic and administrative posts have been filled with people who are ideologically close to the ruling party. Congress often did the same. But in the past, those appointed had professional attainment to their credit, whereas many appointees today lack academic credentials or achievement.

Barring the brief period of Emergency, academic freedom in India was not throttled by the state at least as far as central universities were concerned. There are no instances of seminars being monitored, academic books being banned, or the imprisonment of public intellectuals and academics for their views. However, the covert and overt forms of pressures on academic institutions headed by different political parties including the Congress were commonplace, especially in state universities. But even then, there was no concerted threat to academic freedom or dissent which is at risk now. Evidence of this risk comes from restrictions on freedom of scholars who want to do research on India by way of visa denials, besides pressing lawsuits and suspending professors in universities on various grounds. Far from nurturing critical thinking, there is constant interference with critical enquiry and research. The Ministry of External

Affairs released guidelines for holding online international conferences, seminars, and activities. Institutions are now required to request prior permission if the subject is centred on the security of the Indian state or 'clearly related to India's internal matters'. The directive was later withdrawn following a strong opposition from scientists and academics.

Changes in syllabi and the exclusion of several important ideas, movements and books from university syllabi on non-academic grounds have become common. Publishers have been compelled to withdraw books and references to Jawaharlal Nehru expunged from textbooks in BJP ruled states. There's a long list of seminars, lectures and events that have been cancelled, meetings have been disrupted. University administrations have acted against organizers after an event, as in the case of seminars in Ramjas College, and colleges and universities in Jodhpur, Bhopal, and Lucknow and so on. Cancellations also happen when affiliate organizations of the Hindu right protests events in an aggressive and militant manner. Authorities buckle under pressure. The order to celebrate Christmas Day as Good Governance Day in all Central educational institutions – including Navodaya Vidyalayas and Central Board of Secondary Education affiliated schools, the 45 Central universities, the IITs and the IIMs– was an early indication of this.

Academics have been penalized for critical thought, scholars have been 'reprimanded by universities' for criticizing the government. The *Times Higher Education Supplement* (London) reported that in some cases academics were given the sense that 'we are noting who from which institutions' are indulging in actions such as signing petitions. They were called into meetings with university officials after publicly criticizing government policies. One academic who was called for such a meeting said administrators gave her the 'impression' she should be careful about what causes she is seen to support. A teacher in Kolhapur Institute of Technology's College of Engineering, was asked to go on leave because some students in her objected to her comments in the classroom. She was harassed for countering statements in her classroom that Muslims are rapists and never get punished for their crimes. To avoid things getting out of hand, she told them that rape is not limited to any religion or community and rapists don't have any religion or caste. What she said was recorded, then doctored and circulated on social media, leading to her being forced by college authorities to go on leave and there is even a police investigation against her. Ashoka, a private university on the outskirts of Delhi has faced criticism after one of its faculty members resigned following a row over his academic paper that suggested potential electoral "manipulation" on several seats during the 2019 general elections. The university administration was accused of stifling academic freedom after it distanced itself from the research paper, thereby 'forcing' his resignation.

A related aspect of this phenomenon is a deliberate under-emphasis on humanities and social sciences that open the mind and encourage students and teachers to think critically. But their significance has been reduced partly because they are seen as less useful in a world where economic calculations matter most, but also because they are seen to be more critical disciplines and therefore bring trouble for university administrations. Humanities and social sciences provide a crucial source of critical reflection and concern for the lives and interests of others that simply cannot be provided by an education system concerned only with technical skills that have immediate economic application. 'By de-emphasizing the liberal arts, we are devaluing and weakening democratic citizenship...A healthy democratic society needs independent-minded and creative individuals, who have the character and confidence to resist arbitrary authority and hierarchical attitudes,' argues Martha Nussbaum, in *Not for Profit: Why Democracy Needs the Humanities.*

Unlike the social sciences, history doesn't suffer from under-emphasis or neglect because rewriting history is an essential for imposing one single ideology in academic institutions. So, a concerted attempt is being made to replace the study of India's syncretic history with mythology and the rich diversity of Indian philosophy with Hindu theology. School textbooks are rewritten by removing references to Mughal history, Gandhi's opposition to Hindu nationalism, and the 2002 Gujarat massacre. This is in stark contrast to Nehru's writing of Indian history, for example, which as David Kopf states, was done in a way 'to preclude even the slightest nationalist bigotry and distortion'. The Hindutva forces lack the expertise to produce an Indian history that will meet even minimum standards of historical research, hence, they produce history by administrative fiat and by reorganizing educational syllabi through the New Education Policy introduced in 2021 and changing textbooks to reflect a view of history gleaned from mythology and religious texts or appropriating conservative icons from the nationalist pantheon to compensate for their conspicuous absence from the freedom struggle.

The UGC issued a directive to the vice-chancellors and principals of colleges and universities to hold lectures on the theme of 'India: The Mother of Democracy' on Constitution Day. In his speech, the Prime Minister referred to India as the 'mother of democracy', citing examples of a democratic ethos from Hindu texts and history, even though there is no evidence to support this claim. Democracy is a modern institution that emerged together with nationalism and secularism. India established democracy after Independence but this was not preordained by the ideas and practice of democracy centuries before. But gullible thinking must be popularised by glorifying the ruling dispensation and its ideological proclivities.

## Sarkari film industry

From the realm of academia to the hub of popular culture - Bollywood, the Hindu right has sought to control every institution and to an extent managed to overpower the founts of dissent, pluralism and syncretism. The regime did not have to exert much effort in the case of the media as it volunteered to self-censor. More official inducements and various methods including intimidation were needed to subjugate Bollywood that had played a stellar role in promoting India's secular ethos and the hope and optimism of nation-building in the early decades after Independence. When top stars were trolled and intimidated or their films were boycotted, their colleagues looked the other way. Several films stereotyping Muslims fuelled by Hindutva supporters have been produced and promoted officially, often endorsed by the ruling dispensation. Hindi cinema is now fraught with Islamophobia which has infected films and web series, especially productions about terrorism, war and espionage. These films have more to do with ideology than entertainment. The film industry plays a supporting role for the government, amplifies the Hindu right-wing message and sows divisions between communities. But as in academia, everyone in Bollywood has not fallen in line, and hence, there is a greater urge to exert control and snuff out dissent in both spheres.

Bollywood has come under the radar of right-wing social media and official censorship for any content deemed offensive to religious sentiments of the majority community. The Union Minister for Information and Broadcasting even went as far as demanding an explanation from the Central Board of Film Certification (CBFC) on why it cleared a scene involving lines from the *Bhagvad Gita* in the Christophe Nolan's much acclaimed film *Oppenheimer* in 2023. Attempts have been made in the past too to try and control Indian cinema - mostly through the CBFC, that can order alterations or essentially ban movies by refusing to certify them. But in this case the minister asked for cuts after the film had been cleared by CBFC. Certification once given, cannot be revoked. By asking the Board for an 'explanation', the minister was attempting to override the institutional mechanism with a political response. In the process, a blow was dealt to both artistic freedom and due process.

The 'hurt sentiments' argument is often used to claim legitimacy for imposing curbs on free expression. The idea is to control Bollywood which the regime thinks is full of liberals and seculars who need to be weeded out. It was part of the move 'to control and purge spaces seen as controlled by 'left liberals,' or as syncretic and thus unamenable to Hindu-Muslim polarisation', notes Nivedita Menon. This limits the space for religions and ethnic groups in the film industry which was earlier representative of India's great diversity. The regime has used various methods to purge Bollywood of Muslims who dominated it, and of its cultural syncretism and cosmopolitanism which found reflection in the movies.

The clout of the Hindu right has ensured Twitter boycott campaigns associated with the right-wing against some of Bollywood's biggest stars. According to *The Guardian*, 'organized trolling has also been deployed against films and streaming series such as *Thappad*, *A Suitable Boy* and Bombay Begums, particularly for the last two's depictions of interfaith romance. After a scene from *A Suitable Boy* depicted a Hindu girl and Muslim boy kissing, a state-level minister called for a criminal case against Netflix India, which streamed the show.' Aamir Khan's movie *Laal Singh Chaddha* – an adaptation of Tom Hank's *Forrest Gump* – became a target of what is now known as the Boycott Bollywood Campaign, leading the actor to a defensive reiteration of his love for his country. The film fared poorly at the box office. Thanks to the pressure exerted through censorship and right-wing campaigns, Bollywood is glutted with movies and TV shows that align with right-wing politics and revisionist history and mythmaking and films targeting Muslims on the pretext of terrorism.

A culture of self-censorship pervades the streaming industry. OTT platforms are under pressure from the Hindu right to censure shows and they often shelve or don't take up projects that might upset the regime and its affiliates. Executives at Netflix and Prime Video ask for extensive changes to rework political plots and remove references to religion that might offend the

Hindu right and the BJP. *The Washington Post* reports that in the last four years, 'a chill has swept through the streaming industry in India as Prime Minister Narendra Modi's BJP tightened its grip on the country's political discourse and the American technology platforms that host it. Just as the BJP and its ideological allies have spread propaganda on WhatsApp to advance their Hindu-first agenda and deployed the state's coercive muscle to squash dissent on Twitter, they have used the threat of criminal cases and coordinated mass public pressure to shape what Indian content gets produced by Netflix and Prime Video.' Suketu Mehta says Netflix dropped the film adaptation of his book *Maximum City* because the director Anurag Kashyap criticised the government.

So, the cultural and religious right stopped Bollywood from giving messages of social and religious harmony and promoting a pro-poor ethos. And as to the academic community, it has been polarised, making dissent risky for those speaking truth to power.

Based on and excerpted from Democracy on Trial: Majoritarianism and Dissent in India published by Aakar Books.

# 'Bloody Sunday' in JNU

SUCHETA MAHAJAN

2020

As a teacher of history, I have taught about Bloody Sunday, the event which sparked off protests in Russia in 1905. Yesterday, I lived through Bloody Sunday right in the very campus I teach at: Jawaharlal Nehru University. It was a balmy afternoon when my research group met at my house. A student presented a chapter of her thesis, on which there was an extensive discussion. One of the students took photographs of the meeting, saying she would post them on her Facebook page with the ironic caption "lockdown in Jawaharlal Nehru University" to emphasise that academic activity continued.

The students dispersed at around 5.30 pm, mostly headed to nearby *dhabas* for tea. One of them, along with my niece, stepped out towards Sabarmati Dhaba. The Jawaharlal Nehru University Teachers' Association had given a call for a meeting at 4 pm and a sizeable number of teachers were around even at 6.30 pm. My niece saw a group of students, many masked and holding lathis and rods, assembled outside Periyar hostel. She continued towards the *dhaba* only to find herself, other students and teachers set upon by this group. She ran for her life and hid under a table at 24/7, a popular eatery outside Sabarmati. She saw students being thrashed and teachers fleeing to escape this armed mob – which included women too. Large stones were hurled. To escape, many students ran into neighbouring Sabarmati hostel for shelter. The masked group chased them into the hostel, battering everything in their way, from windows to doors – creating scenes of terror. As many as 15 students took shelter in a room and prevented the door from being broken down by the sheer weight of their bodies.

Later, I met one of the mess workers from the hostel who had escaped being beaten by locking himself in an office room. One of my colleagues, Sucharita Sen, had also been hit by a stone on her forehead and was admitted to the trauma centre at AIIMS. JNU Students' Union President Aishe Ghosh, clearly a target, was hit on the head, and bled profusely. I began to receive calls from students who were holed up in their hostel rooms, fearing attacks. Apart from recognised students from left groups, many Muslim students sought advice on what to do. I advised them to stay in their rooms until the situation settled. But rather than settling down, trouble came from another quarter as militant, Bajrang Dal type groups mobilised from surrounding villages like Munirka and Ber Sarai, amassed at the main gate, and now posed a threat to the safety of all JNU's residents.

We rushed to the main gate on a call from the teachers' association. The situation was ugly. Slogans such as "*Goli se uda do saalon ko*" (blow them off with bullets), "*tukde tukde gang waalon ko*" rent the air, punctuated with "Bharat Mata Ki Jai". I felt as though I was in a gladiatorial arena, awaiting with dread the bloodthirsty mob which might be "allowed" to push their way in. The popular 'Azaadi' slogan associated with Kanhaiya Kumar was inverted to "*Naxalvad se Azadi*", "*Naxalvaadiyon se campus mukt karo*". While standing at the gate, I had a strange sense of déjà vu. It seemed as if were back in 2016 when popular anger was being whipped up by organisations linked to the ruling party against alleged 'anti-nationals' and supposed seditionists at JNU. It fed into the agenda of the BJP and its cohorts to whip up aggressive nationalism around supposed threats to the nation. JNU was to be invoked as the enemy within, just as Pakistan was the enemy without.

It reminded me of a larger reality – that today was part of a continuum of assaults on the university, which curiously began within days of the present Vice Chancellor taking office. I have been privy, as the head of my centre, to the systematic hollowing out of the institutional edifice of the university, including the highest bodies such as the Academic Council, as well as the ignoring, mocking at and suppression of voices expressing differences, let alone dissent. I remembered how it was only the courts to which we had turned which gave us some redress. I have spent the last three years as a petitioner in the court and every month, many of us teachers contribute to a legal fund to monetarily support the teachers and students who have moved the courts.

All this while, on Sunday, we were frantically calling those who we knew in the media and in the police to intervene. I wrote in a JNU alumni group that we needed support, including the presence of sympathisers in large numbers. Soon, groups of students and teachers from Jamia and Delhi University began to reach Jawaharlal Nehru University. Gradually, they outnumbered the groups baying for our blood. We could now turn to escorting marooned students to their hostels or outside campus. In all this, the security personnel were glaringly absent. When my husband came into the campus at 6.30 pm, there were many police personnel at the main gate, but none where they were required. The police later said that they had been asked not to come in by the Vice Chancellor. The police was given permission to enter only after images of the reign of terror streamed continuously on television channels. We were somewhat relieved when very senior police officials, including a JNU alumnus, personally directed operations.

This raises many uncomfortable, unanswered questions about the attitude of those responsible for the functioning of the university. Was it merely the apathy of the administration towards the privations of certain sections of students and teachers seen by them as troublemakers, or was there complicity or connivance by the administration as is perceived by students and teachers?

Whatever the answer to that is, there is a clear failure of leadership at the university. Let alone leading from the front, no responsible official of the university was to be seen anywhere. I stop and ask myself: was this unexpected from an administration which has only carried out the wilful destruction of the university? Had not the Vice Chancellor, as perceived by students and teachers, been appointed to do the bidding of the powers that be, namely, to destroy this university, which was seen as a beacon of the values of the constitution?

When I walked back home much past midnight, it was not with an injury from a heavy stone which hit me on my forehead as it did others, but a heavy heart, as if a big stone had settled on it.

Cry, my beloved campus! Cry, my beloved country!

# Delhi University: Microcosm of a Police State

RAAZ

November 2024

On the sunny morning of 23 October 2024, the courtyard of Delhi University's arts faculty was swarming with more police officers than university students. We all know how this story is going to go. By afternoon, 11 students had been detained. Their crime? Attempting to enter their university library. You may believe this is an exaggeration for dramatic effect. But, as far as anyone could see, this was the extent of the criminal act. Still, let us understand the relevant context.

The central library of the arts faculty is an important resource for students, but one that is brimming with issues. Since September, there have been appeals to the administration for the implementation of basic reforms – reinstating 24-hour access to the research floor, opening the computer section and providing clean drinking water, among others. However, the librarian steadfastly ignored these, first by denying that the problems persist despite the hundreds of student signatures pointing to the contrary, and eventually by refusing to meet with the students. This spurred students in the library movement to give a protest call for 2 p.m. on 23 October.

At 11 a.m., two students wanted to access the library for their regular use. 'It was our routine study session in the morning. But we were stopped by the security. The librarian was standing there, surrounded by his staff and security forces. He said that we students specifically were banned from using the library for three days', says Rajveer, a fifth-year PhD scholar in the Punjabi department. Rajveer and her classmate were selectively targeted for speaking on behalf of the students. They were denied entry into the library despite showing their college identity card and library card, and eventually detained. 'The night before, I had got a call from my head of department (HOD)', Rajveer continues. 'He tried to intimidate me and said we should not protest. A person from the National Assessment and Accreditation Council (NAAC) was coming to inspect the college for annual rankings and our dissent would spoil the department's reputation, the HOD said. I told him that if the librarian would meet with us and hear us out, we would not need to protest. We are not doing this for fun, we only want our issues resolved.'

We see a strong case for unauthorised detentions by the police in violation of the Bharatiya Nyaya Sanhita (BNS) Sections 126 (on wrongful restraint) and 127 (wrongful confinement), acting on the mala fide intentions of the Delhi University administration. Nevertheless, the story continues to unfold. At 2 p.m., students gathered to speak with the librarian regarding the detention of fellow students and to submit a revised memorandum with signatures from more students. Once again, they were stopped at the gate by university guards and police officers. This time, the arguments ended in violence. Students were physically held back and dragged across the ground. In the process, the clothes of female students were torn. 'There were more than 100 officers at the arts faculty that day. Our necks were grabbed. My hair was pulled. All this arrangement was done for a few students because the administration is so scared of the students going to talk to the librarian', says Ravjot, a member of Bhagat Singh Chatra Ekta Manch (bsCEM) who was brutally detained.

'Students were physically held back and dragged across the ground. In the process, the clothes of female students were torn.' The agitation drew in a crowd of bystanders, many of whom took videos and decried the assaults of the police and the guards. 'The police were threatening the students to leave the library. It was as if the students were the intruders. The way the guards and police behaved with girls was extremely bad', Safvan, a bystander who intervened to shield a female student from police aggression, adds. In the end, it took more than 50 university guards and police officers to detain seven students. Nine students were apprehended – seven members of bsCEM involved in the library movement, and two bystanders, including Safvan. The detainees were taken 55 km away to the Nangloi station, where they were held and interrogated until late evening.

Such incidents are by no means unique in universities at present. To enter a library is a crime. To enquire about detained comrades is a crime. To ask that the central library of the national capital's premier public institution meets basic standards of functionality is a crime. The question must naturally arise: How does the justice system of the world's largest democracy allow this?

To understand this, we must turn to a jarring feature of the Indian Constitution: Article 22 (3)-(7), pertaining to preventive detention. These provisions invert the underlying logic of the justice system: instead of punishing a guilty person for a crime, they allow the lock-up of an innocent person to prevent them from committing a crime in the future. The glaring contradiction between preventive detention and the fundamental right to life and personal liberty under Article 21 has been obvious since the very founding of this republic. In the A K Gopalan versus State of Madras (1950) case, then Supreme Court Justice M Patanjali Sastri referred to this provision as a 'sinister-looking feature' and stated that 'preventive detention laws are repugnant to democratic constitutions and they cannot be found to exist in any of the democratic countries of the world'. The reason for the exceptional nature of such laws is the flagrant violation of fundamental democratic rights: presumption of innocence, due process and fair trial. Criminal law recognises four stages in the commission of a crime – intention, preparation, attempt and execution. In essence, preventive detention allows the state to label a person 'criminal' based on perceived intention alone.

These authoritarian provisions have a rich colonial legacy as descendants of the infamous draconian Rowlatt Act (the protest which resulted in the inhumane massacre at Jallianwala Bagh). This was noted by the Supreme Court in April 2023 in Pramod Singla versus Union of India case. Former Justice Krishna Murari stated, 'This act of protecting civil liberties, is not just the saving of rights of individuals in person and the society at large but is also an act of preserving our constitutional ethos, which is a product of a series of struggles against the arbitrary power of the British state.'

But the transfer of this arbitrary power from the British to the Indian state has blurred the line between preventive detention and wrongful detention to near vanishment. In the 74 years since the A K Gopalan case, the enabling provisions of the 1950 Preventive Detention Act have only evolved into an ever-expanding list of easy tools for state overreach and oppression of individual liberties. The most infamous among these are the (repealed) 1971 Maintenance of Internal Security Act (MISA) under which thousands were detained during the Emergency, the 1980 National Security Act which was upheld despite the Court's acknowledgment of the vagueness and uncertainty of its provisions, and the leading threat to democratic rights today – the Unlawful Activities Prevention Act (UAPA), a sugar-coated death sentence that has even bypassed the explicit constitutional safeguards which apply to standard preventive detention laws.

The vanquishment is also greatly aided by the normalisation of this once- 'sinister' feature: the familiarity and inevitability of such police response, the fact that we all knew how the story of the Delhi University students was going to play out. This has been acknowledged by the Supreme Court in September 2023 in the Ameena Begum versus The State of Telangana case: 'It requires no serious debate that preventive detention, conceived as an extraordinary measure by the framers of our Constitution, has been rendered ordinary with its reckless invocation over the years, as if it were available for use even in the ordinary course of proceedings.' Justice Dipankar Datta further emphasised the specificity of the grounds which warrant preventive detention, viz., the disturbance to public order: 'The specific activity must have an impact on the broader community or the general public, evoking feelings of fear, panic or insecurity.' It is a matter of great irony, therefore, that in the case of the library incident, the fear, panic or insecurity among the general student body was not caused by the detained students, but by the aggression of the state authorities themselves.

The altercation on 23 October was by no means an isolated incident. Indeed, it was only three weeks earlier that student leaders Shahreyar Khan and Annan, who were standing in opposition to the Akhil Bharatiya Vidyarthi Parishad (ABVP) in the student union elections, were brutalised and detained by the Delhi police. Shahreyar told journalists how he was picked out, beaten with lathis and boots, and abused with communal slurs such as, 'Mulla' (pejoratively term for Muslims in India), '*deshdrohi*' (anti-national), and 'terrorist'. 'I repeatedly told them I was a patient of sarcoidosis, under treatment at Patel Chest Institute, but they ignored me', he reports.

Shahreyar's treatment underscores the material reality of the nature of the police: authorised for the commission of legal violence, dancing on the strings of ABVP leaders, the Delhi University administration and the Hindutva fascist state. 'Police are nowhere to be found when someone is harassed on campus, but when they want to suppress the political engagement of students, suddenly both the police and the cameras start working. Students don't need the protection of the police, but protection from them', says Ravjot. The purported role of the police in our society is to serve and protect justice. Here, we must ask the crucial question: justice for whom? The job of the police is to keep peace, but the peace for whom? As it stands today, the police are the greatest destroyer of peace for the Indian masses, and the greatest inflictor of injustice against the student activists, the *kisan* (farmer), the *mazdoor* (labourer), the trade unionist, the Dalit and the Minority.

At Delhi University, anyone who resists the terror of the police or questions the tyrannical administration is ostracized. 'As a student activist, I am treated like an outsider on my own campus', says Gurkirat, a student at Cluster Innovation Centre who was violently dragged and detained on 23 October. 'They want Delhi University to be a market for selling degrees and propagating the ruling ideology. This administration that promotes saffronisation programmes on campus, threatens, harasses and detains us brutally when we try to speak up for even our very basic democratic demands. Even when we are not doing any protest or programme, the guards specifically stop us at gates, check our bags, etc. The police force roams freely while our mobility on the campus is restricted.'

The authority of the police over students on their own campus is being increasingly institutionalised, most recently under the guise of the anti-ragging policy. In their press release dated 25 July 2024, the Delhi

University proctorial board announced new measures to 'ensure the maintenance of discipline and prevention of ragging', which includes, 'placing of police pickets outside every college' and codifies the administration's ability to seek out the police's violence, 'whenever the situation warrants direct intervention by them'. The statement goes a step further, authorising the police to patrol the campus and take 'speedy action in case of any untoward incident', thereby creating a provision for arbitrary and extrajudicial action by the police against students, which the administration can then conveniently ignore.

Nearly every pattern of oppression, violence and fascism laid out so far – the unconcern for Shahreyar's medical condition, the criminalisation of bsCEM students for speaking against the wrongful detention of their comrades, Delhi University's deployment of police in plain clothes inside the university and outside the premises of each college – can be seen in their most vicious form in the case of the recently martyred Delhi University professor and political prisoner, Dr G N Saibaba. Prof Saibaba was a teacher of English at Ram Lal Anand College of Delhi University. He was paraplegic since age four, 90 per cent disabled and confined to his wheelchair. Yet, his mind was free, empathetic and radically committed to people's justice. This was the brain that was too dangerous for the Indian state. He was arrested in 2014 for 'alleged links with Maoists', his real crime being vocal opposition to the Indian state's displacement operations against Adivasis for corporatisation of their land under the genocidal Operation Green Hunt. He spent 8.5 of the next 10 years in prison along with five other co-accused, where he was subjected to intentional and ruthless medical negligence.

Following the death of the Adivasi-rights activist and Saibaba's co-accused, Pandu Pora Narote in August 2022 after he was denied critical medical care, Saibaba's advocate Nihalsing Rathod prophesied, 'Narote's death, in its own right, implies that the institutional murder of G N Saibaba is a virtual inevitability'. This foregone conclusion was realised on October 12 of this year, and Prof. Sai passed away a mere seven months after his acquittal.

At the public meeting for G N Saibaba held at the Delhi University's arts faculty on 15 October, former professor Nandita Narain from St Stephen's College recalled the inhumanity of the police during his arrest. 'He was abducted by plain-clothes officers and dragged off his wheelchair by his left arm and thrown around like a sack of potatoes. He was not allowed to use the toilet for 48 hours. He eventually lost the use of his left arm, and then his right arm. He was actively disabled by the state and its agencies.' The excessive cruelty of the police was even acknowledged by the Bombay High Court in 2015, which criticised the police for 'working blindly' and treating the ailing professor 'like an animal'. Here again, we see the complicity and the true loyalties of the Delhi University administration, from Sai's eviction to the raid of his university residence to his suspension and the refusal to reinstate him following his acquittal. 'Teaching was Sai's entire life. I will not forgive the vice-chancellor. He did not even reply to Sai's letter', said Prof Narain.

Delhi University today is a microcosm of the increasing militarisation across the entire country: the ever-increasing list of political prisoners who are incarcerated for years without trial and the codification of the police's impunity in the three new criminal codes.

Courtesy: The Leaflet

# Stifling dissent in Jamia

MARYAM HASSAN

February 2025

Following several years of oppressive rules and regulations, a wave of protests erupted in one of India's leading minority institutions, Jamia Milia Islamia, on 10 February 2025, bringing students in conflict with the administration of this deemed university in Delhi. The administration responded with heavy police deployment, invoking the law to curb demonstrations. Faced with archaic property defacement laws and charges of 'unlawful assembly' and 'mischief' under the new criminal codes, students, nevertheless, continue a push-back for free speech. Following the prohibition of protests and slogan-shouting on the campus, the university which played a crucial role in mobilising agitations against the Citizenship Amendment Act in 2020, has again become a hotbed of state repression. While students are detained and served with show-cause notices, groups called for a university-wide boycott of classes. As tensions flared up, police patrol rapidly increased, strict identification checks have been put in place, and altercations have left students navigating an atmosphere of uncertainty.

For many, memories of the forceful entry of and brutal crackdown by Delhi police in the campus following a confrontation with student protestors in December 2019, remain raw. In August 2022, a memorandum was issued, noting that some students with 'political agendas' were holding 'protests, *dharnas* and boycott campaigns on the campus for their malafide and political interests', therein disturbing the 'peaceful academic environment' of the university. More than two years later, in November 2024, a second memorandum was released – allegedly in response to student protests Prime Minister Narendra Modi – which prohibited protests and slogans on campus without the administration's permission. It noted that students had also protested 'other law enforcement agencies of the country on the issues which are not related to the academia' as well as to the university.

Soon after, on 20 December 2024, Jamia's 'Property Department', warned against the defacement of property including writing, painting, and putting up posters without permission. While the Property Department's mandate, on the face of it, is to upkeep campus infrastructure, it routinely fines and threatens legal action against students for 'property defacement', which includes putting up posters, *graffiti* or even paintings. In its 20 December notice, the Department warned of a fine of up to Rs 20,000 for 'defacing' university property and warned of forwarding students' names to the police for prosecution under State and central laws. It also informed, in a matter-of-fact way, of the decision to install more CCTV cameras around the 239-acre campus. The notice brazenly threatens students of prosecution under the Delhi Prevention of Property Defacement Act, 2007, a law which has been routinely invoked by the Delhi police to charge and harass student protestors. 'The notice is emblematic of a broader tendency within institutions to frame dissent as something inherently disruptive rather than a form of engagement or dialogue', says Shah Kulsum Shaikh, a former Jamia student who led the *graffiti* scene during the 2019. Section 3 of the Act provides for a fine of up to Rs 50,000 or a year of imprisonment for putting up posters or painting on walls. Just between 2020 and 2022, the police registered a whopping 1,468 cases under the 2007 Act, and arrested 929 protestors. The department also threatened to charge students under Section 324 of the Bharatiya Nyaya Sanhita, 2023. The provision allows imprisonment for up to five years along with fine for 'mischief'. Of even more concern is that *it is a cognisable charge* – the police could arrest and start investigating without a judge's permission. These office memoranda, by threatening hefty penalties such as expulsion, fines, and rustication have created an atmosphere of suppression where students risk serious consequences for dissent. Wrapped in the clothing of disciplinary measures, their implications on free speech and political engagements on campus are grave.

The February protests began with students condemning the administrative repressions which included the issuance of the memoranda and the circulation of show cause notices against two PhD students of the varsity's Hindi department, for allegedly organising a demonstration last year, commemorating the 2019 police violence in the campus. Tensions escalated in the early hours of February 13 when Delhi police detained more than 10 students from the protest site. By the time they released them the next day, the fear of shrinking campus security had already settled in. The university campus has witnessed increased police deployment with security personnel standing at the campus gates in large numbers. A rapid action force vehicle is stationed at the campus frequently. For students, it is an intimidating, everyday site. 'Our University is our second home and their presence feels like an intrusion into my personal space', says Archana Aggarwal, a student of the AJK Mass Communication Research Centre at Jamia Millia Islamia. 'It does not make me feel safe at all.' Archana generally commuted to the university through motorbike riding apps such as Uber and Ola. 'Usually, they allow the bike rider to drop me inside the campus. But since 11 February, they have not been allowing that. They are also very strict about our ID card.' Another student, preferring to remain anonymous, says, 'I have been a Jamia student since high school and never before have I encountered such stringent measures.' 'In case of a missing ID card, many students were asked to go back to their house to get it, despite having a copy of the same on their cell phones. This leads to disruption in our classes', the student adds.

Frequent altercations broke out between the students and the guards over these measures. The conflict escalated on 11 February 2025, when a physical brawl ensued between two guards and a student. According to some people who witnessed the incident, this happened after the student failed to show his identity card. Several students blocked that gate and began protesting the manhandling of students by the guards. Soon after the protests at the gate, a scuffle ensued between two groups of students. The police were quickly deployed on the scene, but accounts suggest they did little to pacify the conflict. According to *The Jamia Review*, an independent media organisation at the university, 'the police did not enter the campus and curb the situation'. A student of the varsity and an eyewitness to the account, Kashif (name changed) told the university-based outlet, 'After the altercation between guards and students, a group of individuals arrived, demanding protestors to clear the campus. But what authority do they have? Many of them have campus bans for past misconduct yet enter freely without ID checks, unlike us, legally students. It seems the administration sent them to break up the protest.'

People I spoke to suggested that the disrupting students belong to informal blocs with a history of inciting hostilities on campus. A few hours after this clash, the same group created a campus-wide ruckus. 'With the gates of the campus closed, we were trapped inside, running all around in a state of panic and confusion', Archana recalls. Imtiyaz, a student from the human resource management department recalls that the ruckus went on for thirty to forty minutes. 'It exposes significant loopholes in how administrative authority was functioning', he says. Some students have alleged that the disturbance appeared as a deliberate move to undermine student activities. 'The timing and nature of this ruckus makes it clear, it was orchestrated to distract, divide, and delegitimize our struggle', a student activist alleged. 'The real culprits are those in power who manufacture these divisions to weaken the struggle.' Unlike other central universities in Delhi, Jamia has continued without a student union since 2006. Formal accountability is difficult to pursue. 'The administration's refusal to allow [a student union] creates an authority gap, letting these factions run without accountability and threatening campus security', a student protester, associated with the left-wing Student's Federation of India (SFI) says.

In the early hours of 13 February, around 14 students – nine women and five men – were reportedly detained from the protest site. A video circulated from that day, shows them being hustled into police buses. As major protests erupted, they were released within the day. However, the next day, the administration, reportedly, publicly displayed a list of 17 students who were accused of organising a sit-in protest on 10 February. This list detailed their names, emails, phone numbers, political affiliations, and photographs. 'I have been getting calls and messages since the morning', says Sonakshi, one of the protesters whose details were displayed. She adds that some individuals on the list were neither active participants in the protests, nor had any political affiliations. 'This is a complete breach of privacy and leaves us vulnerable and exposed to attacks. We can even be lynched', she says. The Internet Freedom Foundation condemned this act calling it a 'blatant violation of privacy'. The group noted that the actions not only 'infringed upon the fundamental rights of these students', but also created 'a chilling effect on free speech and peaceful assembly'.

As journalists huddled outside the university's gates, the list was surreptitiously taken down. On 15 February, the administration denied displaying the student's details, blaming 'anti-social elements' for the 'name-and-shame' act. It also said that a committee had been constituted to investigate the matter. The police were quickly deployed at the scene, but accounts suggest they did little to pacify the conflict. On 12 February, like many others on the list, Sonakshi had faced suspension letters from the chief proctor's office for 'breach of discipline'. The detailed suspension order noted that Sonakshi and other students violated Jamia's 'rules and regulations', which included provisions under an 'Ordinance 14' – which prohibits the 'disobeying the instructions of teachers', 'causing damage, spoiling or disfiguring to the property/equipment of the university', and any conduct 'considered unbecoming of a student'. Ordinance 14 prescribes students to be punished with fine, campus ban, expulsion and rustication. 'I had been regularly attending my classes in the morning and it was only after the classes that I participated in the sit-in protest. How can we disrupt classes if we, ourselves have been attending them?', asks Sonakshi. 'Despite several requests for a meeting, the proctor has refused to engage with us', she adds.

The suspension order also suggested that the student's conduct was in violation of Sections 324, 189 and 356 of the BNS. Section 189 entails the punishment for 'unlawful assembly', putting students under the threat of imprisonment for up to six months with fine, while the last provision refers to defamatory actions. It also, rather expectedly, threatens to charge the students under the 2007 property defacement law, just as the office memoranda had warned. The order does not detail how these charges are to be substantiated and how they are specifically linked to the student protesters. The grounds of prosecution are broad and unverified.

Various departments of the university released statements of solidarity with the protesting students and called for a boycott of classes. They demanded the suspension orders and disciplinary actions to be revoked, for the student's details to not be displayed, and for the 'constitutional right to gather peacefully to be reinstated. Sant Kumar, a PhD student from Jamia's English department says, 'In the absence of a student union, the responsibility falls upon us to stand with our peers and uphold the truth. They cannot silence everyone through suspensions'. Kumar is sure that their demands can rebuild an academic space where the right to free speech and discussion can thrive.

On February 19, several students of Jamia, alongside other student groups such as the All-Indian Student's Association and the Jawaharlal Nehru University Student's Union protested the Jamia actions at Jantar Mantar. A press release of the SFI said that on 25 February, over a hundred students protested in front of the history department seeking a withdrawal of the show-cause notices and suspensions. They also called for a revocation of the office memoranda issued in August 2022, and November 2024 which prohibit protests. The demands were forcefully submitted, and the administration's response is now awaited.

When I last spoke to her, Kulsum had become weary of the administration's swift use of the law to suppress expression. 'The balance between freedom and decorum is not about suppressing one for the other. It is about recognising that the very act of suppression – whether through fines, censorship, or removal of works – undermines the essence of freedom itself', she explained. 'Rather than maintaining decorum at the cost of creative and intellectual expression, the administration should seek a more inclusive, democratic way of allowing these voices to be heard while also respecting the need for shared public spaces.'

Courtesy: *The Leaflet*

# A Teacher Laments

SHERNAVAZ BUHARIWALLA

Recently I burnt my books
And tore my Ph.D.
What a waste that career
of half a century.

Teaching is so boring
Learning is a pain
Knowledge is recalling
Ancient texts in vain.

No more of that for me
I'm tired, don't you see
How soothing it would be
To slide into illiteracy.

I sought the B. J. P.
To placate my sensibility.
That lettered trinity
My mascot hence will be.

*Bartan Jhadu Pochha*
Is the assigned task for me.
*Bartan Jhadu Pochha*
My destined end shall be.

My *Bartans* will gleam so bright,
My *Jhadu* will sweep so white
My *Pochha* will bathe and dry
All excrements of earth and sky.

They say dissent is sedition
And protests revolution.
Reasoning is blasphemy.
Is a housewife to office bound
Booked for bigamy?
It's all so bewildering
So baffling, so perplexing
The mind, powerless to see
Or grasp a new vocabulary.

Withdraw me into my den with
*Jhadu* and *Bartan* to attend.
It's lockdown for you and me
Remove the cobwebs instantly.
Thus, are we fortified.
Ishwar Allah reconciled

*Bartan Jhadu Pochha*
Show the way to all of us
*Bartan Jhadu Pochha*
Will defeat the virus.

# The Big Con: Modi's India
and the New World Order

PANKAJ MISHRA

May 2023

Early in January, Gautam Adani, an Indian businessman and associate of India's Prime Minister, Narendra Modi, was the world's third richest man. By the end of the month, he had lost much of his fortune, after being accused by the US-based research investment firm Hindenburg Research of pulling the 'largest con in corporate history'. Facing allegations of fraud and a stock-market rout, he appeared in Haifa on 31 January, smiling for pictures with Benjamin Netanyahu and hailing the Abraham Accords brokered by Jared Kushner as a 'gamechanger', as he took charge of Israel's largest port. Adani's 'liberation' of Haifa, as Netanyahu put it, brings closer the prospect of a rail link between Israel and its new friends in Saudi Arabia and the Persian Gulf. His 'strategic purchase', for which he paid a staggering $1.2 billion, also limits Chinese influence in the region. And Adani had his own reasons to smile. Standing next to Netanyahu, who had just name-checked his 'good friend' Modi, Adani was showing that he still had allies in high places.

The day before, a company controlled by Abu Dhabi's royal family had pledged to invest a further $400 million in his floundering flagship business, Adani Enterprises Ltd. He hoped to raise $2.5 billion through a stock offering: Indian tycoons close to Modi had promised to buy shares, although mutual funds and retail investors were keeping a fastidious distance. Modi stonewalled questions in parliament about his partnership with Adani, which began decades ago in Gujarat; regulatory agencies in India conspicuously failed to investigate Adani's use of offshore shell companies; and his supporters took to the airwaves to allege that white people just couldn't bear to see India make progress.

In the weeks since then, Adani's spectacular fall has continued: among other reverses, he had to cancel the $2.5 billion share sale, and no longer sits near the top of the list of the world's richest men. In his glory days, he would tweet that it was 'fascinating to hear from President Emmanuel Macron at Chateau Versailles' or that he was 'Honoured to host Boris Johnson, the first UK PM to visit Gujarat, at Adani HQ'. His social media feeds have now gone quiet. Adani was not only a beneficiary of the new political and economic order devised by Modi to consolidate Hindu supremacism in India. The neglected details of his frictionless rise show that after their calamitous romance with Russia's oligarchy, Western politicians, journalists and bankers facilitated the ascent of another hyper-nationalist elite with dubiously sourced wealth and an extreme aversion to the rule of law and civil liberties.

A day after Adani showed up in Haifa, Jo Johnson – Boris Johnson's brother and a former *Financial Times* journalist, who was elevated to the House of Lords in 2020 after a decade in the Commons – abruptly resigned from Elara Capital, a UK investment firm that according to Hindenburg Research is complicit in the Adani Group's practice of inflating stock prices through shell companies in Mauritius.

Johnson isn't the only one afflicted with buyer's remorse. Norway's largest pension fund, KLP, recently abandoned all its shares in Adani Green Energy Ltd. France's TotalEnergies, Adani's largest European collaborator and the main source of his credibility among foreign investors, has put a green hydrogen partnership with him on hold. The asset management unit of J.P. Morgan Chase has, in Bloomberg's words, 'wiped its ESG portfolios clean of their exposure to the Adani empire'. Bangladesh, which had agreed to pay dramatically high prices for electricity from Adani's tax-free coal-fired power station in India, is now asking to renegotiate.

Prompted by these developments, Western journalists have been busy investigating Adani, looking into the opaque sources of his funding in offshore entities in Mauritius, the Bahamas and Cyprus, and the role of his 'elusive' older brother Vinod. At least some of these facts have been known for a long time. For two decades, Indian journalists have faced down legal threats to track the intertwined rise of Modi and Adani.

When Modi was barred from travelling to the United States and the European Union because of his suspected complicity in the anti-Muslim pogrom in Gujarat in 2002, and many Indian businessmen recoiled from him, Adani worked hard to rehabilitate his associate. Since becoming prime minister in 2014, Modi has repaid the favour: he turned Adani into India's biggest operator of private airports and ports, as well as its leading producer of power from coal-fired plants. While presiding over an environmental crisis – India suffers from toxic smog, heatwaves, dry riverbeds, falling groundwater reserves and land subsidence – Modi has helped Adani, a fossil fuel tycoon, position himself as India's champion of decarbonisation.

Last year the head of Sri Lanka's largest electricity board was forced to resign after confessing to parliament that Modi had put 'pressure' on the island's then president, Gotabaya Rajapaksa, to award a renewable energy project to Adani. A jaunt to Australia alongside Modi expedited Adani's plan to open a huge coal mine – and secured him the promise of a massive loan to enable this from India's biggest bank. The Wangan and Jagalingou indigenous peoples, who live near the proposed mine, warned many Western financial institutions against investing in the site, with the help of an online campaign, #StopAdani. But Adani still managed to fund it – in part, it has recently become clear, by using stock from his 'green' companies as collateral. A visit to Dhaka with Modi resulted in the deal to sell electricity – generated by burning his Australian coal at his environmentally hazardous plant in India – at inflated prices to Bangladesh, one of the country's most vulnerable to climate change.

Modi has counted on sympathetic journalists and financial speculators in the West to cast a seductive veil over his version of political economy, environmental activism and history. 'I'd bet on Modi to transform India, all of it, including the newly integrated Kashmir region,' Roger Cohen of the *New York Times* wrote in 2019 after Modi annulled the special constitutional status of India's only Muslim-majority state and imposed a months-long curfew. McKinsey's global managing partner, Bob Sternfels, recently said that we may be living in 'India's century'. Praising Modi for 'implementing policies that have modernised India and supported its growth', the economist and consultant Nouriel Roubini described the country as a 'vibrant democracy'. But it is becoming harder to evade the reality that, despoiled by a venal, inept and tyrannical regime. *India is Broken* is the title of a disturbing new book by economic historian Ashoka Mody.

The number of Indians who go to sleep hungry rose from 190,000,000 in 2018 to 350,000,000 in 2022, and malnutrition and malnourishment killed more than two-thirds of the children who died under the age of five last year. Meanwhile, Modi's cronies have flourished. The *Economist* estimates that the share of wealth held by billionaires in India that derives from cronyism has risen from 29 per cent to 43 per cent in six years. According to a recent Oxfam report, India's richest 1 per cent owned more than 40.5 per cent of its total wealth in 2021 – such statistics are more often associated with the notorious oligarchies of Russia and Latin America. The new Indian plutocracy owes its swift ascent to Modi, who audaciously clarified the quid pro quo. Under the 'electoral bond' scheme he introduced in 2017, any business or special interest group can give unlimited sums of money to his party and keep the transaction hidden from public scrutiny.

Modi ensures his hegemony by forging a public sphere where sycophancy is rewarded and dissent harshly punished. Adani last year took over NDTV, a television news channel that had displayed a rare unwillingness to broadcast hate speech, fake news and conspiracy theories. Human Rights Watch has detailed Modi's onslaught on democratic rights: 'the Hindu nationalist Bharatiya Janata Party (BJP)-led government used abusive and discriminatory policies to repress Muslims and other minorities' and 'arrested activists, journalists and other critics of the government on politically motivated criminal charges, including of terrorism'. In February, as the BJP's official spokesperson denounced the BBC as the 'most corrupt' organisation in the world, tax officials launched a sixty-hour raid on the broadcaster's Indian offices in apparent retaliation for its two-part documentary on Modi's role in anti-Muslim violence.

In March, the opposition leader, Rahul Gandhi, was sentenced to two years in prison and expelled from parliament to put a stop to his persistent questions about Modi's relationship with Adani. Such actions are at last provoking closer international scrutiny of what Modi likes to call the 'mother of democracy', though they haven't come as a shock to those who have long known about his lifelong allegiance to Rashtriya Swayamsevak Sangh, an organisation that was explicitly inspired by Nazism and culpable in Gandhi's 1948 assassination.‡ The defamation campaign against George Soros and the conspiracy-fuelled crackdown on India's leading think tank, the Centre for Policy Research, are only the latest in a series of measures – bribing opposition politicians to defect; unleashing mobs to attack opponents on the streets and on social media; subverting the judiciary and the education system; denouncing same-sex marriage as a cause of 'complete havoc' – that are making India safe for oligarchy and unsafe for nearly everyone else.

There is nothing unique about this amalgam of domestic repression, ideological messianism and state-pampered oligarchy, or its legitimation by Western political and financial institutions. In Russia, despotic rulers helped loyalists amass vast private fortunes by showering them with privatisation deals, banking privileges, government contracts, and tax and trade concessions. Western corporations and banks channelled tainted Russian money into the pool of global capital, and law firms and PR companies made New York and London safe for Russian oligarchs. Bill Clinton's secretary of state complimented Boris Yeltsin on his 'superb' work after he ordered tanks to fire on the Russian parliament in 1993. George W. Bush, Tony Blair, Gerhard Schröder and Silvio Berlusconi helped launder the blood-stained record of Yeltsin's chosen successor. In 2001, Blair told the journalist, Anna Politkovskaya, who had been investigating Putin's war crimes in Chechnya, that 'it's my job as prime minister to like Mr Putin.' (Politkovskaya was murdered in Moscow in 2006, on Putin's birthday.) In *Putin's People,* Catherine Belton describes many occasions when the Russian president was confirmed in his assumption that the West's 'financial interests would outweigh concerns about his regime's abuse of the law and democracy'.

Those interests account for another ethical and cognitive breakdown. Visiting New Delhi in December to explain to readers of the *New York Times* why 'Russia's war could make it India's world,' Roger Cohen quoted Arundhati Roy – 'Hatred has penetrated into society at a level that is absolutely terrifying' – then glossed: 'That may be, but for now, Modi's India seems to brim with confidence.' The Western rush to embrace Mr Modi's India isn't only fuelled by the profit motive. The mollycoddling of yet another exponent of crony capitalism and ethnic-racial supremacism is increasingly driven by the imperatives of the new Cold

War: the Biden administration's resolve, deepened by the war in Ukraine, to contain China. Adani's lavish purchase of the port of Haifa came after the US put pressure on Israel to forbid his Chinese rival, the Shanghai International Port Group, from managing a port frequented by the Sixth Fleet of the US navy.

A persistent problem, however, for strategists and propagandists of the new Cold War is that Modi's path to power was paved by grisly – and well-documented – violence. The Foreign Office was not alone in concluding in 2002 that he was 'directly responsible' for the killing of more than a thousand Muslims in Gujarat. In 2005, George W. Bush's State Department invoked the 1998 International Religious Freedom Act to deny Modi's diplomatic visa application and revoke his business visa under the Immigration and Nationality Act. In April 2012 the then State Department spokesperson Victoria Nuland upheld the ban. Yet by September 2014 he was being shown round the Martin Luther King Jr Memorial in Washington DC by Barack Obama, and in June 2016 he addressed a joint session of Congress about his and America's shared 'philosophy of freedom'.

Rupert Murdoch anointed Modi as India's 'best leader with the best policies since independence'. Addressing packed stadiums in India and the US with his 'loyal friend', Donald Trump confirmed Modi's place in a global far-right constellation. But it was liberal and centrist politicians, businessmen, economists and journalists in the West who piled up casual untruths about Modi and his India. 'There is something thrilling about the rise of Narendra Modi,' Gideon Rachman, the chief foreign affairs columnist for the

*Financial Times*, wrote in April 2014. As Modi arrived in Silicon Valley in 2015, just as his government shut down the internet in Kashmir, Sheryl Sandberg declared she was changing her Facebook profile to honour him. In 2019, Bill Gates ignored a letter from three Nobel Peace Prize-winners, including Iran's Shirin Ebadi, protesting his decision to 'give a humanitarian award to a man whose nickname is the "Butcher of Gujarat"'. In January, Twitter and YouTube agreed to enforce the Indian government's ban on the BBC documentary on Modi's complicity in anti-Muslim violence.

For *Time*'s 2015 list of the hundred most influential people, Obama recalled talking to Modi about the teachings of Gandhi and Martin Luther King. He described Modi as if he were a character in a Horatio Alger story: born in modest circumstances but now the leader of the 'world's largest democracy', Modi reflected 'the dynamism and potential of India's rise'. Obama, the first Western leader to embrace Modi, became the only American president to visit India twice, once as chief guest at the Republic Day parade. Less than a year after leaving the White House, he was back in India on a speaking tour, praising Modi's Adani-fied efforts against climate change at a 'leadership summit' organised by a pro-Modi newspaper (the same shindig recently paid Boris Johnson £260,000 for a speech, no doubt its bargain basement rate).

Like the Russian elite, Modi and Adani have succeeded in bending the moral arc of politics and journalism towards greed. Jo Johnson, who had to disentangle himself with haste from Adani's global cash nexus, was, as a reporter for the *Financial Times*, a rare practitioner of sober Western journalism on India, at a period when opinion-making periodicals such as *Time*, *Foreign Affairs*, *Newsweek* and the *Economist* were hailing the country as a 'roaring capitalist success story'. 'Unless India makes a dramatic investment in its human capital,' Johnson wrote in 2006, 'it's demographic advantages will turn into a demographic disaster in the form of a massive unemployable labour force.' His prognosis has become even more menacing today as the country's population overtakes China's, the scope for labour intensive jobs in Indian industry shrinks further, the large middle class long fantasised about by foreign corporations stubbornly fails to materialise, and private investment keeps falling despite lavish government spending on infrastructure. Modi's government has not spent the sums on public health and education that, as Johnson observed, would be necessary for securing a demographic advantage. Instead, it has sought to deploy many of the 'unemployable labour force' as stormtroopers of Hindu supremacism, indoctrinating them in a garishly fabricated version of the Indian past and equally kitsch daydreams of its future as a world guru. Baron Johnson of Marylebone, a dabbler in Adani's honeypot, turned to describing how the 'new India' was 'helping shape this young century'. Such U-turns occur frequently in the global networks of journalistic, academic, business and geopolitical opportunity forged by Modi and his oligarchs. (The crudity of manoeuvre can still be breath-taking. While visiting Adani at his headquarters in Gujarat last year, Jo Johnson's brother Boris took time off to plug JCB, the day after the company's bulldozers were photographed demolishing Muslim-owned properties in Delhi. JCB's owners paid for some of Johnson's wedding last year and the disgraced former prime minister currently lives in a £20 million house in Knightsbridge owned by the wife of the company's owner, Anthony Bamford.)

Yet private avarice, which Putin identified as central to public life in the West today, does not entirely explain the whitewashing of Modi or the greenwashing of Adani. Ideological delusion also plays a role. In the mainstream Western narrative shaped during the Cold War, India – with its regular elections – starred as a counterexample to many authoritarian and anti-Western countries. The tattered fable about Indian democracy is being urgently revamped as the Biden administration pursues its new Cold War against Chinese and Russian autocracy. Walter Russell Mead, a leading foreign policy commentator, argued in the *Wall Street Journal* in March that the US should pursue greater intimacy with Modi's party since it 'will be calling the shots in a country without whose help American efforts to balance rising Chinese power are likely to fall short'. As in the first Cold War, such strategic calculations, while keeping arms manufacturers and Beltway think tanks busy, are impervious to observable facts. Over the last year, while the West repeatedly sanctioned Russia, Modi turned the despoiler of Ukraine into India's biggest supplier of oil as well as military hardware; his government has urged state-owned corporations to explore the possibility of buying stakes abandoned by Western companies in Russian energy concerns. In recent months, India has also suffered humiliating military defeats and losses of territory to China while becoming economically ever more dependent on imports from that country. No matter: India is now firmly fixed in the Cold War imagination as a military as well as democratic counterweight to the free world's autocratic adversaries, and Western policymakers and commentators trumpet the country's virtues even more loudly. Speaking at a meeting of the anti-China military coalition QUAD, Biden complimented Modi for 'making sure democracies deliver, because that's what this is about: democracies v. autocracies'. Attending Biden's Summit for Democracy with Netanyahu in March, Modi invoked 'our sacred Mahabharata' and 'our sacred Vedas' while insisting once again that 'India indeed is the mother of democracy.' As New Delhi prepares to host a G20 summit in September, Western officials and opinion-makers echo his claims for India's democracy, using words like 'largest' and 'vibrant'. Both adjectives were deployed by a State Department spokesperson as he tried to avoid commenting on Modi's crackdown on the BBC. Visiting India in early March, Italy's far-right prime minister, Giorgia Meloni, described Modi as the 'most loved of all world leaders'. Australia's new prime minister, Anthony Albanese, joined him in a lap of honour in an improvised chariot at the new Narendra Modi cricket stadium in Gujarat. Such flattery helps Modi to project himself domestically as a universally revered icon, and further demoralises the political opposition. It encourages his fan base to think that Hindu superpowerdom is imminent – a demagogic vanity that is certain to be disappointed and to degenerate into vengeful xenophobia of the kind that fuels Putinism. Fawning on a Hindu supremacist even as his supporters clamour for a genocide of Muslims in India also helps to entrench lies and propaganda in the public life of Western societies. Adani's business empire may or may not turn out to be the largest con in corporate history. But far greater threats to civic morality, let alone to democracy and global peace, are posed by those who peddle the gigantic hoax of Modi's India – the first big fraud of the new Cold War.

Courtesy: *London Review of Books*

# Hindutva and Zionism
## ideological cousins

VIKRAM VISANA

The results are in for India's general election. The country's prime minister, Narendra Modi, has won enough seats to stay in charge for a third consecutive term. But his Bharatiya Janata Party has suffered big setbacks and is gearing up for coalition talks having failed to win an outright majority for the first time in 10 years.

The BJP is premised on Hindutva, a Hindu nationalist ideology. Devised in the early 20th century, the politics of Hindutva insist that the country's national identity be built around those who consider only India's geography sacred. Muslims and Christians, whose holy sites lay in the Middle East, were therefore considered second-class citizens.

Modi foregrounded Hindutva in his election campaign. He falsely accused the main opposition party, the Indian National Congress, of basing their manifesto on the ideology of the Muslim League, the party that championed the partition of India in 1947. He weaponised demographic anxieties around marginally higher Muslim fertility rates to claim that the opposition planned to redistribute wealth to "infiltrators" who "have more children".

But Hindutva doesn't stop at India's borders. Hindu nationalists have used the ongoing conflict in Gaza to vilify other Muslims globally. BJP troll farms have spread disinformation and anti-Palestinian hatred online, and Hindu nationalist groups in India have organised pro-Israel marches.

Where does this curious Hindutva-Zionist solidarity spring from? One origin is from the earliest Hindu nationalists who modelled their Hindu state on Zionism. Hindutva's founder, Vinayak Damodar Savarkar, supported majoritarian nationalism and the rooting out of all disintegrating forces. These included Muslims who supported electoral quotas for their community and left-wing internationalists.

As a result, he even condoned the Nazis' antisemitic legislation in two speeches in 1938 because, as he saw it: "a nation is formed by a majority living therein". Yet Savarkar was not antisemitic himself. He often spoke favourably of the tiny Jewish-Indian minority because he considered it too insignificant to threaten Hindu cohesion.

In fact, Savarkar praised Zionism as the perfection of ethno-nationalist thinking. The way Zionism seamlessly blended ethnic attachment to a motherland and religious attachment to a holy land was precisely what Savarkar wanted for the Hindus. This double attachment was far more powerful to his mind than the European model of "blood and soil" nationalism without sacred space.

Today, Hindu nationalists perpetuate this legacy and still look to Zionism as a uniquely attractive political ideology. To Hindu nationalists, some Zionists were engaged in a project to reclaim their holy land from a Muslim population whose religious roots in the region were not as ancient as their own.

In a similar way, Hindutva's supporters saw it as engaged with a Muslim population that it vastly outnumbered, but which had significant cultural power. This power came through the Mughal dynasty that ruled much of India from 1526 to the establishment of the British Raj in the 19th century.

This idea was further popularised by Savarkar's ideological successor, Madhav Sadashivrao Golwalkar. In 1947, Golwalkar wrote that Zionism was the "attempt at rehabilitating Palestine with its ancient population of the Jews ... to reconstruct the broken edifice and revitalise the practically dead Hebrew national life".

Just as the Palestinians had to make way for those whose claims of ancient sacred space took primacy, so too, in Golwalkar's view, did "non-Hindu people of Hindusthan" must be "wholly subordinated to the

Hindu nation". Part of this process today has been redefining citizenship and delegitimising Muslims.

In 2018, Israel passed a law that rebranded the country as "the nation-state of the Jewish people" and delegitimised its non-Jewish citizens. Similarly, India's controversial Citizenship Amendment Act in 2019 eased paths to citizenship for immigrants from several religious groups, but not Muslims. Coupled with rhetoric associating millions of Indian Muslims with illegal immigration, human rights groups argue that this law could be used to strip many Muslims of their Indian citizenship.

Hindu nationalists have also stoked a culture war to consolidate "Hindu civilisation" and sweep away symbols of Islam. This is very much in keeping with the wish of Israel's far right to rebuild Solomon's Temple on the site of the holy Temple Mount in Jerusalem, where al-Aqsa mosque compound currently sits.

In 1969, a Zionist extremist burned the south wing of al-Aqsa. And in 1980, the fundamentalist group Jewish Underground plotted to blow up the Dome of the Rock, an Islamic shrine at the centre of the compound. A similar project of demolishing mosques and building temples in their place was suggested by Savarkar and Golwalkar. Hindu nationalist organisations focused their attention on Babri Masjid mosque in Ayodhya, since this was the mythical birthplace of the Hindu god, Ram. The co-founder of BJP, Lal Krishna Advani, led a national campaign in 1990 to build a new temple – a proposal that had been prohibited by the Indian supreme court for decades. But the fervour the campaign unleashed resulted in a Hindu nationalist mob demolishing Babri Masjid mosque in 1992. And after a new Indian supreme court ruling in 2019 gave permission, a temple was built on the site of the destroyed mosque and inaugurated by Modi with great ceremony in January 2024.

A few months later, in May 2024, Israeli national security minister Itamar Ben-Gvir declared from al-Aqsa mosque compound that a Palestinian state would never exist. As he did so, his entourage prayed illegally on the contested site of the Temple Mount. Hindu prayers are offered from the site of the demolished Babri Masjid and hundreds of other mosques in India now find themselves under threat. Hindu nationalists are petitioning courts to deliver land administered by Islamic trusts to the majority Hindu community. As Modi embarks on a third term, he may look to complete the task of making India an exclusive Hindu holy land – albeit with a more powerful opposition than before.

*Courtesy:*

**THE CONVERSATION**

# Hindutva cements "Muslimness"

APOORVANAND

Should or do Muslims of India need to change their approach? This was one of the questions I got after I spoke about the approach of Nehru in his *Discovery of India.* Was the questioner a Hindu or a Muslim? I needed to know the context it was asked. I needed to understand what the questioner wanted to ask. When we say the approach of Muslims, do we mean the approach of Muslims in religious matters, social matters, public matters or in political matters. How do we find out what the approach of Muslims is? We need to know whether the term Muslims adequately covers all Muslims. We are talking about approximately 204,760,392 Muslims, all "separate individual men and women, each differing from the other, each living in a private universe of thought and feeling". The approach of each one of them should be different in many matters. Yes, there is something that binds them together which creates a Muslimness, common to this multitude. Yes, there is the thread of Islam they believe in, which binds them but apart from that their social background, their class status, their education is different which affects their approach towards life. And Islam also has different sects. So, when we club these different Muslims together by asking if they need to change their approach, are we even asking the right question? Before answering the question, I realise how a common Muslimness has been created in India reducing these 204,760,392 Muslims to their identity of Muslimness. Be she or he a judge, or a millionaire, or a clerk, or an administrator, or a teacher or a student, they cannot escape this Muslimness. They have been robbed of their individuality, their uniqueness.

This Muslimness has been manufactured by the violence of the politics of Hindutva. We were having this conversation in the city of Pune. The very city where in 2014 'first wicket' was felled after Narendra Modi took over as Prime Minister. This is how the murder of Mohsin Saik was described by his killers. He was killed because his looks, his appearance provoked and incensed the murderers so much that they killed him. That was the beginning of lynching of Muslims on various pretexts. We need to understand the import of the murder of Mohsin Saik. Mohsin was a software engineer. He had a professional identity. He must have had a unique personal identity. But that was not the reason for his murder. As the court said he was killed only because he was a Muslim. It was his murder that made his Muslimness visible. What could he have done to prevent his murder?

Physical attacks on Muslims became commonplace. The expression of Muslimness became an issue. Whether it was your looks, attire, eating habits, religious practices, anything became a problem for a section of Hindus. This section is becoming larger and larger. Whether you wear hijab or abaya, whether you offer prayer in any open public space, take out religious processions, some Hindus, will take offence, and attack you. If you sell meat or name your shop in a religious agnostic way or use 'Hindu' names, you can be attacked. If you seek to do business in a 'Hindu' area you can be attacked, as Tasleem realised while selling bangles in the gullies of Indore. If you are demonstratively Muslim, you are under threat. You can return your home safe but may not return in one piece or not return at all. It all depends on the way Hindus behave with you, those you encounter on train, in clubs, colleges, parks and offices. It is not your actions but their acts which make you aware of your Muslimness. We have heard it so many times from so many people that in these ten years they have been made to feel like Muslims. Earlier they were not conscious of their Muslimness in the way they are now. Not their choice. Not their doing. It is Hindus, not only from the RSS or BJP, but from outside their fold too, who make Muslims realise that they are firstly and lastly Muslims.

If you do not come across identifiably as a Muslim, that can also become an issue. That is what the UP police and Government told the businessmen: they all must identify themselves clearly and loudly. They are disallowed to use not only 'Hindu' names but also names which can confuse people. For example, Sonia or Pintu or Sunny. They must display their Muslimness so that others can decide what to do with them. And then there are BJP leaders like Narendra Modi and his followers claiming that they are there to save Hindus from Muslims who keep growing in numbers and tend to lure Hindu women.

This is how Muslimness is created. Anyone from the Muslim community across sects, classes, castes, and gender can become a target of this anti-Muslim hatred and violence. I understood that the questioner in Pune was speaking from within this identity. And he was asking if Muslims need to change their approach. Change their approach for what? To stop Hindus from attacking them, from entering their houses, from stopping their prayers, from stopping them from conducting their business? What do Muslims need to change in themselves so that they are allowed to live peacefully and with dignity? What should Muslim do to end laws which target them especially the anti-Triple talaq law or CAA or the so-called freedom of religion laws or the anti-love jihad laws across states which criminalise Muslim men forming union with Hindu women? What should Muslims change in themselves to prevent calls for their slaughter in so-called *Dharma Sansads*, by Hindu religious figures? What are Muslims expected to change in themselves so that the RSS and BJP officials from the PM to ministers stop abusing them or stop spreading hatred against them?

What change do Muslims need to bring in themselves so that the Hindu mobs stop attacking their mosques, their houses? For Hindu saints to stop abusing them in their *'satsangs'* what is it that Muslims need to do. What step Muslim need to take so that the political parties start recognising the atrocities against them and speak clearly about it? What do they need to do to persuade political parties to give them adequate representation?

I guess all this must have been there in the mind of the gentleman who asked the question: Should Muslims change their approach? How, in which direction? What has been the general approach of Muslims in these matters which has now become part of their lives? What have they done when faced with violence of various kinds? What did Bilkis Bano or Zakia Jafri do? What is the family of Junaid and Pahelu Khan doing? Their approach has been the constitutionally given legal approach. They keep knocking the doors of different courts. Even when in most of the matters they suffer injustice, they do not give up. Like Zakia Jafri. Or Bilkis Bano. When faced with calls for violence they, like Mohammed Zubair, flag them in public and appeal to the police and authorities to act. This insistence on justice is resented by the authorities and even the courts. But Muslims have not given up on the Indian judicial system. Muslims are investing more in education. More Muslims are entering professional fields, trying to qualify for civil and police administration. Is this not what we expect all communities to do? From

OBCs to Dalits, we encourage them to be seen in these positions. Muslims are trying to do that. But even this is seen with suspicion and resentment. From TV anchors to the RSS chief, all allege that it is a collective conspiracy to infiltrate and capture the state structure.

Politically, the approach of Muslims has been to cast their lot with the Hindu masses. They vote for liberal and 'secular' parties. They have voted for the Congress party, for the socialists, for the Communists, even for a party like Shiv Sena. If we look at the pattern from 1952 to 2024, Muslims vote for the parties for which Hindus vote in majority. That changed in 2014. But it was not the fault of Muslims. A critical number of Hindus voted for the BJP which actively professes and practices anti-Muslim politics. Muslims cannot be expected to vote for a party which vilifies them and which does not believe that they are equal citizens in this country. Muslims cannot be expected to vote for a party which does not believe in secularism. What we can say with confidence is that Muslims have not gone for a "Muslim" party. Indian Muslims will never encourage an Islamist ideology.

A lot is said about the absence of leadership in Muslims. But Muslims, at least in the political field, never wanted a Muslim leader. They have chosen Jawaharlal Nehru, Indira Gandhi, Jaiprakash Narayan, Lohia, V P Singh, Mulayam Singh, Lalu Prasad, Jyoti Basu, Mamata Banerjee, Arvind Kejriwal, even Uddhav Thakre as their leaders. They have opted for Akhilesh

Yadav or Rahul Gandhi. All non-Muslims. Muslims have always taken an open, liberal stand.

Socially Muslims are not homogenous so they do not have one single approach to social and religious matters. There will be conservative elements and elements which are more open in religious matters. Are they becoming more religious and is this a problem? If we look at other religious communities, we find religiosity increasing there too.

What then is the answer to the question: Do Muslims need to change their approach? If a society wants to move forward; it can do so only by regularly examining its approach in different fields of life. So, the question applies to all communities, not only Muslims. All of them need to keep rethinking their approach and change it when needed. But to stop marginalisation, persecution, violence, and injustice against themselves it is not for Muslims to change their approach. It is for the state, for the executive authorities, and the courts to change their approach. It is for the RSS and BJP to change their approach. It is for Hindus in general to change their approach. The concern and anxiety behind the question can be understood but to address that it is largely Hindu society which needs to change its approach.

# Obituary of a Culture

ASHIS NANDY

May 2002

The massive carnages at Rwanda and Bosnia have taught the students of genocide that the most venomous, brutal killings and atrocities take place when the two communities involved are not distant strangers, but close to each other culturally and socially, and when their lives intersect at many points. When nearness sours or explodes it releases strange, fearsome demons.

Those shocked by the bestial or barbaric nature of the communal violence in Gujarat would do well to read some accounts of the carnages in Rwanda and Bosnia. In both cases, the two communities involved were close to each other and ethnic cleansing took the forms of a particularly brutal, self-destructive exorcism. And the same thing happened during the great Partition killings in 1946-48. The ongoing death dance in West Asia, with the Arabs and Israelis locked in an embrace of death, is another instance of the same game.

Gujarat was being prepared for such an exorcism for a very long time. It is a state that has seen thirty-three years of continuous rioting interrupted with periods of tense, uncomfortable peace. During these years, a sizeable section of Gujarat's urban underclass has begun to see communalism and rioting as means of livelihood, quick profit, choice entertainment, and as a way of life. Riots have, in addition, ensured temporary status gains for this underclass; they are considered heroes in their respective communities during riots and for brief periods afterwards – an important reward for persons at the margins of society.

Rioting everywhere is pre-eminently an urban disease. Demographers of riots – from Gopal Krishna to Asghar Ali Engineer, and from P.R. Rajgopalan to Ashutosh Varshney – have shown repeatedly that it is even more so in India. The icing on the cake is that the urban middle class in Gujarat is now the most communalised in the country; it has become an active abetter and motivator of communal violence. Sections of it participate in the loot enthusiastically, as we have seen in the course of the recent riots; those that do not often participate in the violence vicariously.

(For the last hundred years or so, the so-called non-martial races of the subcontinent – Bengali *babus*, Kashmiri Muslims and Gujarati upper castes, for instance – have had a special fascination for violence, particularly if someone else was doing the fighting and risking their lives. However, in recent years, this fascination and the search for redemptive violence, which bestows heroic stature by being expiation for one's own 'passivity' and 'effeminacy', have often found direct expression in public life.)

Unlike in places like Uttar Pradesh, cities matter in Gujarat. Urbanity is a crucial presence in Gujarat's political life. The state has fifty cities, many of which have already become cauldrons of communal hatred and paranoia. The result is that Gujarat is now a classic instance of the urban-industrial vision, decomposing and spitting out in a blatant form the violence that the vision has always hidden in its belly. The state has not only been riot-prone but at war with itself. Even after the present riots die down – available data show that riots last longer in Gujarat than in other states – it would be at best a temporary truce. Tension and hatred will persist and both sides will remain prepared for the next round. Gujarat is and will continue to be an arena of civil war for years.

This situation has come about not because the Inter-Services Intelligence or the ISI of Pakistan – omnipotent, omniscient and omnipresent like God himself, according to many Indians – has planned it that way. Nor because the minorities have been the main victims in the recent riots. This situation of civil war has arisen because minorities now know that they cannot hope to have any protection from the state government. Lower-level functionaries of the state government have been complicit with rioters many times and in many states. But this is probably for the first time after the anti-Sikh riots of 1984 that the entire state machinery, except for some courageous dissenters among the administrators and in the law-and-order machinery, has turned against the minorities. The minorities of Gujarat are by now aware that, for good or worse, they will have to prepare to protect themselves. This is a prescription for disaster. It will underscore the atmosphere of a civil war and create a new breeding ground for terrorism. More than Operation Blue Star, the anti-Sikh riots spawned terrorism in Punjab in the 1980s; the two decades of rioting in Gujarat has by now similarly produced the sense of desperation that precedes the breakout of terrorism.

In the early 1960s, when I first went to Gujarat as an adolescent student, it was difficult to believe that Gujarat could ever have a major riot. People talked of riots that had taken place in the past and the state did have a history of small riots and skirmishes. Many Ahmedabadi Hindus seemed afraid and suspicious of the Muslims, but they were afraid and suspicious mostly of non-Gujarati Muslims, many of them labourers in the huge textile industry of Ahmedabad. They took the Gujarati Muslims, a large proportion of them business castes, as a part of Gujarat's landscape, though there was clear social distance. In retrospect, the picture was remarkably similar to that of Cochin, which I studied a few years ago as a city of religious and ethnic harmony.[2]The only difference probably was the more than moderate dislike for the Muslim as representing a *tamasic* principle in Ahmedabad's predominant Jain-Bania culture. That dislike was, however, 'balanced' by a similar dislike for the westernised outsiders congregating in the new, fashionable institutions being established in the city. Traditional Ahmedabad kept away both.

The 1969 riots began to change the city radically, though at the time the changes were not that obvious. Like all riots in South Asia, that one too was organised, and it was organised with great managerial panache by the RSS. The violence paid rich dividends. So did the imaginative hate campaigns unleashed by the Vishwa Hindu Parishad and the RSS. Together they gave a kick-start to the process of ghettoisation of the Muslims and the growth in the power of Mafia-like bodies in both communities, always itching for a fight and acting like protectors of the Hindus and the Muslims at times of rioting.

However, the growth of this criminal sector was disproportionately high among the young, unemployed Muslims. Understandably. The existing social distance between the communities had already acquired another tone. Facing discrimination in job situations and housing, many among the unemployed Muslim youth began to take to professions in which slum youth everywhere in the world specialise – illicit distillation, drug pushing, protection rackets and petty crime. And they always seemed ready for street violence. The situation worsened once Ahmedabad's famed textile industry collapsed. The changing political culture of the city ensured that this collapse, too, affected the Muslims more.

The dragon seeds sown by the 1969 riots have sprouted over the years. Gujarat's regular annual harvest began to include gory communal clashes and mob violence. We saw the full flowering of this culture during the Ramjanmabhoomi movement. As the great charioteer Lal Krishna Advani moved through Gujarat, he left in his wake a series of riots in which, according to Achyut Yagnik, for the first time, women and children were seen as legitimate targets of attack and atrocities. Riots were now becoming more brutal and barbaric.

During the last decade, Gujarat kept up with that tradition. In the ongoing riots, women and children have not only been attacked but also often killed with a sadistic glee that will be inconceivable in a civilised society. Even in the attack on *karsevak*s at Godhra, the one that precipitated the riots, it now transpires that the main victims were women and children. The following is an extract from a widely circulated eyewitness account, which some of the readers might not have seen. It is written by an IAS officer: 'Numbed with disgust and horror, I return from Gujarat ten days after the terror and massacre that convulsed the state. ... As you walk through the camps of riot survivors in Ahmedabad, in which an estimated 53,000 women, men, and children are huddled in 29 temporary settlements, displays of overt grief are unusual. ... But once you sit anywhere in these camps, people begin to speak and their words are like masses of pus released by slitting large festering wounds. The horrors that they speak of are so macabre, that my pen falters... The pitiless brutality against women and small children by organised bands of armed young men is more savage than anything witnessed in the riots that have shamed this nation from time to time during the past century...

'What can you say about a woman eight months pregnant who begged to be spared. Her assailants instead slit open her stomach, pulled out her foetus and slaughtered it before her eyes. What can you say about a family of nineteen being killed by flooding their house with water and then electrocuting them with high-tension electricity?

'What can you say? A small boy of six in Juhapara camp described how his mother and six brothers and sisters were battered to death before his eyes. He survived only because he fell unconscious, and was taken for dead. A family escaping from Naroda-Patiya, one of the worst-hit settlements in Ahmedabad, spoke of losing a young woman and her three month old son, because a police constable directed her to "safety" and she found herself instead surrounded by a mob which doused her with kerosene and set her and her baby on fire.

'I have never known a riot which has used the sexual subjugation of women so widely as an instrument of violence as in the recent mass barbarity in Gujarat. There are reports everywhere of gangrape, of young girls and women, often in the presence of members of their families, followed by their murder by burning alive, or by bludgeoning with a hammer and in one case with a screw-driver.'[4]

Gujarat disowned Mohandas Karamchand Gandhi long ago. The state's political soul has been won over by his killers. This time they have not only assassinated him again, they have danced on his dead body, howling with delight and mouthing obscenities. The Gandhians, in response, took out some ineffective peace processions, when they should have taken a public position against the regime and the Nazi Gauleiter ruling Gujarat. One is not surprised when told by the newspapers that the Sabarmati Ashram, instead of becoming the city's major sanctuary, closed its gates to protect its properties.

Almost nothing reveals the decline and degeneration of Gujarati middle class culture more than its present Chief Minister, Narendra Modi. Not only has he shamelessly presided over the riots and acted as the chief patron of rioting gangs, the vulgarities of his utterances have been a slur on civilised public life. His justifications of the riots, too, sound uncannily like that of Slobodan Milosevic, the Serbian president and mass murderer who is now facing trial for his crimes against humanity. I often wonder these days why those active in human rights groups in India and abroad have not yet tried to get international summons issued against Modi for colluding with the murder of hundreds and for attempted ethnic cleansing. If Modi's behaviour till now is not a crime against humanity, what is?

More than a decade ago, when Narendra Modi was a nobody, a small-time RSS *pracharak* trying to make it as a small-time BJP functionary, I had the privilege of interviewing him along with Achyut Yagnik, whom Modi could not fortunately recognise. (Fortunately because he knew Yagnik by name and was to later make some snide comments about his activities and columns.) It was a long, rambling interview, but it left me in no doubt that here was a classic, clinical case of a fascist. I never use the term 'fascist' as a term of abuse; to me it is a diagnostic category comprising not only one's ideological posture but also the personality traits and motivational patterns contextualising the ideology.

Modi, it gives me no pleasure to tell the readers, met virtually all the criteria that psychiatrists, psycho-analysts and psychologists had set up after years of empirical work on the authoritarian personality. He had the same mix of puritanical rigidity, narrowing of emotional life, massive use of the ego defence of projection, denial and fear of his own passions combined with fantasies of violence – all set within the matrix of clear paranoid and obsessive personality traits. I still remember the cool, measured tone in which he elaborated a theory of cosmic conspiracy against India that painted every Muslim as a suspected traitor and a potential terrorist. I came out of the interview shaken and told Yagnik that, for the first time, I had met a textbook case of a fascist and a prospective killer, perhaps even a future mass murderer.

The very fact that he has wormed his way to the post of the chief minister of Gujarat tells you something about our political process and the trajectory our democracy has traversed in the last fifty years. I am afraid I cannot look at the future of the country with anything but great foreboding.

The Gujarat riots mark the beginning of a new phase in Indian politics. We talk of terrorism in Kashmir and the North East and proudly speak of subduing the terrorism that broke out in Punjab. The total population involved in these cases, particularly the section that could be considered sympathetic to militancy, has always been small. Even if we believe that Pakistan's ISI and the Indian Army between them have persuaded all Kashmiris in the Valley to support militancy, these Kashmiris add up to only three million, one-third the size of the city of Delhi.

The forces the Gujarat violence might have released are a different kettle of fish. They seem to have done what the Partition riots did. Also, given that they have been arguably the first video riots in India – riots taking place in front of TV cameras – their impact will be pan-Indian and international. The minorities all over the country have seen the experiments in ethnic cleansing and the attempts to break the economic backbone of the Muslim community. The sense of desperation brewing among the Gujarati Muslims is likely to be contagious.

I wonder what we should do with 120 million bitter Muslims, a sizeable section of them close to desperation. Will it be another case of Palestine now onwards, at least in Gujarat? Prima facie, Modi has done his job. The Sangh Parivar's two-nation theory is genuine stuff and has already initiated the process of a second partition of India, this time of the mind. We, our children and grandchildren – above all, the Gujaratis – will have to learn to live with a state of civil war. The Gujarati middle class will have to pay heavily – culturally, socially and economically – for its collusion with the recent pogrom.

Courtesy: Seminar

# Gujarat of the year 2002
# What did it teach us?

SALIL TRIPATHI

February 2022

The death of 59 people in the train compartment at Godhra 20 years ago, and the violent aftermath in which more than 1,000 people were killed, had many lessons for us. And what did we learn from it? We learned to compartmentalise our dead. We learned to be selective in our compassion. We realised the raw power of the hatred that was latent within us, which had been internalised, not allowed to erupt, and when it did erupt, it revealed callous fury which we could not suppress, and which diminished us.

We learned to normalise the idea of revenge. We had done that with other outrages in the past, but 2002 made retribution acceptable. We found that it was all right to provoke others by shouting slogans. We saw that such provocation could lead to retaliation that can be violent. We recognised the rage within us when people were burned in a train, because some of us felt those burned were our people, and those who may have set the train on fire were their people. This idea of us and them got solidified among us.

We were torn between justice and reprisal – justice would happen, but it tended to take time. Revenge was quicker and gave many of us vicarious thrill, sadistic joy. We determined that we may not have full facts but truth was on our side, and so we could act. We began to accept rumours as fact and trusted the spoken word over the printed word, and the printed words discarded any sign of restraint and added kerosene to the leaping flames.

We attacked businesses and property belonging to the other community, because the unrest and violence provided an opportunity to do so. We realised that leaders liked to stoke the fires, by not condemning violence outright, by not providing succor to the innocent who were maimed, raped, or whose homes were looted and destroyed, by not restoring order, by claiming that the administration was still new in a state with long experience in dealing with communal violence, where the bureaucrats would know the standard operating procedures to follow to calm the storm. We saw politicians exploiting a tragedy to rouse emotions.

We did not wish to distinguish between the perpetrator and the bystander, we believed the victims deserved what they got because they acted in a provocative manner. We wanted them to be taught a lesson. We assigned class guilt on a group when a those responsible for an atrocity were few and individuals, not the collective. We decided to overlook the failures of those whose job it was to protect.

We accepted that sometimes, eggs must be broken to make an omelette, even in a city where many preferred to eat omelettes surreptitiously. We also learned that it may not be possible to unscramble an egg, so we began dividing the city into our half and theirs. We created walled gardens, lived enclosed, avoiding interacting with the other.

We also believed that it was OK to say things that were offensive. Our tongues lost any sense of control. We cheered when leaders would say things that might be deeply offensive. We saw the limitations of courts of law in providing justice. We saw how realpolitik could override law, principles, processes, morality, and a sense of fairness.

We learned to forget. We wanted the victims to forgive even though the perpetrators had not expressed any remorse. We wanted to move on, we even urged the victims to move on, even as they surveyed the debris; we would not feel what they felt. We garlanded portraits of Gandhi while our schools ran elocution competition on the topic why Gandhi's assassin should be seen as an idol – this, in a city 80 km. from the waterfront where Gandhi bent low to pick up some salt, defying an unjust tax, and sank an empire.

That we is among all of us – you, me, others we know, the majority, the ones with power, the ones that dominate the society but believe we are persecuted. February 27, 2002, and what followed luridly revealed our collective failure. And we were incapable of seeing it as failure. We became smaller, but we believed we had become bigger. We now live with its consequences without being aware how much we have changed, or what we have become.

Perhaps that veneer was wrong – we were always violent. It took a Gandhi to calm us and to shame us into putting away our weapons and change our vocabulary, ridding our speech of hate. But seven decades have passed since he was killed. We don't seem to need him anymore. We have learned that it is time to move on.

Courtesy: Scroll.in

# Learning from the past
# Lessons for the future

*Githa Hariharan, noted novelist, had a conversation with eminent historian Romila Thapar at the Kerala Literature Festival in Kozhikode in 1018. Romila spoke of the contradiction between religious non-violence and political violence, and the bridge between ancient India and modern India.*

GH: It is a great pleasure for me to be in conversation with Romila, especially because she's a friend and a fellow traveller. And most important in these times, we value the historian who does not fabricate history, but questions those who are distorting it. I do want to preface our conversation by saying that I am here as an interested citizen and a writer. I am not an academic and not a scholar. What we are hoping to do is talk about the past insofar as it is used in the politics of the present. Romila, we used to be told: 'Tell me what your classic is, and I'll tell you where you come from.' Suppose I twist that and say, 'Tell me what your way of looking at the past is, and I'll tell you where you come from in the present.' In other words, what are the different ways of looking at the past to use it in the present?

RT: Now, Githa has asked me about history. I don't really know where to begin because it's a subject that I have read and taught and thought about so much. But let me clarify one thing. I often get people coming up to me and saying, 'You're a historian and there are so many controversies these days, where is the truth?' And I have to say, 'I'm very sorry, but we are not looking for the Truth (with a capital T), certainly not in my case as a historian. What I am looking for is how we understand the past, how we analyse it. And that's as far as I'm willing to go. The past is past. It's over and done with. We cannot reconstruct it as it was, but we can try and understand it. And that is the important issue.

GH: Romila, hearing you frame the study of history, I think of my own school days when we had to study something called 'Oriental History'. Then and now, the official historians have always had an agenda.

RT: Indeed, they have always had an agenda, though that was not recognised early on. But that is the first question we ask today when we pick up a text. Whether it is a Sanskrit chronicle from the pre-Islamic period, or a Persian chronicle, the first question we ask is, 'What is the agenda of the author?' These are new questions. 'Who is the author? What is the agenda? What is the purpose of the text?' And very important, 'Who is the audience the author and the text are addressing?' This gives you some idea of the complications we face now when we look at texts as sources. You don't go to them and come back and say, 'In such and such a text it says this. This must have been what happened.' Not at all. Your next question is, 'If in such and such a text it says this, did it happen? How do we test whether it happened?' This is very important. The agenda does govern the reading of a text. We originally had Orientalists and Indologists who did first-rate work in finding the texts and analysing them up to a point—linguistically—and giving us the information of the texts. Then the agenda changed. Just information was no longer enough. Now historians wanted to know what the approach of the author was. What the purpose of the text was. And so, you had a tradition of colonial historians who wrote at great length about the purpose of these texts and made certain statements. And the nationalists disapproved of some of these statements.

So, a few of the nationalist historians, such as K. P. Jayaswal, R.C. Majumdar and others, questioned what the colonial historians had said. And then my generation came along and said: 'Wait a minute, both the colonialists and the nationalists have made mistakes. They are not reading the texts the way we should read them.' And so, we gave a fresh reading to the text, putting it into context. And that has done something very interesting, which the public is not fully aware of. It has shifted history from being a subject in Indology, where you want information, to becoming a subject in what we call the social sciences, where you want more than information; you want to know the how and the why and wherefore of events. You want to analyse these events. You want to look at the context, and you want to look at causal relationships and logical reconstructions.

GH: Could you give us a specific example of the 'rational social science method' which does not pretend you can reveal the past, but you can sort of put in some pieces and say, 'This is possible'? Does any example come to mind?

RT: The example in which I explored this the most was my study of the Mahmud of Ghazni raid in 1026 on the temple of Somanatha. The Persian chronicles were the only sources that were used for a long time, and they had descriptions of the temple and what was looted. It was very interesting that each chronicle changed the description of what was there. One said it was a Shiva lingam. Another said it was a pre-Islamic Arabian goddess, in a formless form. Somebody else said it was something else and so on. They couldn't quite make up their minds what it was that Mahmud of Ghazni had looted, except for the basic fact that the temple was very wealthy and that it had been raided for its wealth. Then some of us came along and said, 'What about what happened after the raid?' So, we started looking at Sanskrit texts, Jain texts, studies, histories, chronicles of the Chalukya dynasty of Gujarat [contemporaneous with Ghazni's raid], of individual rulers and Sanskrit inscriptions. A totally different story emerged: Somanatha had become a major commercial centre trading with the Arabs and the Persians. The temples were even richer than before and had a lot of land to their name. When the Arab traders came and wanted to build a mosque, the

Somanatha temple donated some land to them. And this is in the century after the raid.

Now this was a revelation. And why did people not look at the Sanskrit text? Because the British colonial writers had divided Indian history into the Hindu period, the Muslim period and the British period. They said the Hindu period ends in 1200, then the Muslim period begins. And in the Hindu period you only read texts in Sanskrit because it's a Hindu period. And in the Muslim period you only read texts in Persian, not realising that the texts and the writing of the texts, and the writing of inscriptions, continued in Sanskrit and Persian—in Sanskrit right up to the nineteenth century.

So, we had to use this kind of information. We had to stop talking about the Hindu-Muslim crisis and begin to look at the temple and commercial relations. We had to ask questions such as, 'What was the nature of these commercial relations? Who were the merchants who came and what was the nature of trade? Who did they mix with? Who did they marry?' And the Arabs, as we now know, set up as commercial settlers along the west coast. They set up a series of communities where they married locally and a new community emerged.

Then somebody said, 'What about the Hindu trauma?' The colonial writers had said a great deal about how Mahmud of Ghazni's raid had created such a strong Hindu trauma that it became the basis of Hindu-

Muslim antagonism for centuries to come from the eleventh century onwards. I went through the Sanskrit texts but could find no reference to this trauma. There is no reference even to the raid, in fact. The texts described the destruction of the temple in various other ways. Then I chanced upon a debate in the House of Commons in 1842. A member in the British House of Commons asks a question: 'Did this raid not create a trauma among the Hindus?' The colonial writers picked this up and began talking about how the raid created a trauma among the Hindus. Then the nationalist historians picked it up, and they too said it created a trauma among the Hindus.

GH: And that brings us to present times. You have spoken of the colonial division of the Hindu period and the Muslim period. That has made today's politics possible — ironically the so-called nationalists today are using a colonial schema. That is one issue. And then this trauma you speak of also seems to have some link with the present narrative of Hindu victimisation, which calls for Hindus to become martial. Would you tell us more about these two strands of the right-wing narrative?

RT:  Let me go back a bit. One thing to keep in mind is that nationalism emerges in the modern period. We cannot talk about nationalism in the Mauryan period or the Gupta period, or the Chola period, or the Mughal period. Absolutely not. Nationalism is a modern concept, and it is a way to bind people together and create a nation. What existed before were kingdoms and states, not nations. Nations come into existence around the eighteenth century. Now, what happens with nationalism in our case is this: we had anti-colonial nationalism, which was a kind of secular nationalism. It was inclusive. It tried to bring all Indians together in a movement which was to try and get rid of colonial rule.

Now, side by side with that, and encouraged by colonial rule, there emerged what we call religious nationalism. It took root via the Muslim League in the case of Islamic nationalism, and the Hindu Mahasabha and such like with Hindu nationalism. Religious nationalism is different from secular nationalism— anti-colonial nationalism—which is inclusive. It brings in everybody as much as possible, whereas religious nationalism caters to a particular religious community. It's confined, it's exclusive.

History is an essential feature of all nationalism. The great European historian Eric Hobsbawm [1917– 2012] has a lovely statement on this. He says, 'History is to nationalism what the poppy is to the opium addict.' It is the source of trying to give people a vision that can bring them together. And because of that, because of the centrality of history, very often what happens is that your religious or your linguistic—or in these days, caste nationalism—tends to create new histories, fantasy histories. These play havoc with genuine history— genuine in the sense of well-researched, well-thought-out history, based on hard evidence, as against histories which are more myth than history.

This is where history becomes a central issue in our kinds of societies. I have often thought about the fact that when I opted to study ancient Indian history—this was in the mid-1950s— everybody would say, 'Oh, you've taken the easy way out because nobody knows about that history. You can say what you like.' Now I find it is the most contested history. It partakes of the nationalist tradition of having a golden age. All nationalist histories have a golden age. With Europe it is, of course, Greco-Roman. And so, in the Indian case too, there is a hunt for a golden age, and the Gupta period becomes the golden age.

The other contestation, or problem, emerges because those of us trying to bring in the importance of evidence—reliable evidence, evidence that has been analysed, evidence in which causal relationships have been examined deeply, evidence based on rational, logical connections—are regarded as 'antinational' because we don't further the fantasy histories that are being put forward.

GH: Romila, let me complicate matters. It seems there are huge absences in our history. I know that all of us would like to say that the freedom movement was inclusive. We are talking of a written history in which large numbers of people are not visible, because of the caste system. You remember we were talking about the first mention of caste in the golden period. So much for the golden period! Could you talk about that, and about how we could express nationalism—in the good sense of the word—as citizens of India? Till Dalits and other large sections of the population have a *visible* history of their own, we will have absences and contentions, such as the one about Bhima Koregaon.

RT: This is a very important point because a lot of nationalist history tended to go by what the texts were saying. So, if the Dharmashastras describe society in a particular way and give much more visibility to the upper castes, there was a tendency for historians to say, 'Yes, that is how society functioned.' Part of the reason for the absences is that those who were not literate didn't produce texts. And so, we must look for evidence of them in the texts of elite groups and upper castes who may mention them. Some do, but not at great length. So, there is a certain amount of evidence that is missing in a direct way, and which needs to be discovered.

There are also other things we must consider. For example, the oral tradition was always dismissed by historians as being impossible, as inexact and indirect. 'Anybody can add anything they like.' And this became a little matter of debate when we discovered that there are many texts that we take for granted where bits and pieces have been added on, and we don't know who added them on, but we can suspect who did because of the message they carry.

The *Mahabharata* is a beautiful example of a text which has constantly been added on to in the past, gradually. In Africa, for example, it was said, 'Oh, there was no history south of the Sahara.' But they began studying the oral tradition more analytically and carefully; they began making a method for the study, and method is crucial in any kind of study. So just as we have a historical method we use, a method was also produced for the oral tradition. Now it is possible for us to go to nonelite sources, and even use the oral tradition to get some idea of what the history might have been.

GH: Romila, let's talk a little more about caste. What are the ways in which this completely extraordinary system of stratification—our negative contribution to the world— emerged, grew and lived? What were the strategies that allowed caste to become an institution that has lasted? Would you tell us how this fits in with the modern historian's paradigm?

RT: These questions are, perhaps, a little difficult because they are still being worked out. So, I would make two points. One is that all societies have stratification. So, it's not very unusual that Indian society also had stratification. The second point I would like to make is that all stratifications are subject to being changed. So, the old idea that we had that caste as varna, as described in Dharmashastra, was something that made society static and was always observed, come rain or shine—this is false! We have enough historical evidence now to say that within each of the four varnas, for example, there were changes, movement up and down. So, we must relook at the whole caste stratification and see what these changes were.

The second point I would like to make is that there's always been this contention between *jati* and *varna*, and *jati* was always treated as a subcaste of *varna*. But now people are beginning to ask the question: 'If we say that the original stratification was *jati*, based on extended families, clan systems, or all these early forms by which society was divided, and varna then came in as a very deliberate design and strategy to demarcate groups of people from each other, are the two things not different?' They play along in a different way. Now, there is an interesting thing about what is called *avarna. Savarna* refers to the four castes that constitute varna. *Avarna* is a group that is not given a status in caste and which is outside society. We have very interesting references to the chandala who was the characteristic person regarded as the *avarna*, always living outside the society. But to begin with, the *chandala* was regarded as lower caste, and that was it.

For example, there's a very interesting dialogue in the *Mahabharata* with the sage Vishwamitra, who's been performing *tapasya* like mad, because he is trying desperately to acquire so much merit that he becomes a major sage. There's a famine in the land. Vishwamitra is desperately hungry. He comes to a *chandala* hamlet. In one of the houses, he sees dog meat hanging, and he's just about to grab it and eat it, he's so hungry. The *chandala* comes out and says, 'Wait, what are you doing? If you eat that meat, you will lose all the *punya* you have been gathering with this intense *tapasya*.' And there's a dialogue in which the *chandala* explains to Vishwamitra, or tells him off, saying, 'This is not *Brahmin dharma*. This is not how you are expected to behave.' And he explains to Vishwamitra why he's saying this is not the way he's expected to behave. Finally, of course, Vishwamitra eats the dog meat and then says he will double down on the *tapasya* and get back his merit. This would be unheard of in the Gupta period, and certainly unheard of today. But there is this dialogue in the *Mahabharata*, some kind of communication which indicates something interesting happening. And coming to the situation of the *chandala* living outside the settlement. By the Gupta period, we have a description from Fa-Hien, a Chinese Buddhist pilgrim who visits India. And he says that they have here a category of people whom they regard as very polluted. Remember, the *Mahabharata* story is not talking about pollution. But now we have a category of people who are very polluted, therefore live outside the settlement. When they come into the settlement, they must strike a clapper so that people will move away since they don't want to touch or be touched by the *chandala*. Again, it's in the Gupta period also that you begin to get references in the Dharmashastra to the *asprishya*, those not to be touched.

And that was the point that I was making, that this is your golden age, an age where lots of admirable things are happening, whether it is in literature or art or philosophy. Certainly, all this makes it a remarkably brilliant age. But on the social side, it was different. And my question has always been, 'What kind of society was it that allowed the two things to co-exist?' This I haven't understood, I must confess.

GH: I remember your telling me that the *asprishya* (untouchables) couldn't leave their situation physically. Religious persecution has seen waves of people going elsewhere, but caste …

RT: They couldn't get up and go for the simple reason that they were regarded as genetically polluted. It is not just the individual who is polluted, but also the child born of *asprishya* parents is automatically polluted. So, there's a genetic pollution. And the thing about the early period of Indian history was that there were no peasant revolts as such, unlike China that had lots of peasant revolts. We had peasant migrations. The peasants were overtaxed, impoverished. They would move into the next kingdom. And this was always feared by the kings because they would lose revenue if the peasants moved. But the untouchable, the chandala, could not move because no other kingdom would accept the polluted person. The other kingdoms didn't want to increase their population of polluted people. So, this category of people who were at the lowest occupational levels, both in terms of artisanal production and in terms of being agricultural labour, were forced to remain where they were. They couldn't get away because of the stigma of pollution. And in some ways, I suppose it is an astute method to keep available a permanent body of labour you can control completely.

GH: What about the medieval *bhakti* movements, limited but powerful protest movements that experimented with fighting caste and this whole system of co-option? The perfect example is Basava [fl. twelfth century] and what happens to the movement he is part of, how it ends up creating one more caste, the Lingayat caste. So, has that always been a kind of a strategy that you see in 'Hindu history'?

RT: You see it in all religions here because this category of polluted people is not restricted to the Hindu religion. It occurs among the Muslims, the Christians, also among the Sikhs. The first question we need to ask about the movements you refer to is, 'Was this a religious movement or a social movement, or a mixture of the two, one using the other, one giving strength to the other?' If you argue along these lines, you partly explain why even important religions not using this idea outside India use it here—they are continuing the social basis of what is going on in

India. And I think that is an important thing to keep in mind, that there is this continuation.

GH: Coming to the present, could we talk about the role of the public intellectual, and the role of university spaces, of educational spaces? Also, what sort of public discourse should we aspire to? That seems to be a huge problem today when we speak of history, literature or culture.

RT: After Independence, there was a strong feeling that we need to envision the kind of society we mean to build. There were two important issues involved. One was, 'Who are we as Indians? What is our identity?' And the other was, 'What is the kind of society we're going to build?' It was quite clear who we are as Indians: We are Indians on a larger scale because we are not divided into religious categories or caste categories or linguistic categories. We are Indian citizens. The new thing at the point of Independence was that we now had a nation, we had a nation-state, and we had citizens. And the relationship had to be that of the citizen to the state, which in a sense cuts out all the other incisive categories that pull people apart. And, of course, despite attempts, we didn't achieve much in terms of forging this relationship between the citizen and the state, because we have arrived at a present point when nobody talks about *citizens* anymore. Everybody talks about majority communities and minority communities, which is entirely a colonial construct; it is entirely antidemocratic. Democracies don't have permanent majorities and minorities separated by a single qualifying factor such as religion or language. The majority and the minority change with each issue under debate. So, there is that distinction. Perhaps the important thing is the question of how we make all our people learn to think. Because that's essential. And it is that critical aspect of education where we have failed. Yes, education may have spread literacy up to a limited degree, but …

GH: Education itself is a troubled site today. They have been saying things like, 'Drop the Mughal period altogether from the syllabus', or 'Darwin was wrong!' We seem to be grappling with new idiocies every day.

RT: But that is partly because in our educational system, we don't do the one basic thing that all good education systems require. And that is to teach the student to doubt accepted knowledge and to ask relevant questions. If you don't question then you have a mindset which says, 'It says so in the book, you learn it by heart and repeat it.' And the crisis today for students is that they're not battling with ideas. 'What grades will I get?' That is the only question they ask. It is tragic. It is the termination of a good educational system when you stop grappling with ideas.

GH: When I think of the JNU with which you've been associated ever since it was founded, I see that this kind of questioning was part of the vision for the University that all of you worked very hard to implement. Despite all odds, even today, you see that in the JNU campus, there are students who speak up and ask hard questions. But what do you do with those in authority who systematically suppress this natural desire to question? What should writers and students and academics do in such a situation?

RT: The central issue is the right of institutions to determine their goals. This right must be exercised within and outside the university—and this is where the question of the public intellectual becomes very important. The right to insist that institutions must not be silenced must have a social backing. We want university education, which is an education that teaches us how to question, how to think, how to move knowledge ahead, whatever knowledge it may be.' But if there are institutions creating impediments to this kind of understanding and questioning, we must question those institutions.

GH: I think that's a good point at which to draw this conversation to a close, since all your comments come together at the point of knowledge, the question of how we seek knowledge, and the understanding that knowledge is not something which is readymade, or something that belongs to a few people. It's something we are all working towards.

From *This Too Is India: Conversations on Diversity and Dissent*, Westland, 2024, pp. 64-79. Reproduced with permission from the publisher and the editor.

# *Ram ka Doosra Banwas*
## The Second Exile

The next piece written by Pratap Bhanu Mehta in 2017 marked the 25th anniversary of 6 December, 1992, the infamous day on which a mob, armed with hammers, assaulted both Hinduism and secularism in Ayodhya. The self-styled Ram devotees demolished the Babri Mosque, with jubilant BJP leaders applauding them. Eminent poet Kaifi Azmi imagines what Ram, coming to the Saryu river and seeing spots of blood, felt on that day. The poem says:

> *Ram turns to the mad men who mobbed his Ayodhya and tells them that the stones they threw at Babar injured his head.*
> *Ram then leaves his kingdom for the forest, going into exile for the second time.*

# *Ayodhya Kand*
## It began on 6 December 1992

PRATAP BHANU MEHTA

December 2017

The 25th anniversary of that fateful day in Ayodhya when the Babri Masjid was demolished brings a sense of foreboding. It was a day when both secularism and Hinduism were assaulted by a mob. The psychological and historical significance of that day is complex. But when all is said and done, it must be admitted that the worst of our political tendencies that were on display on December 6, 1992, are in the ascendant 25 years later. Open majoritarianism and divisiveness is now a dominant cultural and political sensibility. The nature of the act that brought down the Babri Masjid structure, a form of violent vigilantism, is freely accepted in politics. The idea that something nebulous like community sentiment can trump the Constitution, values of equality and individual liberty, and the rule of law itself, is now considered political common sense.

The sensibility that informed the Ram Janmabhoomi movement, a kind of coarse, mediocre, and insecure aggression, has become second nature to politics. The transformation of Hinduism that the events in Ayodhya represented continues unabated. Instead of its highest philosophical aspirations being guided by the plenitude of the world and a blissful realisation of the Self, Hinduism's aspiration became defined by raw assertions of power. Its leadership, if we can call it that, came to be characterised by an odd combination of agitators and new-age hucksters. Piety was replaced by a will to power. The cultural ideal that Ram constituted was finally reduced to a single point. The living reality of Ram, in an effective sense, had till this point never been erased. But by reducing Ram to a crude historical drama, India for the first-time assaulted Ram. That fateful day assaulted the Ram of Valmiki, Tulsi and Kamban and countless other real Rams. They replaced it with the Ram of L.K. Advani and Adityanath and Ashok Singhal. Did faith live or die that day?

Then there was the corruption of all political parties under a feigned faith. As the Congress once again does the rounds of temples, it is worth remembering that it was its duplicity, its double-speak on constitutional values, its attempts to run both Hindu nationalism and Muslim identity politics together that brought us to this pass. Whatever its professed values, its credibility was reduced to a point from which it is still not recovered. The BJP had its ups and downs since the movement, but its organisation and commitment made sure that its views penetrated across a range of civil society institutions. But it is politically reaching a point where it will be hard for it to deny its core supporters the satisfaction of the temple being built. Almost all the elements of building the temple, creating a political momentum, opening institutional spaces, are being put in place. We will give in out of sheer weariness. But the scars of divisiveness will continue.

Indian institutions have never been strong, and riot victims from numerous riots, including 1984, still await justice. But the role of non-elected institutions should come under the scanner. Cases were not swiftly disposed of from the early Fifties, keeping the ground perpetually open for facts on the ground to be distorted. Despite the Liberhan Commission, the leaders in that act of vigilantism have, 25 years later, not been called to account. The psychological message that sends, that you can get away with anything, so long as you can invoke faith, damages institutions. For years, the Supreme Court has tried its old trick of a modus vivendi by deferring the decision. Now the Court has decided to resume hearings in February next year. It will not be appropriate to speculate how it will rule. But it is a fair institutional point that the Supreme Court has damaged its reputation and credibility so much over the last few months that it will have to go the extra mile of care, fairness, and probity to ensure that whatever its judgement, justice is not only done, but seen to be done.

There is no question that on that day, a significant number of Hindus felt, even if briefly, a sense of catharsis. The range of psychological complexes behind that need to be unpacked. At a very immediate level, the rank opportunism of the Congress during the Eighties left the country insecure; from Salman Rushdie to Shah Bano, it was easy to indict the Congress. Thanks to the Rajiv Gandhi years, Nehruvian secularism became a byword for opportunism and corruption, not for liberty and rule of law. So, the symbolic destruction of the so-called Nehruvian order became a live force in Indian politics. The demolition of the *masjid* represented that.

Second, as V. S. Naipaul, one of the few writers who has the depth to go to dark psychological spaces, understood, there were too many suppressed histories in India; and the simple-minded historical pieties and institutional control of the Left-Congress alliance on history could no longer cope with these. The sense that many Indians have, of being denuded of their history and their own power to write it, was and remains widespread. Stories of cultural oppression win out because there is sometimes a comfort in victimhood; it directs attention away from our failings. But more deeply, we could never say: It should not matter what the medieval India story is, let the historians argue it out. But we cannot tie the fate of the present to what happened in the 16th century. It binds us to the past more than it liberates the future. Babri Masjid is the symbol of the tyranny of the past over the future.

Hindutva ideology was constructed by resentment because it saw Hinduism as constituted by three deficits: It has no political centre, its history has been marginalised by others, and it is internally weak and divided. Ayodhya was the cheap psychological recompense for these deficits. It attempted to give a Hinduism a political identity and centre, it attempted to reclaim history, and one could always have a consciousness of strength by targeting minorities. But this sense of lack, once internalised, cannot be easily satiated because it is a flight from reality. It does not have the inner cultural resources to make Hinduism creative and progressive; instead, it sees diversity, creativity, and plenitude as a threat. It has no ethical mooring, because its idea of strength is a crude masculine assertion, not the power of inner conviction. The agitators tied themselves to the yoke of the temple because they felt Ram's presence, his *karuna*, the least.

The events of December 6, 1992, assaulted both secularism and Hinduism. As one sees on the 25th anniversary of the tragedy in 2017, the consequences are still to play out fully.

Courtesy: *The Indian* EXPRESS

# Ayodhya, an Issue not a Town

VIVEK KUMAR

*A widely circulated post in Hindi, translated by Prof. Nivedita Menon and published in Kafila. A 300-year-old Janmasthan temple in Ayodhya, built on land donated by a Muslim zamindar, was demolished in August 2020 to accommodate an expanded vision of the new Ram Mandir.*

They say Ram was born in Ayodhya; in Ayodhya he played and roamed around as a youth, grew into adulthood, was sent from there into exile in the forest, and then returned to rule there. There are temples in Ayodhya to commemorate every moment of his life. Where he played, there is Gulela Mandir. Where he studied there is Vashishta Mandir. Where he sat and ruled, there is a mandir. Where he ate his meals, there is Sita Rasoi. Where Bharat stayed, there is a mandir. There's Hanuman Mandir, Kop Bhavan. There's Sumitra Mandir, Dashrath Bhavan. There are many such temples and all are about 400 to 500 years old. So, these temples were built when Hindustan was ruled by the Mughals, by Muslims.

How strange! How did Muslims permit these temples to be built? They are remembered after all, for destroying temples. Under their very noses an entire town was gradually transformed by temples and they did nothing! What sort of usurpers were these who kept giving land for temples? They must be liars who say that the land where Gulela Mandir stands was given by the Muslim rulers. And certainly, the documents in Digambar Akhara must be fake, in which it is written that the Muslim rulers donated 500 bighas of land for the specific purpose of building temples. And it cannot be true that Nawab Siraj ud-Dowlah provided the land on which Nirmohi Akhara stands. No, the only truth is Babur and his Babri Masjid!

Now it seems Tulsi too was wrong, who was alive around 1528, as he was born in 1511 by the Gregorian calendar. People say it was in 1528 that Babur destroyed a Ram Mandir at the spot where Ram was born and built Babri Masjid. Surely Tulsi would have known about this in his time. Even as Babur was demolishing the birthplace of Ram, Tulsi was writing *"maang ke khaibo, masit mein soibo"* – I eat by begging for alms, I sleep inside the masjid. And then he wrote Ramcharitmanas. How could Tulsi feel no sadness at all for the destruction of the Ram Mandir and the building of Babri Masjid upon its ruins? Surely, he must have written about it somewhere.

Truth and falsehood have lost all meaning in Ayodhya. For five generations Muslims have grown flowers there. These flowers have all been consecrated at the temples, on the deities, on Ram. Muslims have made wooden sandals there since who knows when. Sanyasis, sages, devotees of Ram, have all worn these *khadaus* (wooden sandals) made by Muslims. Sundar Bhavan Mandir was entirely run by one Muslim for four decades. In 1949, it was taken over by Munnu

Mian who remained its manager till December 23, 1992. When sometimes, as it happened, devotees were fewer, and Munnu Mian himself clapped the *kartal* rhythmically during prayers, did he wonder, perhaps, what was the truth and what the lie of Ayodhya?

On every brick of a temple built by Agarwals, is inscribed the figure, 786. All the bricks for building this temple were given by Raja Hussain Ali Khan. What is the truth here? Were the Agarwals who built the temple out of their minds? Was Hussain Ali Khan insane, that he was donating bricks to build a temple? The hands raised in prayer here cannot be identified as Hindu or Muslim, they all come here to worship. The one figure 786 made this temple belong to all. Is December 6, 1992, the only truth? After December 6, 1992, the government took over most of the temples of Ayodhya. They were all locked down. Aarti ended. People stopped going to them. Did the deities seated behind closed doors curse those who clambered up on a dome with the ambition of laying their hands on Ram? From the ancient temples of Ayodhya is there an exhalation of the stink of blood, the blood that was shed in the name of Ram in Ayodhya and in Bharat?

Ayodhya is the story of the transformation of a town into an "issue." Ayodhya is the story of the death of a civilisation.

# Old Ram, New Ram, Hey Ram!

ANAND K. SAHAY

In the newly divided Ayodhya, an old humble pilgrim will be dazzled by the grand Ram Mandir. The true Ram devotee brought up to conjure the gentle, divine image of Ram in the manner made immortal by the sage Valmiki in his *Ramayan* (probably around 2000 years ago), or the much later *Ramcharitmanas* of Goswami Tulsi Das (late 16th century), stands stupefied by the sights and loud tawdry sounds of construction and religious tourist capitalism.

In her article, *Deity to Crusader: The Changing Iconography of Ram*, theatre scholar Anuradha Kapur writes: "Traditional iconography tended to represent Ram, Janaki and Lakshman smiling serenely. Emblematically, the figures represented tranquility, compassion and the *shanta rasa*. The images now available…, the *rasa* in these images is not *shanta.*"

The pilgrim cannot but regard with anxiety – and with thoughts of deviation from the path – the New Ram in the New Ayodhya of New India, presented on the new walls as murals depicting a ferocious Hindu warrior, possibly even a hunter, the defender of ferocious nationalism. In 21st century India, is Ram going to be cyclostyled as a politician?

The mystique of religion flounders here; spirituality hurries to take a back seat in New India's new Ayodhya. Today, the most striking visual of that ancient town where the devout have thronged for centuries can said to be unabashed contractor capitalism running hard to make it count in case the bubble bursts all too soon.

Unseen hands of contractors and management from the state of Gujarat appear to be just about everywhere in the jobs to be executed, overriding local sentiment, with the river Sarju as a mute witness. On its banks are now moored cruise boats for the anticipated rush of the fancy tourist, not the paddle boats of the humble *Kewat*, the tribe of fisherfolk and boatmen who once had the ear of Lord Ram, the King of Ayodhya, as the *Ramayan* suggests.

The sovereign body in Ayodhya does not seem to be the Government of Uttar Pradesh – even if the chief minister is a *mahant* (Hindu priest) – but the Sri Ram Janmabhoomi Teerth Kshetra Trust or SRJTK. It is an autonomous body created in 2020 under Prime Minister Narendra Modi's guidance in line with the Supreme Court ruling of November 2019 which handed over the title of the land under the demolished Babri mosque to the same set that was castigated by the apex court in sharp terms for destroying the mosque.

This trust was charged with overseeing the construction of the Ram temple around the site of the former Babri Masjid, pulled down with human hands in 1992 by surcharged mobs high on the opium of religion and guided by the BJP's then top leaders. It is also entrusted with the improvement of Ayodhya with an eye to turning it into a Hindu Vatican or Mecca and a mammoth tourist attraction. The Government is eying massive tourism revenue.

VHP vice-president Champat Rai is the SRJTK general secretary and calls the shots in the new temple's management. The VHP is an affiliate of the Rashtriya Swayamsevak Sangh (RSS). The most influential entity for Ayodhya, however, is the chairman of the construction committee of the SRJTK, Nripendra Misra. He served as the principal secretary to the prime minister in his first term and is now after retirement deals extensively with the top engineering and consultancy firms. In effect, Modi's PMO runs Ayodhya, a very special project high on the regime's ideological and potential revenue-index.

The sums projected are impressive. According to a Mint report, the brokerage Jefferies "has recently estimated that a $10 billion makeover of Ayodhya with a new airport, revamped railway station, township and road connectivity will likely drive a multiplier effect with new hotels and other economic activities. It could attract 50 million tourists a year." Activities under the Ayodhya Masterplan have a time horizon that extends to 2031. Real estate is the name of the game.

There is probably no way to test such an exuberant projection, but context can help. Agra's world-famous Taj Mahal nets some six million tourists annually in contrast, and there are other sites of historical and architectural wonder in its vicinity. If Ayodhya were to raise eight or 10 times that number, it will probably have to upstage the tourist arrivals of several leading international destinations taken together.

Faizabad district – now renamed Ayodhya in a burst of religiosity – with its principal town of the same name, was the original seat of the Oudh (Awadh) nawabs, who later shifted to Lucknow. The city thus has a flavour of that past. The entire district and those around it constitute the agricultural hinterland of this region of Uttar Pradesh. In this backwater, industry (MSME and large included) has an annual turnover of under Rs 25 crore, according to relatively recent data of Union MSME ministry, and a workforce of about 30,000. A generally poor area has been dragged into the 21st century.

Can a standalone, modern temple of a particular faith, lacking universal appeal, in a relatively less developed part of the country, justify projections based on international tourist arrivals, presumably made up in large measure of well-heeled NRIs? Fancy hotels, glittering airport, and a very modern large railway facility in a backward region with limited demand, appear somewhat incongruous.

The government drummed up support to transport people to Ayodhya from various parts of the country in the weeks following the Ram temple consecration by Modi. The ruling party MPs and MLAs were assigned quotas to send people to Ayodhya. The railways laid out fast trains called "*Astha*" (faith) specials. Many passengers appeared to be genuinely simple, religious folk, others like mobilised political cadres. Members of a VHP group from western India said each of them paid Rs 1,800 for the train journey both ways and one day's stay in a comfortable tent city, erected to promote state-inspired religiosity. The railways had slashed all concessions in fares, including for senior citizens. But the neo-pilgrims mobilized for the Ayodhya campaign benefited from moderated fares.

There were vociferous complaints of people's homes and small businesses bulldozed to widen roads in the entire temple complex of Ayodhya. But the most conspicuous local grumble this writer encountered during a visit to Ayodhya concerned the contractors. We came across guards of a security company from Gujarat called *Kavach* charged with managing a section of the river ghat. According to one complaint, tribal workers were transported from Gujarat to work on some underground cable-laying. Has Uttar Pradesh exhausted its capacity to supply even the basics to mount an effort to modernise itself? The question and its implication hang in the air.

Guided to its final moments on January 22, Modi inaugurated an unfinished temple, practically on the eve of the national elections, with a rousing speech linking religion with nation in the presence of India's business, film, and sports stars. His role as a priest, the timing of the event and the consecration of a half-built temple were openly criticised by true Hindu leaders. So, Modi's political project was opposed both by the liberal Hindus as well as a section of devout religious scholars. Besides them, those who were noticeably absent were the ordinary Ram devotees of the ancient town of Ayodhya.

The project that surreptitiously commenced in 1949 with the insertion of Ram's idol inside a 500-year-old mosque was at last complete. History reminds us of Hitler ordering a "one-thousand-year Reich". This is a moment of triumph for political Hinduism – the unveiling of the unfinished temple, touted in BJP's national convention in New Delhi as a singular "achievement", an unleashing of the (doubtless Hindu) nation's "consciousness", a harbinger of "one thousand years of Ram Rajya".

The story of Ram is traditionally cherished in every Hindu home. His love of all beings, his poise even in war, his concern for his people, even at the expense of disregarding his wife Sita, his glowing beauty which gets culturally underlined as the metric for performance of duty, are celebrated as popular theatre in the form of *Ramaleela* across the villages, towns, and cities of North India. In recognition of this, the Muslim poet and future philosopher of Pakistan, Mohammed Iqbal, had given to Ram the title of *Imam-e-Hind*. That Ram appears to have gone missing in Ayodhya in the time of Modi.

Courtesy: *The Wire*

# Saffron is a political colour

APOORVANAND

January 2024

The colour sported by the Chief Justice of India while in Gujarat recently has become one that is associated not so much with spirituality as with hatred and violence. I have three kurtas in different hues of saffron. It is a colour I do not dislike. But after 2014 it has become increasingly difficult for me to wear those kurtas. I did not stop wearing them suddenly but gradually they have gone into disuse. There is a reason behind it. After 2014, thanks to WhatsApp and other social media platforms, I started getting images and videos of saffron-clad goons attacking Muslims. Beating them up, torturing them, killing them. I also saw goons with saffron *pattas* and stoles storming areas where Muslims lived, attacking, violating houses, mazars, and mosques. Saffron very rapidly became a colour associated with hatred and violence against Muslims. It has been used as a competitive colour, often to oppose Muslims. How can one forget instances of Hindu boys and girls wearing saffron turbans and scarves only to oppose the hijab-wearing women?

India braces for a potent brew of majoritarianism and authoritarianism in 2024. I also see young people sporting the colour in kurtas, stoles, and turbans as a sign of assertion or perhaps religious dominance. I see the colour suddenly being adopted by universities and other institutions, in hoardings and publicity material, as the theme colour in public functions. Politics of exclusion. The saffron colour has morphed from being just a colour to one that announces your association with an ideology, a politics that is narrow, which tries to create a group identity of Hindus, not the traditional one based on inclusion, but one based on exclusion of those who do not belong. On my campus and on other campuses, I see the colour flaunted by those who regularly indulge in violence against students who dare to have their own voice and who refuse to speak in the language given by a party. I also see it being used or worn by those who seek to associate with the not-so-newly minted idea of "nationalism". I have seen many new converts to the RSS ideology donning saffron to publicly announce their affiliation. I have seen the colour used by Vice Chancellors, teachers, and students to announce their loyalty to a particular ideology. If you sport a saffron *patta*, you are less likely to be charged by the traffic police for violation of traffic rules. They are aware that saffronised people belong to the party and it is better not to mess with them.

The colour evokes a feeling of subservience, mob mentality, and violence, but whatever it does, it never evokes sacred emotions or thoughts or the idea of sacrifice and renunciation that Indians and Hindus traditionally associated the colour with. It has now become a colour of domination. It has a threatening air. I feel that it has become something like the infamous Swastika of the Nazis. So, after 2014, every time I have touched one of my saffron-hued kurtas, a thought has crossed my mind about the reaction it could evoke in a Muslim's mind. How would I be seen? Would I look threatening? I often ask myself: am I overreacting? Am I exaggerating? At times, my wife chides me for giving up a colour. I have seen my friends wearing it, claiming they will not allow the colour to be usurped by violence or by Hindutva. But it sounds unconvincing to me. If I enter a Muslim locality wearing this colour, I will be looked upon with fear and suspicion. Imagine five, or even two, saffron-clad persons entering such a locality. Imagine the menace the colour will instantly acquire. So, this is my decision: I will not let this colour touch my body again. I do not want to be part of the Hindutva group identity. These thoughts came to my mind when I saw our serving Chief Justice of India (CJI) wearing a spotless saffron kurta as he visited a temple in Gujarat. It also struck me that his wife wore a saffron stole. Or a shade of it, as some friends suggest. They were on a pious mission. Visiting temples. But wearing saffron is not an essential uniform that must be worn when one visits a Hindu sacred space. I belong to a Hindu family and we come from Vaidyanath Dham or Deoghar. It is a popular pilgrimage place for the devotees of Shiva. I have never seen devotees wearing saffron while visiting the Shiva temple there.

Saffron does not automatically lift you to a spiritual plane. If anything, in recent times, it does the opposite. Moreover, I saw the Chief Justice walking on a red carpet, which is a very worldly touch. The CJI was walking to the deity in his capacity as the CJI, which explains the red-carpet treatment. One can say it is the CJI's personal choice and we are unnecessarily reading too much into it. But when you wear the colour in these times, it is to make a point. To underline your religiosity publicly, a religiosity which has political overtones. The CJI did not leave it there. According to media reports, he referred to the *dhwaja* atop the Dwarka and Somnath temples, the two temples he visited during his two-day visit to Gujarat, and said, "I was inspired this morning by the *dhwaja* at Dwarkadhish ji, very similar to the *dhwaja* I saw at Jagannath Puri. But look at the universality of the tradition in our nation, which binds all of us together. This *dhwaja* has a special meaning for us. And that meaning which the *dhwaja* gives us is—there is some unifying force above all of us, as lawyers, as judges, as citizens. And that unifying force is our humanity, which is governed by the rule of law and by the Constitution of India." Ramachandra Guha has rightly criticised him for mixing religion with the Constitution. "For the Chief Justice of India to claim a congruence between the flag that has traditionally flown above Hindu temples and the modern text that is the Constitution of India is tendentious and misleading (to say the least)," he wrote in a recent column. The

CJI is doing this at a time when another constitutional authority, the Prime Minister, is asking the whole nation to celebrate the inauguration of the Ram temple being built on land that belonged to the Babri Masjid, after its criminal demolition was overlooked in an act of judicial innovation. Mr Modi is calling it an end to the 500-year-old exile of Ram. The wait has ended, and we know for whom. Prime Minister Modi performs *Bhoomi Pujan* rituals for the construction of the Ram *mandir* in Ayodhya on August 5, 2020.

Large sections of Hindus appear to have been misled. And the CJI cannot shy away from his responsibility. It was he and his fellow judges who dragged the Indian state into this religious act. It was an unprecedented decision to ask the state to facilitate the building of a temple, which was the symbol of the victory of a divisive politics. It cannot be the job of a secular state to be involved in the construction of a religious place. This act, like the "Hindutva is a way of life" judgment of the Supreme Court given by a predecessor of the present CJI, has obliterated the separation of religion and state. The CJI and his brother judges waxed eloquent about the secular fundamentals of the Indian state. They quoted the 1991 Places of Worship Act (which ensures status quo of religious places) to assert that what they were doing with the Babri mosque could not be repeated. But very soon, the CJI upheld an order by the Allahabad High Court and allowed the Archaeological Survey of India (ASI) to investigate of the Gyanvapi mosque in Varanasi. Thus, when the same CJI so touchingly talks about "Dwarakadhishji" and "Somnathji", he makes a statement. It is again not an innocent statement when he says, "When I visited Somnath ji this morning, I was deeply moved that this is the first temple in India that has a zero-waste facility. Let us be inspired by making every court system in the State a zero-waste facility. It is then that we will be truly inspired by the ideals of these great temples, which dot the landscape of Gujarat...." It is a political statement. We are being asked to take inspiration from the *Dharma Dhwajas* to ensure justice and from the zero-waste facility of Somnathji to ensure cleanliness. Religion, cleanliness, unity: who mixes up all of these?

When the CJI laced his speech with Gujarati, Prime Minister Modi applauded him. There were other times when CJIs who would have been embarrassed by endorsement from a political authority. They would have shied away from publicity. CJIs are not supposed to be public figures. Popularity can be harmful. So, they consciously turn reclusive. As many senior lawyers have commented, politicians must know the people and talk to them. Judges do not have to talk to the people to do their job. They must keep a conversation with the Constitution alive. Leaving it and turning to the masses leads them to do what they did in their judgments on Babri mosque and Jammu and Kashmir.

Courtesy: Frontline

# Policing and Politics

KEKI DARUWALLA

October 2018

A policeman's lot is not a happy one--over worked, overregulated by laws that give him little respect—statements before police officers carry no weight in court-- and bullied both by higher khaki echelons and politicians. There is of course light in this gloomy picture, excuse the sarcasm. The Policeman has started reveling in the power granted to him by law, also what he has usurped from the books. Obtaining search or arrest warrants forms no part of his concerns. You didn't stop your car when I asked you, buddy! Take that, and two constables, unsupervised by anyone responsible, shoot the Apple executive, Vivek Tiwari dead in Lucknow. Who gave them license to shoot? What made them so trigger-happy? This needs to be traced to the pro encounter policies of the Chief Minister, who stated after the event, "This was not an encounter. The guilty will not be spared". The Chief Minister obviously thinks that 'encounter' is a decent legal term approved by the Constitution!! It is a dirty word Yogiji. It means that police has circumvented judicial process and killed someone, perhaps innocent, and often, in cold blood.

'Encounters" should be taboo. According to press reports, Sixty-seven people have been killed since Mr. Adityanath Yogi took over. In these 'gun duels' only suspects fall. Police parties come out unscathed. Superior marksmanship obviously! The police in many states have been accused of an anti- minority bias. When eight inmates escaped jail in Bhopal, the police surrounded them the next day and shot the unarmed guys. That evening the Chief Minister Madhya Pradesh felicitated the team openly, Reception shown on TV. The macho strain, and the communal bias fostered and encouraged by politicians, has now passed on to women police. We saw how a Meerut policewoman beat up a girl for hobnobbing with a Muslim, by today's yardstick, an almost anti-national crime. Remember over a year back the DGP UP wanted to try cow- slaughter cases under the National Security Act!

It is unfair to blame BJP for anti-Muslim bias in the police. Events in Hashimpura are close to three decades old, where UP's Pradeshik Armed Constabulary (PAC) killed forty odd Muslims and threw them into a canal. Very little happened to the perpetrators who continued to get their increments and promotions in this "elite" force. Successive governments turned a blind eye to these happenings and accountability became a casualty.

The frightening thing is that this is the first time we see the state meddling in individual criminal cases, and in defence of alleged criminals. A Senior and bold Prosecutor Ms. Rohini Salian is told to go slow on bomb blast accused. The NIA denies this but the prosecutor names the SP (Suhas Warke) who told her to take it easy in an affidavit in the High Court. Take the Sohrabuddin and Ishrat Jahan alleged fake encounters. The Gujarat government has behaved over the last decade as if the state itself was in the dock and not DIG Vanzara and co. In the post Godhra riots one could understand that the Gujarat state was in fact the accused. It later appointed officers allegedly involved in the encounters, to high posts. P.P. Pandey, behind bars for sixteen months in the Ishrat Jahan encounter case, was appointed Director General Police in April 2016. Not only that he was given extensions, till the Supreme Court, on a petition by the respected Julio Ribero, sent the DG on overdue superannuation on April 2nd, 2017.

To trot out other cases, take the killing of Pehlu Khan, a dairy farmer carrying cows legally. He was killed by the vigilantes in April 2017 in Alwar. The SP spoke up that he was a cow slaughterer, without any proof or investigation, the same day. The Minister Minority Affairs Mukhtar Abbas Naqvi stated that the way the incident was being projected, no such incident took place. The lynching was all over the Television. What is to be noted is that the minister spoke up in defence of the assailants.

To pick out at random inflammatory statements by politicians, T Raja Singh of BJP (Hyderabad) threatened to behead those against the Ram Temple.

One cannot realise what effect such rubbish has on men in police barracks.

A sociologist, Nandini Sundar, sympathetic to the plight of the tribals in Maoist land, got almost charged with murder, till better sense prevailed. An Inspector general Police of Chhattisgarh railed against her on TV! There is a considerable anti-intellectual strain in both the police and the party in power. Kobad Gandhi rotted in jail for years under the Congress regime. This strain is very much in evidence today as the Maharashtra police zeroes in on five activists, accusing them of harbouring evil designs on the person of the Prime Minister.

# Swamy and Friends

KEKI DARUWALLA

*Remembering Father Stan Swamy, SJ (1937-2021)*

Beyond the Gangetic plain and the Jumna,
they had their world, women dancing in the night
tapping their earth-and-sky-world into rhythm;
their days ruled by taboo and totem
long before Freud had heard of them;
cults flowered, and shamans held the long stick

Civilisation advanced with Surf and powdered milk;
amulets and talismans were plucked from their hair, a
rout of the adivasi, and they were told that the
cosmos was ruled a trinity: Brahma, Vishnu and
Shiva; others came, white-skinned, and their trinity
had a Holy Ghost jungle-folk didn't know what to do
with. (The state knew what to do: it shot their King,
Pravir Chandra Bhanj Deo)

Socialists jumped in and told them of their rights
to land and livelihood—trouble was they
didn't know what rights were. Then guns came in,
and modern saints – Kobad Ghandi, Stan Swamy.
Kobad was kept in Jail for ten years in the
days of Sonia G and Somnolent Singh.

The anti-secessionist state was born
as Modiji came into power, strong state.
If you had no *mai-bap*, you were left to fate;
no bail, more jail. If accused, you fried.
Only votaries of Human Rights cried.
Young women of Pinjra Tod spent 13 months
in Tihar. Stan Swamy died.

Nothing will happen, those who wrote lies
in charge sheets, those who denied him bail,
those who were heartless in jail and didn't let him
have a straw to drink they just let him sink.

On his death bed, let it be noted
they'll all be promoted.

*(Stan Swamy was a Catholic priest and a tribal rights activists,
the oldest person in India to be charged with terrorism. He was
denied bail despite his serious health issues. While incarcerated,
he died on July 5, 2021.)*

# 'Prisoner No. 626710 is present'
# Curious case of Umar Khalid

SAGARI CHHABRA

September 2024

Some years ago, I was early for a meeting at the Constitution Club and seated with my notebook, pen in hand. Just then, a young man walked in with a flustered expression on his face. He sat a few rows behind me and muttered, '*mujh pe goli chali hein* - a bullet has been shot at me'. I must confess, my first reaction was to ignore the man dismissing it as a hallucination. Then he said, '*kisi ne mujhe maarne ki cheshta ki hai* – someone has tried to kill me.' At that point someone in the hall went up to him and inquired. Then he shouted out aloud, 'This is Umar Khalid and someone has tried to kill him!'

Immediately there was a furore and many people encircled Umar Khalid. A guard came and proceeded to lock everyone inside the hall. His argument was that if a bullet had been fired, everyone here was a witness and must not be allowed to leave. Prof. Apoorvanand, with calm demeanour, explained to the guard that the bullet had been fired outside on the road and that we were only trying to find out what had happened. The police was called and Umar Khalid marched off to have his statement recorded but I was distressed. The Club near the Parliament is in a high security area and I had never heard of such an incident before. This did not augur well for democracy, human rights, law-and-order and students' rights as Umar Khalid was a well-known student leader doing his PhD at Jawaharlal Nehru University. Much later, Umar Khalid was arrested under Unlawful Activities Prevention Act on grounds of sedition and has been behind the bars without trial for over four years! To arrest a young person and to put him inside a prison without bail or a trial is a travesty of both freedom and justice and all the constitutional values.

When I heard that the well-known film director, Lalit Vachani who is known for his earlier documentaries, *'An Ordinary Election'*, *'The Boy In The Branch'*, *'The Men In The Tree'* and *'The Play Is On'* was screening his new film, *Prisoner No. 626710* is present, I felt I must go and watch the film. A man seated on the front row was noticed taking pictures of members of the audience. When called out by a woman that he cannot take her picture without her permission, he said, *'mein sevak hoon aur mujhe bola gaya hein* – I am a helper and have been told to do this.' When asked who told him to do so, he said the police had asked him. In democratic India, a film audience is photographed by someone for the police!

The film was a revelation, with speeches of Umar who says, 'if they give us hate; we will give them love. They will give us stones; we will give them flowers.' Nowhere did I see hate or 'sedition' emanating from the young scholar. His friend, Banjyotsna Lahiri, talks about the Shaheen Bagh movement and what was spoken by the grandmothers, daughters and young people. It was a people's movement like the *Narmada Bachao Andolan*, Right to Information and the Right to Food campaigns. Here the people's voices, and power were unleashed against the Citizenship Amendment Act that discriminates on the ground of religion.

The documentary film also shows hate speeches by two BJP leaders who are saying, *'desh ke gadaaro ko, goli maaro saalo ko* – the country's traitors, shoot the …' and another who says, *'Jab tak Trump hein yahan hum kuch nahin kahenge. Uske baad agar yeh sarak khaali nahin kee toh hum nahin sunenge* – till Trump is here we won't say anything but after that if these roads are not emptied, we will not listen to anybody.' Lalit Vachani's camera is unobtrusive but revelatory. What follows are CCTV footage of the Delhi riots showing the crowds entering the minority area. The scene is juxtaposed by Shudhabrata Sengupta's narrative. He is a friend of Umar Khalid and calls himself a 'messy elder brother'. Banjyotsna's photos of her memorable times with Umar Khalid and her account of their meetings in the jail through a screen and the books

Umar chooses to read, the first being *Suitable Boy* by Vikram Seth are heartrending. We are witnessing something here; a young man being accused of sedition, his friends visiting him in jail and his bail – which is his right – being systematically denied. Four years is a long time to take away anyone's freedom. The film raises questions: what is seditious about Umar Khalid and why is the state incarcerating a young man without a trial? If this could happen to Umar Khalid, a young man with a PhD and a student leader from JNU with a group of committed friends, it could happen to just anybody.

The idea of the gulag is a chilling one. Anyone could be picked up and called an 'urban Naxal' - a new addition to the lexicon - or 'seditious' and be put away. Even the British Raj did not use sedition to this extent Any of us can be turned into a prisoner number.

Courtesy: Mainstream

# The Battle *after* Dussehra

PRATAP BHANU MEHTA

October 2018

Vijayadashmi (Dussehra) is supposed to be a moment of empowerment, both literally and metaphorically. Ravana has been vanquished; Sita has been rescued; and the embodiment of perfect virtue, Ram, is about to end his exile. But we know from all Indian epics that the moment of triumph is just a smoke screen — the public celebration of a victory that is about to prove pyrrhic. This is usually recognised in the case of the Mahabharata, where the victory over the Kauravas is followed by carnage and suffering on an unprecedented scale; even the redeemers die ignominious deaths; and the human condition is fated to be like Ashwathama — an interminable walk through an existence that has neither hope nor redemption. There is a reason immortality is a curse.

But the Ramayana, even in the moment of its triumph, is no less melancholy. In the Mahabharata, the cumulative weight of resentments and past karma weighs down the future so much that you know any moments of respite will be more like paper boats, washed away by an over-determined past: Curse upon curse, sin upon sin. The Ramayana, and the moments of triumph in it feel even more melancholy precisely because Ram is the embodiment of full virtue. And yet, triumph turns into tragedy. The tragedy, of course, centres on the figure of Sita.

The Ram-Ravana conflict is given so much prominence, as that site of public hope, that moment of redemption and liberation. But, very frankly, it reads like a sideshow in the beating heart of the epic: The Ram-Sita love story, and a genuine love story it is. What happens after the victory, including Uttarakanda, is central to the meaning and sadness of the text. On this narrative, the Ramayana becomes exactly the opposite: Not the victory of good over evil, but the permanent triumph of injustice. Ram, that embodiment of virtue, encounters an immovable injustice that diminishes him.

Vijayadashmi is melancholic because the real and deep evil will surface only now, after the political triumph over Ravana has been achieved. An unspeakable injustice will be meted out against Sita, who as Ram knows, and everyone knows, has done nothing to deserve it. The psychological ordeal is probably even worse: Ravana had abducted Sita. But now she is repeatedly the accused. Her virtue does not get protected against being defamed; she can be, with impunity, meted out punishment by her defamers. Her treatment is the point at which every single virtue breaks down: He was supposed to redeem even "impure" women like Ahalya; here, even the embodiment of purity gets punished. The compassionate saviour who is supposed to rehabilitate everyone turns on the just. The punishment is cloaked in some high principle of kingship: Ram wants to retain the confidence of his subjects. He sacrifices everything for the sake of dharma. But this is rubbish. There is no dharma here. Ram went into exile against his subjects' wishes, so popular acclaim is not the issue here. Sita has also already undergone an unjustified trial, but that equivalent of due process seems nothing in the face of innuendo and rumour.

She can be criminally defamed, while her accusers and those meting out punishment will not see justice. In Sita's case, malicious gossip has more authoritative status than the public trial. If dharma can be held hostage to the vagaries of public opinion, it is not clear what that dharma is. Ram, the embodiment of virtue, becomes a full coward, who cannot even look Sita in the eye, and must resort to subterfuge to banish her. Yes, his personal commitment to her, his absolute fidelity, his practising austerity himself to make amends, is never in doubt. But that amounts to roughly nothing. Rama suffers, but he does not do justice.

The act of Sita's banishment is the *reductio ad absurdum* of the epic. The easily visible political evil of the battle between Ram and Ravana is easy to resolve.

It takes all our public energies. But the evil implicit in the accumulated weight of culture seems almost impossible to confront. Ram has no confidence in his own truth. At every moment he repudiates her, he does so by accusing her. When she is vindicated, he turns around to say that this was necessary so that she could be publicly seen to be vindicated. Ram must hide behind her unjustified trial, and in the end, behind the testimony of Valmiki. Sita is guilty even if proven innocent; her accusers are believed even if they have not proved anything at all. It was Valmiki's greatness that he left these questions hanging. There is no sugar-coating the outcome. There are no theological acrobatics (the distinction between Ram the avatar, and Ram the man). Many later writers, like the great Bhavabhuti and Dinganga, wanted more Bollywood endings: Ram and Sita are united; separation would be for love to admit its own defeat. But while the outcomes are happier in these plays, the ethical dilemmas are not really resolved. Ram is not quite absolved. Sita repeatedly calls Ram "merciless". The threat in their works comes from the fact that it is not the rulers' fault: It is the people who are without any restrictions (*loko nirankush*). The people here is not people understood in a democratic sense; it is the norms of the people. That Ram who can vanquish Ravana cannot vanquish cultural norms; for this he needs outside assistance, the help of poets and seers.

Ram is reduced to pathetic self-doubt over truth. Sita puts him out of his misery and constant vacillation, by settling the question of her truth, once and for all, by returning to her mother Earth. Of course, Ram is in a sense broken by this grief. Rescuing Sita from Ravana was easier, rescuing her truth from cultural norms, the weight of public opinion, almost impossible. In fact, there is something so merciless about those cultural norms that they invert everything: Due process becomes injustice, the accusers become the accused.

While Ram and Sita may be theologically incomplete without each other, the weight of gender norms makes their union impossible. It is almost as if Valmiki ends up saying: The battle that ends at Vijayadashmi was a cake walk. The battle that comes after is the one Sita will have to fight alone: There is no redeemer like Ram who will fight this battle. The conventional truth is not her ally. Sita will one day take the initiative. And then see all other truths fall by the wayside.

Courtesy: *The Indian* EXPRESS

# Religious identity commodified

BHABANI SHANKAR NAYAK

In the 1959 Hindi movie *"Dhool Ka Phool" (Flowers of the Dust)*, there is a song written by Sahir Ludhianvi and sung by Mohammad Rafi, which can be translated as: *"you will neither become a Hindu nor a Muslim; you will become a human being, a child of humanity."* Another song of the 1976 Hindi movie *"Maha Chor" (The Great Thief)*, conveys a similar sentiment and can be translated as: *"I am neither Hindu nor Muslim; I don't know my religion, but I know that I am a human being."* This song was written by Anand Bakshi, with music composed and directed by R. D. Burman, and memorably sung by Kishore Kumar. There are thousands of such examples of songs and movies that not only represented the progressive popular culture of that era but also celebrated the promise of a secular India.

Odisha was no different. Hindus, Muslims, Christians, Buddhists, Jains, followers of other religious sects and spiritual cults, as well as atheists, lived together in peace and harmony. Odia people continued to observe their respective religions quietly, without overt public displays of their religious practices. *The Car Festival in Puri* has long been a mass celebration symbolising the deep-rooted secular values of the state. However, the socio-political landscape is changing with the forward march of Hindutva politics, where even cars are becoming Hindu. Such advertisements and the association of cars with Hindu identity are part of the commodification of culture and materialisation of identity driven by capitalism and accelerated by the influence of Hindutva politics. On January 2nd, 2025, the logo of a Honda car bearing Hindu identity was prominently displayed on the national highways of Bhubaneswar. Such an unusual sight would have been unimaginable just a few years ago. Hindutva politics has advanced slowly but steadily and finally seized state power. It has worked relentlessly to reshape Odisha's historically secular culture into a divisive Hindutva line. This transformation is being facilitated through the commodification of human identity, narrowing it along rigid religious lines.

All forms of human identity emerge from self-reflection, material and non-material conditions, and individual choices. These personal individual identities often evolve into collective or group identities, shaped by individuals' interactions and socialisation within one or multiple value systems, practices, and environments. As a result, both individual and group identities are inherently fluid. These fluidities were transformed into permanent structures in society with the help of religious, political, cultural, economic, and social ideologies. These ideologies are constructed in ways that either promote connection or create exclusionary practices, depending on the mutual convenience of governing elites. Political patronage of identity—whether through access to resources or discrimination in everyday lives—determine whether identity politics becomes progressive or regressive. The dominant identity politics of white supremacists or Hindutva represents a regressive form of dominant identity politics, while identity politics centered on caste, race, gender, and sexual orientation is progressive and emancipatory identity politics. Emancipatory identity politics, or identity consciousness, poses a challenge to the growth of capitalism and its popular culture. Therefore, it becomes essential to transform and commodify dominant identities to undermine the emancipatory politics of marginalised communities. This is achieved by promoting a dominant popular culture centered on the commodification of human identity, where an individual's worth and identity are determined by possessions such as brand of cars, size of houses, or price of accessories.

Hindutva politics across India has accelerated this reactionary political and cultural process. Writing "Hindu" on a car is not merely an advertisement for Hindutva politics; it is part of a broader capitalist strategy aimed at consolidating commodified individual identities through consumer goods. Labelling cars as Hindu, Muslim, Christian, Chinese, American, German, Indian, or Italian does nothing to improve wages for workers in car factories, garages, or showrooms. The branding of cars with a specific religious or political ideology does not alter the exploitative working conditions faced by these workers. However, the creation of a commodity identity through Hindutva politics has accelerated a culture of commodity fetishism, where objects are imbued with political meanings to shape social and economic relations in line with the needs of capitalism and its mass culture.

This process marginalises the working-class culture, which is rooted in both material and non-material realities, by replacing it with a consumer-driven identity politics that serves capitalist interests. It promotes a mass culture where both producers and consumers are marginalised, driven into an environment of perpetual insecurity.

The glorification of one's identity, driven by dominant political narratives, ultimately erodes the collective foundations of identity built on solidarity and its social meanings over time. Therefore, Hindutva politics and its cultural values align with the demands of capitalism and its culture of commodity identity. In contrast, these ideologies are in direct opposition to the core values of our society, which are rooted in human connections and everyday needs that extend beyond objects and commodities in the market. This cultural project of Hindutva capitalism is neither accidental nor new. A similar transformation is depicted by Charles Dickens in his novel *Great Expectations*, published in 1861. Set in 19th-century Victorian England, the novel explores the transformation of life and society in Kent and London. The making of identity into a commodity for all forms of market is a social, cultural, and economic project. Hindutva politics in India follows a similar path, creating a pathologically restless society where insecurity and dominant identity politics give political dividends for the governing elites who serve capitalism. Hindutva politics is not an Indian ideology, and it has no place in Odisha.

The defeat of Hindutva politics depends on the dismantling of its mass culture of commodification, capitalist alienation, and fear mongering. In this context, it is crucial to pursue alternative politics where commodities like cars do not define human identity but instead serve humanity, promoting health and happiness.

Courtesy: *countercurrents.org*

# Cultural "cleansing" sullies India

AVAY SHUKLA

April 2017

Dadri is back with us. Earlier this week a group of *"gau rakshaks"* stopped a truck carrying cows in Alwar (Rajasthan), beat up the occupants and killed one of them. The police registered a case against the Muslims for cow smuggling and arrested all of them. Only a case of "manhandling" was lodged against the killers and none arrested. The Home Minister of Rajasthan defended the vigilantes and said they were needed to curb crimes against the cow! A Union Minister even denied the incident in Parliament! It was only after a national outrage that the police registered a case of murder.

It now emerges in the media that the cows were not being smuggled at all -- the truck had the necessary permit from the administration to transport the cows! Meanwhile, the count for people killed by *gau rakshaks* has gone up to ten. *Gau raksha* is big extortion business now, as a sting by Srinivas Jain of NDTV some time back showed. Cows are seized on roads and markets and released only on payment of ransom disguised as " service charges."

This is not an isolated case, but one that keeps repeating itself in practically all (mainly) BJP ruled states over the last couple of years. Nothing ever happens to these vigilante goons who are vociferously defended by Ministers and senior BJP functionaries. The police is thoroughly compromised if not complicit. The frenzy is maintained by deliberately provocative measures such as amending laws to provide for life sentences for cow slaughter, or by Chief Ministers publicly stating that those who kill cows will be " hung". The ban on illegal slaughterhouses in UP has gone completely out of hand: hundreds of meat shops have been forcibly shut, not only by the administration but by " gau rakshaks", some have been burnt (Hathras), and thousands rendered unemployed. Restaurants and hotels serving legal meat have been intimidated into shutting shop, on the ostensible ground of Navratras. Over 500 of them were ordered to close in Gurgaon, right under the nose of the central govt. Shiv Sainiks boast on prime-time TV how they shut down the shops, but no action is taken against them. The Haryana Government announced that all meat and egg shops shall have to shut on 9th April (Mahavir Jayanti). This sets the stage for more closures on other Hindu festival days and gives another handle to these *bhakts*. Cow slaughter was legally outlawed in 1955, then why this frenzy now? Nor is this distorted and venomous cultural nationalism limited to cows and beef. It is now being extended to the policing of young boys and girls, under the garb of " anti-Romeo squads". An intensification of the Valentine Day bashings by outfits like the Ram Sena, has been conferred legitimacy by being made state policy in UP. Now it is being adopted by the police of other BJP-ruled states. Even Delhi has announced that it will set up such squads. The result is a repugnant invasion of privacy, police high handedness and corruption, and the emboldening of the same goons: visuals of innocent couples being mercilessly beaten up or dragged to police stations and released after paying bribes are a sickening constant on news shows. And generally, it is the couples against whom action is taken, not the ones who harass them.

The same goondaism, without any force of law, is being displayed on matters relating to singing of the national anthem, films that do not conform to a particular version of history or mythology, any questioning of the strait-jacketed " nationalism" invented by the ideologues of the ruling party, or any " offence", imagined or otherwise, to the Hindu religion. Those who do not toe the line are beaten up. film sets destroyed; police let loose. Most of our corporatised media have been effectively silenced and do not protest beyond depicting a stray incident or two. These vigilantes are beginning to resemble the Hitler Youth or Mussolini's Black Shirts, and it is time to worry where we are headed. Over the last two years an environment of intolerance, hatred and anger has been created and lumpen elements are being insidiously encouraged to take the law into their own hands. What cannot be done legally is sought to be implemented through fear and intimidation, with the state machinery generally standing by as silent or complicit spectators. There is no law which prohibits two members of opposite sexes from meeting in a public place, and there cannot be. But to do so today means risking life and limb. There is no law which says that legally acquired buffalo meat or mutton cannot be sold, but to do so in large swathes of the BJP controlled " Hindu heartland" means inviting trouble and worse. There is no law which permits self-styled groups to enforce existing or imagined laws- but the police allow them a free run. A way has been found around the laws. The BJP has become adept at speaking in two voices: one in Parliament and one on the streets. Of course, the Prime Minister's voice is never heard except at election rallies.

Vigilantism draws sustenance from two factors: one, the belief that its own value systems are superior to those of others, and two, the confidence that its practitioners will not be caught or punished. The BJP is providing justification for both, and for the moment it appears to be reaping the benefits. But this is a dangerous game and can quickly get out of hand. Hatred can develop a momentum of its own and, like a fire, feeds on itself. The increasing incidents of assaults on Africans or people from the north-east stem from the same vigilantism: it doesn't matter whether they are racist or not. These are hating crimes based on contempt for others' culture. When you constantly reiterate that your own culture is the only one that counts, when you show complete intolerance and contempt for what others eat, drink, wear, worship or who they consort with, when you believe that you have the right to use violence to force others to conform-that is cultural, or worse, ethnic vigilantism. When the Government allows lawlessness to exist to suit its own purpose, sooner or later it will spawn total criminality, and this is happening now daily.

The stand of the BJP was clearly demonstrated through a powerful symbolism last year: when one of the Dadri accused died in jail (of natural causes), his body was draped in the national flag, he was declared a "martyr", and his funeral was attended by a Union Minster who even donated Rs. 10 lakhs to his family, One remembers the poignant words of the Urdu poet:

*Ab kahaan jaoge dhoondne mere katil ko,*
  *Mere katl ka ilzam mujh par hi daal do.*
[Where will you now go to find my killer,
  Put the blame for my murder on me.]

Courtesy: *View from [Greater] Kailash*

# Social tensions rising

MAHENDRA VED

Indian society is at a tipping point. Citizens sensitive to their social and political surroundings struggle to balance their traditional cultural systems with new social dynamics introduced by globalisation and a new kind of domestic politics. Social unrest and mass protests are increasing in frequency and magnitude. Two major causes are the mixing of religion with politics and economic stress caused by the people migrating from countryside to seek work in the cities.

See the front page of any newspaper any day, and you will read about violence that is verbal, visual and actual. Most of it is directed against critics and political opponents. Warnings are issued to select communities and castes. Hateful discourse and 'othering' of people who do not agree with the dominant discourse have become the order of the day.

We witness what is called "bulldozer justice" of properties of those perceived as the wrongdoers by the law-keepers destroyed before or without judicial intervention, let alone disposal of the case. The judiciary at the lower levels gives the impression of being influenced by the administration and lawmakers who have their own biases. The higher judiciary has been found in many cases to shut out appeals and redressal and once the two layers of justice have taken a stand, the judiciary at the highest level finds it difficult to undo the impairment of justice at the ground level. In sum, bold observations, many critical of those in power, are of little help when they do not eventually find a place in the final verdict. When they do, the government doubles down with an appeal for revision. Those affected get little or no help. In some cases, armed and emboldened by the judicial verdict, the authority doubles down on the victims.

The actual issues affecting the public get drowned in a discourse that is cleverly diverted to issues that do not affect the citizen's daily life. They are meant to appeal to sentiments – social, religious, regional, and linguistic, and when this is consciously done, the collective voice drowns the specific issues like unemployment, rising prices of things of daily needs, bad civic amenities and more.

This is where media's role comes in. Newspapers and television channels have become the barometer of the heat generated, thanks to the social tensions that are on the rise. But redressal rarely forthcoming. Verbal violence spreads fast through social media. Of course, cell phones allow access to the digital world and any hate crime once filmed, cannot be easily suppressed. This is happening even as the media struggle to toe the 'official' line drawn by the media owners, many of them guiding remotely the editorial policy through their hand-picked editors. It is a far cry from the owner leaving the editorial task to the editor. It has also given a go-bye to the age-old principle of news being 'sacred' and comment being 'free'.

The so-called objectivity comes in camouflaged form. Known terms like 'secular', 'inclusive' 'progressive', 'nationalist' and many more have been appropriated and given quite the opposite twists and turned into pejoratives and terms of abuse. Adherents and advocates of the earlier meanings and perceptions are ignored or trolled.

It is not surmising that many discerning readers and viewers have veered away from the media. Except, of course, those who look for entertainment from the media featuring television anchors who dish out news and views amidst a cacophony of loud sounds. Indeed, the media that is supposed to inform, educate and entertain has placed itself in the entertainment-first role to grab the TRPs. The advent of technology and funds from investors who wish to acquire economic and political clout has helped. The last two elections, without going very far into the recent past, are proof enough for this. From the look of it, this is unlikely to change. There are enough eyeballs, to be grabbed by providing infotainment.

The media organs mostly raise rather than reflect social tensions. They have no solution and only exacerbate tensions. More than the mainstream media, their website portals and social media extensions are engaged in a discourse that is making society volatile and more prone to violence.

Joining this lop-sided discourse that does the citizenry no good, of late, are serving government officers holding high, even top positions, keeping their jobs secure by pandering to the views of the powers that be. The orders come from the political leadership that encourages public statements by public servants that defy social norms, the law of the land and even the Constitution. This was once the 'preserve' of the political class, especially the elected representatives who enjoy immunity from the law; now it has spread to the executive and the judiciary. Sections of the judiciary have joined, delivering judgments with clear, barely concealed, objectives of winning political favour, even political office. In the last Lok Sabha elections, a few bureaucrats and judges crossed the line, got political office and even won elections.

This naturally sends a depressing message to those who want to serve with diligence and without political bias. Such officials are threatened by the presence of young vigilantes roaming the roads and storming the courtrooms and police stations and the meetings organised by their critics. Cultural events are targeted and university campuses have become battlegrounds of conflicting political ideologies.

In the new ethos that has begun to seep in slowly, but surely, non-issues like what to wear and what to eat find prominent space at the cost of the day-to-day problems. The elections – India has a few every year – have become 24x7 exercises that significantly add to social tensions. Their outcome impacts politicians, but not the day-to-day lives of the people who vote in increasing numbers but find themselves socially and economically struggling. When a hyped-up political system fails to deliver on the economic front or does so only selectively leaving out a vast majority of people, a rise in social tensions is the inevitable outcome.

# Communal Tinderbox

HUMRA QURAISHI

The bias against Muslims has spread to all regions and all sections of society and administration. Even some in the judiciary have been affected. The utterances of a sitting judge of the Allahabad High Court in December 2024 could be termed alarming. Blatantly communal. One can imagine the trickle-down effect of such bias expressed against the minority Muslim community.

Communally surcharged comments, with abuses, get publicised. Several Right-Wing parliamentarians target Muslims with obnoxious comments and get away with it. The political rulers never apologise because they themselves use hate speech to advance their political career! It is frightful how television debates feature shrieks, counter screams and even physical violence, never focusing on issues ha matter. Spokespersons of the Right-Wing political parties don't even bother to camouflage their anti-Muslim tirade! The Right-Wing targets the Muslim community and its faith through social media organs. The gullible are fed this anti-Muslim diet, as the political mafia continues to flourish by using hatred. The current political pollution is destructive. The poor are becoming poorer and weaker ever so hapless. Unable to even raise a finger at those who persecute them. Masses are distracted so that they don't cry out for *roti* and *rozgaar*! Human cries fill the atmosphere! It is getting much too dangerous to see the Right-Wing Agenda unfolding. Mosques and historical structures are being targeted by the Hindutva brigades under various alibis. Now they are questioning the very basis of the *dargah* of Khwaja Moinuddin Hasan Chisti, Gharib Nawaz, in Ajmer.

Interaction between families of Hindus and Muslims has declined. Deep divisions have hit us as never before. After all, Hindus and Muslims can only talk or walk or eat together if they reside in the same block or work or study together. The Hindutva brigades thrash Muslim men if they dare to befriend Hindu women. The bogus Muslim appeasement theory is floated to discredit the Opposition. A great majority of Indian Muslims have a humiliating experience. They face obvious discrimination vis-à-vis employment, housing and education.

Communal toxicity started increasing since L K Advani undertook the rath yatra in the early 90s, which culminated in the destruction of the Babri Masjid. The situation has worsened since then. From 2014, when the Right-wing government came, the hounding of Muslims got intensified. Today, there is a feeling of hopelessness. Why should the largest minority community of this country be reduced to this second or third-class status as citizens. Our administrators sense the bias and discriminations but do nothing to provide any relief to the victim community. They too are responsible for pushing the Muslim not just into a ghetto but making him or her insecure about future. There is a definite pattern to the hounding of Muslims on the pretext of beef buying and cooking and cow slaughter. The lynching of Mohammad Akhlaq in Uttar Pradesh's Dadri has been followed by several similar tragic incidents. One of the victims was a 13-year-old boy killed in the open. The Minority Commission kept quiet. In the autumn of 2016, in district Faridabad, on the outskirts of New Delhi, two young men were thrashed and forced to eat cow dung and drink cow urine! It was painful to see the plight of the four young Kashmiri students in Rajasthan's Chittorgarh region where they were made to stand as though they had committed some heinous crime. They had just bought 300 grams of mutton from the local market. That was enough to trigger off rumours that it was beef! Summer of 2017 saw the blatant killing of sixteen-year-old Junaid Khan on a train. He was killed by fellow train passengers and 'beef eater' comments hurled at his fractured skull. The 'beef scare' continues. I attended the marriage festivities of two middle-class Muslim families and there was no trace of a single meat dish. Pure vegetarian fare. The hosts said: "Who will prove to these goondas that its mutton or chicken. Didn't want anyone to disrupt the wedding." Muslims are not the biggest buyers and consumers of meat in India and the meat industry is controlled and run by non-Muslims. Why is it that Central and State ministers from the Northeast can openly talk of their beef-eating traditions but Muslim cattle grazers and traders are lynched in public on the beef alibi?

Today, many more Muslins are humiliated at workplaces, many more Muslim children are bullied in schools, many more Muslim families are moving into ghettoes. There are countless incidents of the goon brigades targeting Muslim men. A special clause in the rules for punishment for crimes seem to have been introduced, especially for Muslims. It is called "Bulldozer Justice". Justice or Injustice! How many more homes will get bulldozed in the country? Bulldozing of homes is a barbaric rejoinder to crime, as not just the alleged culprit is punished but her entire clan. And in the latest case in Rajasthan's Udaipur, even the landlord's home was not spared! Was there any valid justification of bulldozing the landlord's home, whose tenants were the family of the school-going teenaged boy who had stabbed his class fellow with a knife he was carrying to school? The sarkari version is along the strain that the landlord's house was built on an unauthorized stretch of forest land. But the basic fact that emerged is that it was built years ago with the relevant official documents, and in that locality many homes have remained untouched, un-bulldozed! Relevant queries do come up: which government department gave the valid go-ahead sanction to build that house which was bulldozed? And with that supposed sanction, is it not illegal to pull down a built structure, with a mere one day's notice? Where and how the victim, in this case an auto rickshaw driver, is to survive with his entire family, in this roofless-homeless condition? Why is it that homes of the minority and disadvantaged communities can be so easily targeted. In fact, Bhasha Singh, political commentator and U-tuber, raised a pertinent point in one of her recent talks: why homes and properties and abodes of the convicted rapists and murderers with Right-Wing slants are not bulldozed!

BJP's double standards trouble the minorities. Young Muslims ask me that if the BJP can show an artificial concern for their "Muslim sisters" by harping on social ills like the "Triple Talaq", why does it not show concern for the widows of Vrindavan and Varanasi and for women dying on account of dowry related tortures. "We Musalmaans cannot talk! No question of dissent as any charge can be thrown at us! We fear criticising even the local goons, but Hindutva leaders are nurturing their *senas.* Why can only Hindus raise their brigades? If Musalmaans had done what Karni Sena or Shiv Sena does, their entire families would have been ruined." Muslims also point out that double standards prevail even when a serious crime such as rape is reported. Different treatment is meted out to rapists if they are connected to the ruling brigades or if they rape during rioting and pogroms. During the Gujarat pogrom and the Muzaffarnagar riots, Muslim women were raped. Threatened by the political mafia, the victims and their families sat subdued and quiet.

Encounter specialists are set free. New Delhi-based lawyer-activist Vrinda Grover often represents victims of police atrocities and violence. After meeting Shamima Kauser (Ishrat's mother) and her children, seeing the case file about Sohrabuddin's murder, she was clear that this "encounter" was not just a crime committed by trigger-happy cops, but part of the State-sanctioned violence against Muslims unleashed in the pogrom of 2002. Vrinda says this pattern of targeting Muslims and demonising them as the enemy must be eliminated. The political leaders, administrators, police and Intelligence Bureau in Gujarat, all suffer from the anti-Muslim bias. Provocative communal remarks are made regularly by the BJP leaders but they are never arrested or thrown out from the party. The likes of Sangeet Soms, Sadhvi Niranjans, Giriraj Singhs, Katiyars, Sakshi Maharajas and Togadias openly threaten the minority community, yet they move around freely. The VHP and Bajrang Dal held arms training camps in Greater Noida, Varanasi, Ayodhya and other places but those properties were not bulldozed. L K Advani, Murli Manohar Joshi and Uma Bharti, who were seen gleefully hugging each other when the Babri Masjid was being destroyed by the *kar sevaks*, were allotted prime slots in the Government.

One ought to look at what is taught in the RSS schools. The former Delhi University Prof. Nalini Taneja once read out aloud several of the provocative passages from the textbooks taught in the RSS-run schools. The history books reflect the RSS view of history, designed to use history for its sectarian agenda – "Aryans are the original inhabitants of India, Indian civilization is essentially Aryan civilization, the ancient period of history when Hindu rulers ruled was golden! The coming of the Mughals brought darkness, and Golwalkar, and Savarkar are amongst the greatest freedom fighters. Muslims as a community are traitors. Hinduism is synonymous with nationalism. Also, caste, child marriages and *sati* tradition are defended. Muslims, Christians and Parsis arc called foreigners. Urdu is referred to as a foreign language." The hatred for religious minorities is drilled into the children. Ministers in the BJP-ruled States of the country pass orders for the government school children (including those from the minority communities) to sing *Vande Mataram*, to do *Surya Namaskar*, and to read scriptures of a particular religion.

Whatever the chance the Muslim community has of its survival is because of the liberal Hindus. Amidst hopelessness, faint rays of hope are seen when Hindu, Sikh and Christian citizens speak out in support of the targeted Muslims.

Courtesy: *Mainstream*

# Fragile democracy makes minorities anxious

JOHN DAYAL

India's civil society and religious minorities fear that the Modi Government's endeavour to domesticate the Supreme Court and the Election Commission will irretrievably disturb the delicate equilibrium between constitutional institutions, taking India far away from the unique democracy it sought to be.

A billion-strong Hindu theocracy with a nuclear muscle is the dream of the militarist Rashtriya Swayamsevak Sangh (RSS), which delegated Narendra Modi to national mainstream politics. Modi, who parachuted as chief minister of Gujarat at the turn of the century, has not been able to wash off the infamy of presiding over a pogrom against the state's Muslim population in 2002. Modi became the Prime Minister in May 2014 riding an acrid election campaign targeting Muslims as anti-nationals. He won a second term in 2019, and a third in 2024, albeit in a coalition, on a similar platform.

Mahatma Gandhi was assassinated on January 30, 1948, by Nathuram Godse, a fanatic Hindu supremacist who thought the 'Father of the Nation' was soft on Muslims. This he had learnt from V D Savarkar, once a campaigner against the British and later their apologist, and "Guru" Golwalkar, a founder of RSS. Both envisaged an India where the Hindu ruled as he did in the mythological golden age. Muslims and

Christians, if they wanted to reside, had to accept second class citizenship. Ironically, life sized portraits of the Mahatma and Savarkar face each other on the cylindrical walls of Parliament. Temples are built to the glory of Godse.

Narendra Modi has done his best to assassinate the character and diminish the political contribution of Jawaharlal Nehru, the man who laid the foundations of a credible democracy with the potential of science, technology, and academic excellence. Modi has not fully succeeded in photo-shopping Nehru out of public memory, but at times he seems to be getting there. The only visual one sees in the country is the visage of Modi, on billboards of various sizes, his silver beard too waxing and waning as he appears now as a paternal and benign philosopher king, and then a general commanding vast army, and occasionally the scientist-engineer holding the wheel of the ship of state. A generation of young Indians entering their twenties has seen no other political face. They dare not ask him for jobs. Now at the peak of his powers, and described dictatorial by his critics, Modi has an Election Commission eating out of his palms, and a rubber stamp Council of Ministers. Islamophobia is combined with a tirade against Christians for luring Hindus to the church by dollar driven conversions.

The targeted hate against Christians has led to violence against children, women, men, and clergy, Catholic and Protestant, in small towns and villages in the states of Chhattisgarh and Uttar Pradesh. The threat to make these states "Christians-free" must be taken seriously. Human rights groups such as Open Doors, Persecution Relief, United Christian Forum, and the Evangelical Fellowship of India estimate the number of violent incidents against

Christians could be possibly as high as 1,500 in 2024. Christians have staged protests in almost every major metropolis against the massacre of the Kuki Zo tribals, all Christians, at the hands of the plains-bound Meitei in the north-eastern state of Manipur. More than 250 are dead, and over 70,000 displaced. Over 350 churches are destroyed. Civil society warns of a national health crisis in the children and young living in the refugee camps run by small churches in the hills inhabited by the Kukis. In early 2023 at least 2000 Christians fled their villages in Chhattisgarh as mobs yelped for blood. The Christians were offered the choice of life as Hindus, In cases of sectarian violence, the police, most often than not, victimizes the wounded, and would rather not register a case against attackers unless civil society raises a red flag.

Rapidly weaponized laws against conversions have made a mockery of the rule of law. "Cow-protection" lynch mobs terrorize Muslims, occasionally killing Christians as well. *Ghar Wapsi* gangs mainly target Christians, with their mission to convert old and new Christians to the Hindu fold. The laws permit the conversion to Hinduism. The police and civil authorities help along.

A timid civil society, with only isolated individuals of courage, and no real powerful institutions, cannot counter the thousand sharp cuts on the body politic. Every valiant Harsh Mander, Fr. Cedric Prakash, lawyer Colin Gonsalves, or Teesta Setalvad and Kavita Srivastava are countered by a National Human Rights Commission and a lapdog national media. Mander, who has escaped death twice from Covid and complications of the heart, is hounded by the federal investigating agencies seeking to indict him for conspiring against the state or cheating. Teesta is currently out of jail on bail ordered by the Supreme Court. Her crime: enabling a Muslim woman, Bilkis Bano, gangraped in the Gujarat 2002 violence by her neighbors who also killed her children and many relatives, to seek justice in a court of law.

The scenario alarms activists, church leaders and the intellectual, but it quite fits into the fantasy of Hindu Rashtra, a larger theocratic state eventually spanning the south Asian landmass and undoing the 1947 Partition of British India. The racial memory of that has fueled Muslim-Hindu violence over the decades, and the India Pakistan military confrontation. Christians are collateral damage. They are seen no more than political trash remaining from the colonial era, and new followers of Jesus Christ as purchase of the rich West. Death, injury, and vandalism are dismissed as occasional and unconnected. International, even United Nations' statements on targeted hate and violence are dismissed as interference in the internal affairs of the world's most populous democracy. Political observers and social activists have long warned that any attempt to change the "secular" nature of the Indian state, especially guaranteed by its Constitution, will be disastrous. This is not just to save the large Muslim and Christian minorities, estimated to be now collectively close to 250 million in a 1.30 billion nation, but for peace in the subcontinent where both India and Islamic Pakistan have an undisclosed number of nuclear warheads and delivery systems.

Stopping the sword play between Modi's cohorts and the Supreme court is critical in this. The independence of the judiciary, now safe in the collegial system of choosing fresh talent to the High Courts and the Supreme Court without political meddling, in turn protects the Constitution from political and executive sorties to cut into its core structure of freedoms, equality, and fraternity. One of India's most celebrated judges, Madan Lokur, said that suggestions made by the then law minister Kiren Rijiju to the Chief Justice of India about how judges for the High Courts and Supreme Court should be chosen are "unacceptable". They would, if implemented, "damage and undermine the independence of the judiciary". Justice Lokur said: "It's a veiled attack on the Constitution through the medium of the judiciary". The Constitution stands in the way of the Rashtriya Swayamsevak Sangh's endeavour to establish a Hindu Rashtra. The Prime Minister used a Constitution Day function by the Supreme Court to say "the whole world is looking at India with a lot of hope amid its fast development, fast-developing economy." He drew attention to the first three words of the Preamble, 'We the People', and said it "is a call, trust and an oath. This spirit of the Constitution is the spirit of India that has been the mother of democracy in the world".

Modi's words are beguiling and the people watch in trepidation Modi pushing India into a different direction. For the common people, especially religious minorities, Adivasis, Dalits and the teeming rural and urban poor, the grand words in golden letters in a book, or etched in stone, translate into a simple right to live in security, with the means to bring up a family with dignity and chosen faith and ideology. They do not want to look over their shoulder every so often to see if the next attack comes from the police, or a crazed majoritarian mob.

# Freedom of (Hate) Speech

GURSIMRAN KAUR BAKSHI

June 2024

The India Hate Lab had warned that 2024 would be a 'critical year' for hate speech in India. The Association for Protection of Civil Rights, a non-profit and non-governmental organisation, found that violence against religious minorities in India attained an "institutional character". This is because it is frequently carried out by the State actors. Where non-State actors are the perpetrators, they do so with the open and tacit support of State officials. Political leaders (56 percent) are the primary contributors to hate speeches in India followed by religious leaders (22 percent).

Hate speeches are made at public rallies, press conferences and assembly sessions. There are no systematic efforts made to record or document the ever-increasing widespread hate crimes against religious minorities. While atrocities against Dalits are recorded under the Schedule Castes and the Scheduled Tribes (Prevention of Atrocities) Act, 1989, there is no similar legislative framework for other religious minorities. Since 2014, incidents of lynching on the pretext of so-called cow protection have increased exponentially in the BJP-ruled states as per the statistics by IndiaSpent database, which records cow vigilantism violence. Such incidents increased significantly since the BJP came to power in 2014. These attacks are often carried out by far-right groups such as the VHP, Bajrang Dal and local *gau rakshak samitis* (cow protection committees). A large proportion of victims are Dalit and Muslim men.

The primary factor behind hate crimes was the religious identity of the victim, provocations during religious processions and celebrations of festivals. Other factors behind violence and hate speech are religious conversions, cow slaughter and disputes over places of worship. There were confirmed 72 reported incidents of hate crimes (55) and hate speech (17) against religious minorities in the first quarter of 2024. The Union Government is empowered to notify religious minorities under Section 2(c) of the National Commission for Minorities Act, 1992. As per it, Muslims (14.2 percent), Christians (2.3 percent), Sikhs (1.7 percent), Buddhists (0.7 percent), Jains (0.4 percent) and Zoroastrians (0.006 percent) have been notified as religious minorities.

The report does not use the word 'hate speech' which is defined by the UN Strategy and Plan of Action as "any kind of communication in speech, writing or behaviour, that attacks or uses pejorative or discriminatory language with reference to a person or a group on the basis of who they are, in other words, based on their religion, ethnicity, nationality, race, colour, descent, gender and other identify factors". There is no universal definition of hate speech under international human rights law. The report uses the term 'hate crime' which encompasses hate speech as well. As per the report, hate crime is a criminal act committed against individuals because of their race, religion, colour, national origin, sexual orientation or other personal traits. Calls to violence are outlawed under various statutes in India, including the Indian Penal Code (IPC), 1860. Hate speech incidents could be tackled Sections 153A (promoting enmity between different groups on grounds of religion, race, etc) and 295A (outraging religious feelings) of the IPC and under the Information Technology Act, 2000.

As per the report, the religious identity of the victim is a major reason behind the incidents. The report finds that 83.3 percent reported victims of hate speech violence are male, while only 16.7 are female. In one reported incident, a 13-year-old Muslim boy was attacked with a knife because of his religious identity in an area of Jaipur. In the first information report (FIR) registered by the local police, it was stated that religious slurs had been used against him by a group of boys. Since December 2021, Muslim girls have been barred from entering their pre-university in Udupi, Karnataka. In 2022, the Karnataka government issued a Government Order stating that all government schools will follow a prescribed dress code.

The hijab ban eventually led to the closure of many educational institutions indefinitely and in some cases created serious safety concerns for Muslim female students who were attacked for wearing hijabs. When the aggrieved Muslim girl students approached the Karnataka High Court, the court upheld the ban. When it was challenged before the Supreme Court, they gave a split verdict on October 13, 2022. Eventually, the new government led by Chief Minister Siddaramaiah last year indicated his willingness to withdraw the ban. While the status of the ban remains unknown, a report by the People's Union for Civil Liberties has found that more than 400 Muslim female students were denied entry or were suspended as a consequence of the hijab ban. While many female students changed their schools, or dropped out, some of them lost their academic year while waiting for the Supreme Court to form a larger Bench to hear their grievances. In January 2023, the Hindu College in the Moradabad district of Uttar Pradesh denied entry to Muslim female students clad in the hijab and burqa. The students alleged that the college administration had compelled them to remove their head scarves at the university entrance.

The report finds that religious festivals are increasingly becoming weaponised by Hindutva groups to target the minorities. The identity of the victims is grouped during the celebrations of festivals and processions. During the consecration of the Ram Temple at

Ayodhya, nine incidents of violence were reported on January 22, 2024. The consecration was followed by large-scale processions and celebrations across the country. Six incidents were reported after the consecration. Around the Holi festival in March, seven incidents of violence were reported. In Bijnor, Uttar Pradesh, a Muslim man along with his sister and mother were harassed by a mob celebrating Holi. In a video that went viral on social media, the mob was heard saying: "This is a 70-year-old tradition. Don't you know by now that this will happen if you come to Badi Bazar?" The Hindu mob tried to beat the man when he resisted the attack. The men tried touching his mother and sister inappropriately and chanted *"Har Har Mahadev"* and *"Jai Shri Ram.* One of the assailants was identified as Aniruddha while three others were minors. They were eventually arrested. A Muslim auto-rickshaw driver was brutally assaulted and beaten and colour was forcefully applied on him by a group of Hindus celebrating Holi in a gated colony Champaner Society in Ahmedabad. The group after learning the identity of the rickshaw driver allegedly set his auto-rickshaw on fire and shouted Islamophobic slurs.

On February 8, the Haldwani Municipal Corporation demolished Maryam Masjid and Abdul Razzaq Zakariya Madrasa in Banbhoolpura locality in an anti-encroachment drive. Consequently, clashes broke out between police officials and locals following which a curfew and shoot-at-sight orders were imposed. Seven people were killed, 31 were arrested and over 90 detained. The local police registered an unnamed FIR against 5,000 individuals. However, the estimates of those killed and injured are much higher than the State's figures, the report suggests.

The Association for Protection of Civil Rights found that the demolitions were carried out against the backdrop of the "*land jihad*" propaganda. The state government led by Chief Minister Pushkar Dhami and radical right-wing groups created divisive discourse in the name of protecting Uttarakhand's "*devbhoomi*" (land of the gods). Two youths, one Hindu and another Muslim, were involved in the abduction of a minor Hindu girl in Purola block of Uttarkashi district. Although the police registered an FIR under the Protection of Children from Sexual Offences, 2012, the incident was given a communal makeover by the *Devbhoomi Raksha Abhiyan*, a right-wing Hindu group. It circulated posters asking Muslims to leave the town. The DRA called a *mahapanchayat* for the protection of "sisters, daughters and ancestral heritage" against Muslims. As a consequence, 44 shops belonging to Muslims were closed. Posters threatening "*love jihadis*" with dire consequences if they do not vacate their shops were found in Purola block and Barkot. The Rashtriya Swayamsevak Sangh affiliated Vishwa Hindu Parishad (VHP) and its young-wing Bajrang Dal, and Bhairav Sena supported these anti-Muslim protests. Reportedly, they sent a letter to the Tehri district magistrate giving an ultimatum to the 'people of a particular community' to leave Jaunpur Ghati (valley) and certain towns of Uttarakhand. According to the letter, "members of a particular community are continuously roaming around the villages in the garb of ragpickers, ice cream sellers etc. Due to which, the threat to our *beti*, *choti*, and *roti* as well as the heritage of our ancestors is constantly rising." The Hindu Yuva Vahini had organised a *dharam sansad* on December 19, 2021 in Delhi where *hate speeches* calling for organised violence against Muslims were made. A similar event was organised from December 17–19, 2021 by Yati Narsinghanand in Haridwar. However, a Supreme Court Bench of Justices K. M. Joseph and Hrishikesh Roy (2022) directed the police to *suo moto* register cases against hate speech even if a complaint is not filed. Any violation of these directions will attract contempt, the court's order stated. An FIR against the organiser was registered and charge sheet filed. In many of the states including Uttarakhand, anti-religious conversion laws have been introduced.

Tehseen Poonawalla and Tushar Gandhi filed public interest litigations in 2018, seeking directions from the Supreme Court for the Union and state governments to deal with the issue of cow violence. One of the issues raised before the court was that many cow protection legislations allowed individuals to act in case of violation of any provisions. The legislation gave immunity from any criminal prosecution if such actions were taken in good faith, for instance, Section 14 of The Rajasthan Bovine Animal (Prohibition of Slaughter and Regulation of Temporary Migration or Export) Act, 1995. The court, however, did not go into the constitutionality of the provisions and focused on implementing preventive measures. A Bench of former Chief Justice of India (CJI) Dipak Mishra and comprising A. M. Khanwilkar and the present CJI Dr D. Y. Chandrachud pronounced its judgment on the matter on July 17, 2018. It issued extensive preventive and remedial measures to the Union and state governments. State governments are required to designate a senior police officer, not below the rank of superintendent of police, as the nodal officer in each district. The nodal officer shall be assisted by one officer of the rank of deputy superintendent of police in the district to take measures to prevent incidents of mob violence and lynching.

The police were directed to register a FIR under Section 153A of the IPC along with relevant provisions against persons who disseminate "irresponsible and explosive messages and videos of having content which is likely to incite mob violence and lynching of any kind." One of the important directives was for the Union and state governments to broadcast on radio, television and other media platforms including official websites that lynching and mob violence of any kind would invite serious consequences under the law. For remedial measures, the court directed the police to immediately register an FIR if an incident occurs and provided that the nodal officer must be duly informed. The court also directed state governments to prepare a lynching or mob violence victim compensation scheme in light of Section 357A of the Code of Criminal Procedure within one month from the date of the judgment. Five years have passed since the judgement was pronounced and there are still legitimate concerns about compliance with the directions. Last year, the Union government informed the Supreme Court that 28 states have appointed nodal officers.

The highest number of incidents reported is that involving physical assault (15) followed by cases of intimidation and harassment (13) and attacks on property (5). Whereas, several incidents involving a combination of the categories were also reported. This showcases the multifaceted nature of hate crimes. The BJP Leader of the Opposition in West Bengal assembly Suvendu Adhikari called a Sikh police officer in Bengal "*Khalistani*".

The northeast Delhi communal violence against the backdrop of the Citizenship (Amendment) Act, (CAA), 2019 and the National Register for Citizens (NRC) on February 23, 2020, coincided with the Delhi Assembly elections. Hate speeches and divisive narratives were made against anti-CAA protestors by BJP legislators

Kapil Mishra, Anurag Thakur and Parvesh Verma. Thakur instigated the participants to raise incendiary slogans and said, "*Desh ke gaddaron ko* (the traitors of the country), the crowd responded "*goli maaro saloon ko* (shoot them)." *Gaddar* was a reference to the anti-CAA protestors. The crowd's response was a throwback to the statement first made by Mishra during a pro-CAA march in Connaught Place on December 20, 2020, when Section 144 of the Code of Criminal Procedure was imposed. On February 23, 2020, Mishra called a pro-CAA rally at Maujpur traffic signal, close to Jafrabad metro station where at least 500 people were staging protest against the CAA and gave a three-day ultimatum to the Delhi police to remove the protestors blocking the traffic. He warned that he would not let another 'Shaheen Bagh' be created in Delhi. In the evening, stone pelting incidents were reported near Maujpur. The BJP MP from West Delhi, Parvesh Verma used another favourite trope of the Hindu Right, the alleged treatment meted out to Kashmiri Pandits by Kashmiri Muslims to rile up the crowd against the protestors. He said, "They will enter your house ... abduct your sisters and mothers, rape them, kill them the way militants had treated Kashmiri Pandits. " The men also tried touching his mother and sister inappropriately and raised Hindu religious chants such as *"Har Har Mahadev" and "Jai Shri Ram".* He added, "Lakhs of people gather there (Shaheen Bagh) and this fire can anytime reach households of Delhi...

People of Delhi need to think about it and decide… That's why today is the moment. "

The findings of the report have also corroborated the report of the Washington-based India Hate Lab. The Department of State of the US released its annual Religious Freedom report, tabulating incidents of violence against religious minorities in India in 2022. The report found discriminatory practices to which religious minority communities are subjected. It rated India as 'partly free' on account of the "discriminatory policies and the rise in persecution affecting the Muslim population ".

Courtesy: *The Leaflet*

# Legal system captured

SANDHYA FUCHS

April 2024

On a crisp winter morning in February 2023, I meet one of my South Delhi neighbours, a lawyer in India's supreme court, in a local cafe. As an avid promoter of religious minority rights, known for his commitment to the principles of equality that were enshrined in the constitution after India gained independence in 1947, I am taken aback by the gravity of the fears this lawyer reveals to me over coffee. He worries not only about the future of India's legal system, but the country itself: International news describes India as the world's largest democracy – but this democracy is rotting from within. Our rule of law is under attack from our own government, and the world does not see this.

The lawyer's pessimism had deepened with the recent news that the Indian government was pushing for a more substantial role in judicial appointments to the supreme court. Weeks earlier, it had blocked the nominations of four new judges proposed by a "collegium" made up of India's five most senior current supreme court judges. The lawyer explained how this collegium had been an important safeguard of Indian judicial independence for the past 25 years.

Now, however, the government was claiming that, "for reasons of transparency", it should have a bigger say in the selection of supreme court judges. A tone of despair in his voice, my coffee companion concluded: This isn't about transparency. This is yet another instance of this government trying to erode the rule of law from within. Soon, we will be a country run by legal mafia authoritarianism.

India is a global power on the rise. In April 2023, the UN announced it had overtaken China as the world's most populous nation. During his visit to the US in June 2023, India's prime minister, Narendra Modi, invited world leaders to a yoga session on the White House lawn. A few months later, he hosted the G20 summit of the world's most powerful leaders in Delhi. Under Modi, India has worked hard to develop a global image as a nation that combines economic and technological innovation with a deep respect for ancient religious practices. This image was cemented by the inauguration of a huge new Hindu temple in the northern city of Ayodhya in January 2024. The inauguration lasted several days and saw diplomats, Bollywood actors and internationally renowned Hindu religious figures flock to pay their respects. But behind these glossy images, a different story is unfolding within India – one that government critics say is marked by exclusion, violence, and the gradual eradication of the Indian democratic project.

Since first coming to power in 2014, Modi and his right-wing Bharatiya Janata Party (BJP) have embarked on an agenda of majoritarian Hindu nationalism. Led by the ideology of Hindutva, which perceives India's history to be inextricably linked with Hindu religious practice, and with the help of a hand-picked committee of advisers, they have pursued a vision of India as a country run by Hindus for Hindus. Over the past decade, India has seen a proliferation of verbal and physical attacks against religious minorities and Dalits (the lowest caste of people in India, formerly known as "untouchables"). Some BJP politicians have described Muslims as "traitors of the nation". Since Modi came to power, lynching of Muslims and Dalits by vigilante groups who condemn the skinning of cattle and the transport or consumption of beef are reported to have increased significantly. At the same time, many civic voices critical of the government have been silenced: journalists, academics and politicians concerned with the increasing repression of minorities and the gradual erosion of India's democratic structure have had their Twitter accounts blocked, their homes raided, and in some cases have been jailed. Recently, Rahul Gandhi, India's principal opposition leader, complained that his Congress party is being "crippled"" by state tax demands leading to the freezing of its bank accounts.

However, one aspect of Modi's growing power has received comparatively little attention: his creeping capture of India's legal machinery. As a legal anthropologist who has spent the past ten years researching human rights and hate crime law in India, I have witnessed the erosion of the country's once robustly democratic legal system by Hindutva forces. The latest example is the BJP's introduction of a new criminal legal structure in India, which will come into force in July 2024.

In Modi's Hindutva version of India, law now exists on two parallel planes. Constitutionally, it remains a secular democracy, committed to the idea of social and political equality. Yet on the level of policing, judicial interpretation, and – increasingly – legislatively, Indian state law has become a site where majoritarian Hindutva ideologies have reshaped ideas of justice and belonging. With Modi an overwhelming favourite to win the Indian general election, which begins on April 19, understanding what is happening to the country's legal system – and how much further it could go in his next term of office – feels important not only for India, but for the world. It illuminates how right-wing regimes are using a playbook to silently dismantle democracy from within, under the veneer of legal legitimacy. This is the story of how you build an authoritarian state, the legal way.

Step 1: Reinterpret existing laws

In February 2022, a human rights activist from the northern Indian state of Rajasthan I'll call Tara* was arrested and sent to jail for four days. Tara told me ten police officers showed up in the middle of the night to inform him that he had been accused of forms of hate speech. Under sections 153A and 295 of the Indian penal code (first introduced in 1860 by the British colonial regime), he was charged with "promoting enmity" between different religious groups and "insulting the religious sentiments of Hindus". Although Tara was eventually released on bail, his time in prison, the brutality he experienced at the hands of the arresting police officers and the threat of further court proceedings have left deep physical and psychological scars. Over the course of multiple conversations in the autumn of 2023, he revealed that he still found it difficult to sleep at night, for fear the police would return and take him away to prison again.

To make matters more confusing, Tara is a devout Hindu. He belongs to India's Dalit community, the lowest in the Hindu caste hierarchy. In his village, many Dalits worship a local Hindu deity, Ramdev Pir – a legendary warrior of the high-ranking Rajput caste who was said to be close to his adopted sister, a Dalit, and therefore is revered both by upper-caste Rajput and Dalit Hindu groups (plus some Muslim followers of the Sufi branch of Islam). But Rajputs in the area would not allow Dalits or Muslims into the local Ramdev temple. Determined to change things, Tara called a meeting to discuss the issue. During the meeting, he publicly proclaimed that Ramdev is a deity who belongs to all Hindus, and even Muslims – not just upper-caste Rajputs. That same night, the police arrived at his door.

When we discussed his treatment, Tara's reflections were nuanced, showing a deep understanding of the changing way India's criminal code is being enforced: The fact that Dalits are discriminated against by upper-caste Hindus is not new in itself … but what we are seeing now under this Hindu nationalist government is that sections of the criminal code are being interpreted in new ways to further exclude communities like Dalits. Now sections like 153A and 295 of the Indian penal code are being used by higher-caste Hindus to claim that marginalised groups who point out exclusion or discrimination are insulting the 'real' upper-caste Hindus.

A prominent human rights lawyer in Delhi describes Tara's treatment as the "Hindutva reinterpretation of criminal terminologies". The British Raj introduced section 153 of the Indian penal code (IPC) to prevent public unrest between different religious communities. But now, the lawyer argues, Hindutva supporters are increasingly "weaponising" it and other sections against minority groups who try to raise awareness about the forms of violence or exclusion they are experiencing: In the Hindutva logic, when a marginalised person points out that they are experiencing violence or discrimination by powerful Hindu groups, this is an 'insult' and amounts to a declaration of hostility against them. Tara's experience is not an isolated incident. In January 2024, police in the north-eastern state of Manipur filed complaints against the Editors Guild of India, again under IPC section 153, for reporting on the ethnic violence towards the Christian minority Kuki-Zo tribes by the Hindu majority Meitei community. According to the complaints, media reporting on the violence was further fanning the flames of conflict between the two communities, so should be prohibited. For Tara, who now spends his time travelling around Rajasthan – both to raise awareness about the treatment of minorities under the Modi regime and because, after his arrest, he no longer likes to stay in his home for extended periods – this is a sign of the very twisted times in India. He complained that Hindus attacking marginalised groups is no longer discrimination in India. But stating that powerful Hindu groups are attacking minorities is now hate speech or incitement.

Step 2: Introduce new laws

The Hindutva political project contradicts the principles of secularism, equality and liberty enshrined in India's constitution, which came into effect on January 26, 1950. Centrally drafted by Bhimrao Ramji Ambedkar, a legal scholar from the Dalit community, the constitution aimed to set up postcolonial India as a democracy defined by profound respect for social, political and religious diversity, and guided by the principle of non-discrimination.

The second element of Modi's strategy is the introduction of new anti-minority laws and criminal codes. He understands that the reinterpretation of existing legal measures is insufficient to build a majoritarian state, where Hindus as the largest religious community can disproportionately determine policy decisions. Therefore, his government has expended substantial resources introducing a series of new legal measures that have gradually pushed Muslims to the social margins. Shortly after being re-elected for a second term in 2019, for example, Modi's government revoked the constitutional autonomy of Jammu and Kashmir, India's only Muslim-majority state. At both national and state levels, the list of anti-minority laws introduced during Modi's reign is bewilderingly long. Just one example is the Prevention of Unlawful Conversion of Religion Act – introduced in India's most populous state, Uttar Pradesh, in 2021 – which has enabled the easy arrest of interfaith couples, especially young Muslim men accused of seducing Hindu women as part of a "love jihad".

But the most blatant anti-minority legislation is the 2019 Citizenship (Amendment) Act (CAA), which denies Muslim immigrants in India the same citizenship pathways as other religious groups. Couched in the language of national protection and Hindu rights, the CAA was quickly declared a "fundamentally discriminatory" law by the UN Commissioner for Human Rights. Critics feared that along with the

National Register of Citizens, launched in 2003 to keep track of all "legitimate" Indian citizens, the CAA would leave thousands of Muslims on Indian soil stateless. Its introduction sparked an outbreak of Hindu-Muslim clashes now known as the Delhi riots, in which at least 53 people were killed (of which 38 were Muslim and 15 Hindu) and hundreds more injured over four days of violence in February 2020.

"One day you wake up and are told that your whole community now officially counts as secondary Indian citizens," Rashid*, a student at Jamia Millia University in New Delhi, told me in 2023. "Then, within the blink of an eye, you are engulfed by violence just because you challenged that assumption. And the police do nothing. Why? Because we all know that the orders from above are to let us Muslim 'traitors' die." Rashid had been part of the peaceful anti-CAA protests in Delhi that began in December 2019. The following February, the situation escalated when Hindu mobs, reportedly unhindered by the Delhi police, began to attack Muslim protesters after some BJP politicians had again publicly called them "traitors". Hindu crowds burned down Muslim homes and businesses, and a video emerged apparently showing five Muslim men being beaten by policemen while forced to sing the Indian national anthem. One of them reportedly died two days later. The impact of the Delhi riots on Muslim communities across India has been profound. According to a Muslim lawyer who works in the supreme court, the introduction of the CAA and subsequent Delhi riots sent not one but several messages to Indian Muslims. First, we are told we don't belong to India in the way other religious groups do. Then, we better not challenge our partial inclusion because it will result in our death. And, law enforcement will not protect us. Finally, we are shown that those who want to help Muslims fight for their rights will see their careers impacted.

Following the Delhi riots, Justice S Muralidhar, a Delhi high court judge, convened an emergency hearing in which he directed Delhi police to file complaints against the BJP politicians who had called the Muslim protesters traitors. Within 24 hours, the Indian government announced Muralidhar's transfer to a different high court, confirming that he would no longer be presiding over the Delhi riot case.

Step 3: Silence the judges

The high court judge's rapid transfer offers a glimpse into the third strategy that India's government has used to cement power and undermine democratic structures: the silencing of a once-independent, critical judiciary.

In April 2023, I returned to Delhi from the UK to conduct ethnographic work on hate speech hearings in the Indian supreme court. I found an apartment in a neighbourhood where many lawyers had their chambers, and soon established a network of local advocates who fed me information about ongoing cases and relevant supreme court hearings. I was at home one day when one of them urgently directed me to watch a livestream of a supreme court hearing. It concerned a petition submitted by a group of concerned human rights and supreme court advocates, which detailed how the government of the Indian state of Maharashtra had repeatedly failed to respond to public and extremely bloody hate speeches by a small group of Hindu radicals. As I watched, the proceedings were intruded on by India's solicitor general, the country's second-highest legal official and adviser to the government. Interrupting the presiding judge, who belonged to India's Christian minority, the solicitor general accused the court of bias for hearing a petition that only involved hate speech against Muslims. He demanded to know why the court was not investigating hate speeches against Hindus: "Let us not be selective!" he chastised the bench. As proceedings descended into chaos, the judge was forced to reschedule the case for another day. The next morning, some news outlets reported claims that this Christian judge had shown pro-Muslim bias, and had even smiled at the suggestion of a possible genocide against upper-class Hindus by Muslims. The lawyer who had submitted the petition was left frustrated and furious by these events:

By the end, no one could even remember that this case was about stopping calls for genocide against Muslims. This is what the government does: create chaos, ignore proper legal procedure, and delegitimise courts through a theatre of distractions.

Step 4: Revise history

According to the authoritarian playbook that has emerged around the world, delegitimising critical courtroom voices is still not enough to dismantle a democracy. To achieve complete control over public opinion, one final ingredient is required: one must use the now-subordinated legal system to promote a version of national history that falls in line with the government's social and political vision. Because when court judgments enter the public record, they have the power to shape public perception and collective memory.

In Modi's India, the best example of this is the supreme court's 2019 ruling in the dispute around the Babri Masjid mosque in Ayodhya, which allowed Modi to inaugurate a glistening mega-temple made of white marble and dedicated to the Hindu deity Ram on this disputed site. It was a ruling which some lawyers I spoke to considered so unconstitutional that it shook their faith in the entire legal system. One up-and-coming supreme court lawyer told me in May 2023: Before the Ayodhya judgment, I was a naive young lawyer fresh out of school who believed that if you present a court with the right evidence, respect the constitution and are argumentatively and procedurally savvy, you win a case. But the Ayodhya judgment broke my faith. He went on to claim that the supreme court had showed "such a complete disrespect for evidence in that case, in order to validate Hindu demands, that [he] almost quit altogether". The lawyer sighed heavily: Judgments matter … They define how ordinary people see the world. And this one has made it very clear to everyone that in Hindutva India, there is no space for Muslim claims.

The Babri Masjid mosque was built in the early 16th century during the reign of the Mughal empire's founder, Babur. But in 1853, a Hindu sect claimed it had been built on the site of a previous Hindu temple dedicated to Lord Ram. After brewing for more than a century, the dispute escalated in the 1990s when the BJP leader, Lal Krishna Advani, spearheaded a national campaign to build a new Ram temple on the site. Inspired by his claim, more than 10,000 Hindu nationalists gathered in Ayodhya on December 6, 1992, and demolished the mosque. Following its destruction, violent Hindu-Muslim riots broke out across India, and more than 2,000 people died.

The dispute over the site ended up in the supreme court which, in November 2019, published a nuanced 1,000-page ruling that, while emphasising the importance of being guided by secular constitutional procedure, observed that "in matters of faith and belief, the absence of evidence may not be evidence of absence". It therefore awarded the disputed plot to the Hindu parties for the construction of a temple, while asking the government to find Muslims a "suitable" alternative plot. Critics of the Ayodhya judgment argue that it gave prominence to the beliefs of one section of the population, and privileged a mythic Hindu version of Indian history over what scientific evidence indicated – thus signifying a new direction in Indian politics and law.

In February 2023, over coffee, my neighbour, the senior lawyer from India's Supreme Court, explained the full significance of the judgment from his perspective: It was more than a clever authoritarian propaganda plot that messes a little with historical claims. Ayodhya was a systematic rewriting of ancient Indian history by the highest court of our land. Many legal experts suggest the Ayodhya judgment was no accident, but the result of a systematic government campaign to fill open positions on the supreme court bench with Hindu nationalist sympathisers. This suggestion is supported by an analysis of supreme court data from 2004 onwards by India's Campaign for Judicial Accountability, which found that the number of supreme court justices who explicitly use Hindu faith-based arguments rather than constitutional ones in their judgments had increased from zero to nine in the years since Modi first became prime minister in 2014. "We still see glimpses of an independent Indian judiciary," the senior lawyer told me when we last spoke in November 2023, "but they are becoming fewer by the day ... I worry that soon our constitutional courts will fall silent."

Authoritarian leaders reshape the nation. Tara, the Dalit human rights activist, is still recovering psychologically from the effects of his midnight police arrest and brief imprisonment. He, along with many of the lawyers I have interviewed, warns that if Modi is re-elected, his BJP government plans to rewrite the Constitution to reflect their vision of India as a country governed by Hindu ideologies and practices. In December 2023, we discussed B.R. Ambedkar, the person with ultimate responsibility for the drafting of India's constitution shortly after independence. "He was a Dalit who had suffered many indignities in his life," Tara reminded me saying that the Constitution is infused with the spirit of equality and social justice for everyone. The attempt to make India a Hindu nation and bend law to this agenda is unconstitutional.

Such concerns have deepened with the Government's announcement in February 2024 that the entire body of Indian criminal law – penal code, code of criminal procedure, and evidence act – will be replaced in July with a new set of criminal codes that will increase police powers and facilitate government surveillance. According to a lawyer who works night and day for the protection of India's most marginalised groups, if the Indian constitution is also rewritten – or "rectified", as one BJP MP recently suggested – then:

India's transformation into a Hindu Rashtra [Hindu kingdom] will be complete. Everything we value about the constitution now, everything that once made India such an exciting democratic project – the emphasis on equality and diversity – will be gone.

At its heart, any authoritarian project – whether in the US, Russia or India – must set out to tackle the country's legal system. To achieve the desired level of control, the project's leaders know they must bring supposedly justice-producing institutions like courts and police into line with their political ideologies, or their ambitions for the country will fail. Most worryingly, as Modi and other authoritarian populists around the world take part in what is dubbed "the biggest election year in history", we would do well to remember that increasingly, even if something is declared legal, it is not necessarily democratic, moral or just.

*(*Some names in this article have been changed to protect the anonymity of the interviewees.)*

*Courtesy:*
THE CONVERSATION

# 'Experts' say what they are told

ANURADHA SAJJANHAR

August 2024

The Modi's administration, over the past two decades, has systematically replaced establishment experts with loyalists, reshaping India's bureaucratic and advisory landscape. This approach has enabled the swift implementation of the government's agenda, but at the cost of diminishing the role of independent expertise in policymaking. In 2008, the BJP instituted its own 'ecosystem' of policymakers in two key think tanks, India Foundation and Vivekananda International Foundation, to build elite support in the lead-up to the 2009 national election. The former vice president of the BJP called this a tactical shift: from being seen as just action-oriented to solidifying its own ideological underpinnings in a policy framework. While the BJP lost the national elections in 2009, it won by a landslide in 2014, and these two think tanks provided personnel for many positions within the central government. Since then, the party and its wide network of supporters have dismantled or co-opted pre-existing advisory committees, universities, and established research institutions.

It must be said that elite experts or institutions do not dramatically shift mass opinion or change waves of party support. But in moments of political change or shifts in dominant perceptions of national identity, intellectuals and technocratic experts often try to re-establish the direct political relevance of their activity, reworking fundamental ideas about society. They 'break the mould' – dismantling, reconstituting, and polarising common-sense understandings of how society ought to be organised. Within limits, intellectuals have a strong hold on public credulity and, particularly, the ability to legitimise paradigms of thought.

The BJP has simultaneously worked to discredit existing establishment intellectuals as irrelevant, elite and detached, while building alternative forms of credible knowledge and expertise. Their relatively new think tanks present an alternative to these institutions, giving the party's political ideology and policy decisions a footprint in already established policy networks. Yet, rather than calling on their grassroots network to develop a bottom-up approach to policymaking, the BJP and its network has mainly replaced one elite with another, albeit one more aligned with the government's worldview.

However, the BJP is not a monolith. Its support base is wide, and champions often contradictory policies. Its political strategies to build support are therefore varied and at times inconsistent, interspersing Hindu nationalism and promises of economic development. The party's tenure has accompanied the discrediting of elite 'intellectuals' and the use of consulting firms, think tanks, political consultants, for its brand management.

Indeed, the last decade has seen an increased outsourcing of the democratic process: an outsourcing of bureaucratic governance to think tanks and global management consulting firms, such as McKinsey, Boston Consulting Group, and Ernst & Young, to name a few, as well as an outsourcing of election campaigns to political consulting firms that use big data to effectively manipulate voters. Earlier this year, Modi's government was revealed to rely heavily on consulting firms make and implement policy, funnelling them millions of dollars. A few months before that, the Indian government was reported to be devising its own democracy ranking index with the think tank Observer Research Foundation. This was in response to India's democracy being named "one of the worst autocratizers" by Sweden's V-Dem Institute, among other global groups.

Modi and the BJP's anti-Muslim rhetoric became more naked and brutal during the 2024 election cycle. They vilified and dehumanised Muslims, calling them infiltrators who are claiming more benefits than they deserve. This stereotype of Muslims 'stealing' from the welfare state has been bolstered by 'experts' from the Prime Minister's Economic Advisory Council recently positing that Muslims birth rates are skyrocketing. Modi made the speech with these infamous claims in Banswara, Rajasthan, where the BJP lost its seat. The BJP candidate also lost in Faizabad, Ayodhya, where it fulfilled a long-awaited desire of the Hindu right-wing, building a temple devoted to Ram over a demolished mosque.

The BJP still received 260 out of 543 seats, undoubtedly a giant margin for a single party. While it might be naive to think that this election proves a rejection of the cultural resentment that Modi's government has legitimised, it shows us that there is still scope for struggle and deliberation in intellectual and expert institutions.

# 'We shall see'

AMIT CHAUDHURI

Students at the Indian Institute of Technology (IIT) in Kanpur sang Faiz Ahmed Faiz's *Hum Dekhenge* in protest and in solidarity with students at Jamia Millia and Jawaharlal Nehru Universities in New Delhi on December 17, 2019 (two days after the police attacks). A member of the IIT Kanpur faculty, Dr. Vashi Mant Sharma, registered a complaint against the protest, saying two lines in particular had hurt his 'religious sentiments': *'Jab arz-e-Khuda ke Ka'abe se, sab buth uthwaae jaayenge / Hum ahl-e-safa mardood-e-haram, masnad pe bithaaye jaayenge / Sab taaj uchhale jaayenge, sab takht giraaye jaayenge'* ('From the abode of God, when the icons of falsehood will be removed / When we, the faithful, who have been barred from sacred places, will be seated on a high pedestal / When crowns will be tossed, when thrones will be brought down') (*The Wire* 2020). Sharma saw this as an allegorical reference to the Mughal invasion of India, which was accompanied by the destruction of idols and temples—the word *buth*, meaning 'idol' or 'figure', plays into this interpretation. The fact that Faiz (1911–84) was Pakistani couldn't have helped, although he'd been a Marxist and an atheist, and his song had been composed as dissent against General Zia ul Haq's

Islamicizing regime in Pakistan. As a result of Sharma's complaint, a committee was put in place at IIT Kanpur, and six students and five teachers were 'counselled', which must mean 'warned, for their role in the protest.

Here's my admittedly cursory attempt to translate the words:

> We shall see—
> It's certain we too shall see
> The day that was promised to us
> And set indelibly in iron
> When the boulder-weight of tyranny
> Will scatter like wisps of cotton
> And under the feet of the reigned-over
> The earth will pound like a heart beating
> And over the heads of those who govern
> Lightning will burn and crackle
>
> When all idols will be vacated
> From the holy places
> And we, the dispossessed and displaced,
> Will be returned to our inheritance,
> Each crown will be flung away,
> Each seat of power brought down
>
> Allah's name will remain; nothing more—
> He, who is present and absent too,
> He, who is both scene and spectator;
> The cry 'I am truth' will be heard,
> The cry that is me as it is you,

And everywhere will reign God's progeny
Which is what I am, as you are.

We are moved by this in a way that we aren't by actionable words. There is an ambiguity of emotion here to do with the phrase 'we shall see', which is inflected with both defiance and defeat (the victorious don't say 'we shall see'); and Allah, who, we are told the moment we are promised the prospect of his ubiquity, is both 'present and absent' (*hazir hai aur gayab bhi*), pointing to the curious sense of annulment we experience in ourselves during the song's prescience of plenitude. Like love, protest implies surrender: a surrender of the personal, during which what is 'present and absent' in ourselves converges. This convergence, in turn, leads to, instead of unequivocal triumph, a melancholy in protest, a melancholy that doesn't paralyze but enables, as this song did for so many in 2020.

The literalism of nationalism allows neither that melancholy nor the contradictory tonality in which it subsists. Neither does the liberal consciousness, which sees the protest poem or song as a *vehicle* for protest rather than a complex experience that exists in and through the texture of poetic language. On January 7, Riyaz Khan, on the *Times of India* readers' blog, identified himself as an 'Urdu poetry lover' and said he was distressed by the way *Hum Dekhenge* had been misread. 'People who are cognizant of the art and nuances of poetry know that in poetry words are not used to stress their literal meaning,' he wrote (Khan 2020). This is a truism of literary criticism and, in the context of the time, a reasonable statement: criticism as an expression of a rationality related to love, the love of 'Urdu poetry', which itself is not unrelated to a wider understanding of democracy, free speech, and *insaniyat*. The first two sentences of Riyaz Khan's biographical note on the blog page describe him as 'basically a mechanical engineer with MBA in International Business. Currently he is director in an Engineering Services & IT headquartered company in Hyderabad.' In keeping with the time of the anti-CAA protests, Khan seems to have been an organic intellectual who emerged from and made his intervention within the system.

Excerpted from *On Being Indian* a new book in the Literary Activism series. The book is *a long essay on the protests that took place from late 2019 to early 2020 against Citizenship Amendment Act.*

# In Ayodhya: God is in details
# Social ethos endangered

SHWETA DESAI

Hindu and Muslim families have lived for decades in and around the newly constructed Ram temple, now a major religious and tourist attraction. The Qureshis and the Sainis speak fondly of their friendship and familial ties. Both say that development projects worth hundreds of crores, muscling into their homes in Ayodhya, are threatening to end their neighbourly attachment.

*"Yeh batana mushkil hoga ki kaun Hindu hai aur kaun Musalman* [It is hard to point out who is a Hindu and who is a Muslim]." Mohammad Shabbir Qureshi, 68, is speaking about himself and his neighbour, Ajay Saini, 52. The two are residents of Ayodhya, and have been friends for the last 40 years in the Durahi Kuan neighbourhood of Ramkot. The families are close, share daily concerns and rely on each other. Ajay Saini recalls, "one time while I was away at work, I got a call from home that my daughter was sick. In the time I could rush back home, my wife informed that the Qureshi family took our daughter to the hospital and

bought the medicines." The backyard where the duo is seated is crowded with buffaloes, goats and half a dozen chickens. Children of both their families are running around, playing and chatting. It's January 2024 and the Ram temple in Ayodhya is getting ready for a high-profile inauguration. A new, heavy, double-barricaded iron grill fence separates their houses from the compound of the temple.

Saini was a young teenager when he and his family moved into the house next to Qureshi in the eighties. He would sell flower garlands for a rupee to devotees visiting the Ram idol in the premises of what was then the Babri Masjid. The Qureshis were originally butchers, the family owned a meat shop on the outskirts of Ayodhya town. Post 1992, after their house was destroyed in arson, the family started a welding business. "Look at these children...they are Hindus...we are Muslims. They are all brothers and sisters," Qureshi says, pointing at a crowd of neighbourhood children of all ages who are playing around them. "*Ab aap hamare rehen sahen se pata kijiye ki yaha kaun kya hai. Hum ek doosre ke saath bhedbhaav nahi karte* [From our everyday living you cannot tell who belongs to which religion. We don't discriminate between us]," he adds. Gudiya Saini, Ajay Saini's wife agrees and adds: "it does not make any difference to us that they are of different religion." When Qureshi's only daughter Noorjehan was getting married a decade ago, Ajay Saini says, "we were involved in the festivities, welcoming and serving guests. We get the same amount of respect as a family person. We know we are there for each other."

Soon the conversation shifts to the Ram temple which they can see from where they sit. It's imposing structure, still under construction, rises into the sky, flanked by massive cranes, all of it covered in a winter haze. Qureshi points towards the imposing structure of the new temple, barely a few feet from his modest brick and mortar house. "Woh *masjid thi, wahan jab maghrib ke waqt azan hoti thi toh mere ghar mein chirag jalta tha*" [There was a mosque there, and at the call of the *azaan* we would light the evening lamp in my house]," he says reminiscing of a time before the mosque was brought down.

But in early January 2024, it is not only the silence of the *azaan* that is worrying Qureshi. "We have been informed there are plans to clear all these houses adjoining the Ram temple compound. In the months of April-May [2023], district authorities from the land revenue department visited the area and took measurements of the houses," Saini told this reporter. Since Saini and Qureshi's house abuts the temple compound and the double barricaded fence. Gudiya adds, "*we* are happy that such a big temple has come up near our house and all this development taking place around. But these things [displacement] are not going to help us," she says." *Ayodhya ka kayapalat ho raha hai, par hum hi logo ko palat ke* [they are transforming Ayodhya by turning us away]."

A short distance away, Gyanmati Yadav has already lost her home and the family is now housed under a temporary thatched hut, covered in cow dung and dry hay. "We never imagined that we would have to give up our house so that Ram can get his temple," says the widow who is trying to hold her family together in their new surroundings. The Yadavs earn their living by selling milk. Her *pucca* house of six rooms adjoined the temple's front entrance in the Ahirana mohalla but was demolished in December 2023. "They just brought the bulldozer and demolished our house. When we tried to show them the documents, house tax and electricity bills, the officers said it is of no use," her elder son Rajan said. That night, the family of four children, an elderly father-in-law and six cattle were left shivering in the winter cold without a roof. "We were not allowed to take anything," he adds. The family has already moved twice before setting up in the tarpaulin tent. "This was my husband's family house. He and his siblings were born here more than five decades ago. But we didn't receive any compensation as authorities said this was *nazul* land [government land], even when we had the documents to prove our ownership," says Gyanmati.

Qureshi and his sons say if provided adequate compensation they will find another piece of land within Ayodhya city's limits, but it won't be a happy move. "Everyone knows us here; we have close relations. If we move out of here and locate to [Muslim-dominated] Faizabad," says Jamal Qureshi, one of Shabbir's younger sons, "then we will be like other common people. We won't be *Ayodhyawasi* [residents of Ayodhya]." A feeling shared by Ajay Saini who says, "our faith is attached to this land. If we are dispatched far, some 15 kms away, then you will take away both our faith and our business." Saini's reluctance to leave his house and move far away is also tied to his work. "I cycle daily for 20 minutes from here to sell flowers at the Nageshwarnath temple near Naya Ghat. I earn between 50 to 500 rupees daily based on the tourist crowd. This is my only source of income to run the family. Any change will mean "longer travel time and additional expenditure," he adds.

Jamal says, "We are proud that such a magnificent temple is standing in our backyard. It has been approved based on faith by the country's highest court, and there are no reasons to oppose it." "But" he adds, "we won't be allowed to live here. We are getting evicted." The families are already feeling the pressure of living in the militarised zone with armed Central Reserve Police Force (CRPF) men milling around, and a watchtower standing guard in the temple's rear compound, close to their house. "Every month, different agencies come here four times for verification checks of residents. If we have guests and relatives staying overnight, then it is mandatory to furnish their details to the police," says Gudiya. Locals are barred from riding on Ahirana *galli* and certain roads near the temple. Instead, they must take a long winding route to reach the central location of Hanuman Garhi. For the grand inauguration of the Ram temple held on January 22, 2024, the road in front of their homes in Durahi Kuan was the route for VIPs like political leaders, ministers and celebrities who came in droves.

The state government unveiled its budget for 2024-25 and dedicated it to lord Ram. "Lord Shri Ram is in the thought, pledge and in every word of the Budget," Chief Minister, Yogi Adityanath said. The budget has allocated more than Rs. 1,500 crore for infrastructural development in Ayodhya including Rs. 150 crore for tourism development and Rs. 10 crore for the International Ramayana and Vedic Research Institute. The temple complex is said to spread over 70 acres of land. The main Ram *mandir* covers 2.7 acres. The entire project draws funds from the Shri Ram Janmabhoomi Teerth Kshetra Trust (SRJTKT). This trust is among the favoured few organisations to be registered under the Foreign Contribution Regulation Act (FCRA) which allows donations from foreign nationals; donations made to the trust by Indian nationals are eligible for tax deductions. Union government largesse can be seen in the flood of funds to develop Ayodhya – Rs. 11,100 crore worth of 'development' projects along with Rs. 240 crore to revamp the railway station and Rs.1,450 crore for a new airport.

After the inauguration, more upheavals are expected. "Ayodhya will experience an estimated daily footfall of over 3 lakh tourists after the opening of the temple," says Mukesh Meshram. He is the Principal Secretary (Tourism) of the Uttar Pradesh government. Preparation for additional visitors will include city-wide infrastructure expansion projects that cut right through old homes and friendships. "The Muslim family living at the corner of the lane, who are our relatives, have already been paid compensation. Their house is partially demolished as it touches the temple fence," adds Jamal, Qureshi's son. He points to around 200 families, including 50 Muslim families, who live in the proximity temple's 70-acre precinct, and who are now on the verge of eviction as the temple trust (SRJTKT) plans to acquire the properties. "Those houses which were in the way of the temple's perimeter have been purchased by the trust and the people have been paid due compensation. There is no plan for additional acquisition," Sharad Sharma, VHP leader said. But locals say the trust is forcefully acquiring land, residential houses and religious places like Fakire Ram *mandir* and Badr mosque.

Meanwhile, the already displaced Yadavs have hung a photo of Lord Ram at the entrance. "If we don't display the poster, they will make it difficult for us to even live here," says Rajan. The 21-year-old left his wrestling training midway to support the family who were being harassed after they lost their home. "Every week, officials and unknown men come here threatening to make us vacate the plot where we have built the hut. We own this land but are not allowed to make any *pucca* construction," he told PARI.

Qureshi recalls the events on and after December 6, 1992, when the Babri masjid was brought down by Hindu mobs and Muslims were targeted in Ayodhya. "My house was burning. It was being looted. We were surrounded by the [angry mob]," recalls, referring to Thirty years later he says, "under such circumstances, people from my locality hid me and kept me safe. I can never forget it till I die, honestly."

The Qureshi family are among the handful of Muslims living in the Hindu-dominated area of Durahi Kuan. "We never thought of leaving. This is my ancestral house. I do not know how many of our descendants have lived here. I am a native resident like the Hindus here," Qureshi tells this reporter, sitting on a metal cot in his backyard. He is the head of a large family including his two brothers and their family as well his own eight sons, their wives and children. He says 18 members of his family who had stayed back, were hidden by their neighbours. Gudiya Saini says, "they are like our family and have stood by us in happiness and sorrow. If being a Hindu you won't help us at the time of crisis, then what should one do with such Hinduness?" Qureshi adds: "this is Ayodhya, you cannot understand the Hindu here, nor the Muslim. You cannot understand how deeply the people mingled with each other"

After their home was burnt down, the family remade parts of the house on a narrow strip of land. The house has three different structures surrounding the open backyard to house the 60 family members. Qureshi's two sons – Abdul Wahid, 45, the second eldest, and Jamal, 35, the fourth – run a welding business and have had a ring-side view of the new temple's construction. "We have worked inside for 15 years, carrying out several welding works including setting up 13 security towers and 23 barriers around the perimeter," says Jamal. They say they work with the RSS, the VHP and all the Hindu temples, and are setting up a watch tower inside the RSS building. "Yahi *toh Ayodhya hai* [this is what Ayodhya is]! Hindus and Muslims live and work with each other in peace," says Jamal.  "Trouble starts only when outsiders come and rake up controversies," Jamal points out.

The families are familiar with the dangers of communal tensions, especially in an election year. "We have seen these dangerous situations many times. We know it is done for political gains. These games are played for a *kursi* [political seat] in Delhi and Lucknow. It cannot change our bonds," Qureshi says firmly. Saini knows his Hindu identity can protect him temporarily in front of a violent mob, like it did in December 1992, when his house was spared and Qureshi's attacked. "If there is fire in their house then the flames will spread to my house too," points out Saini. In such a case, "We will put four buckets of extra water and douse the flames. We know we are there for each other," he said, reiterating about their attachment with the Qureshi family. "We live with each other with lot of love and affection," adds Gudiya.

Courtesy: PARI (People's Archive of Rural India)

# A Madrassa destroyed

UMESH KUMAR RAY

"Burn them!" Mohan Bahadur Budha heard these words during the night of March 31, 2023, when the 113-year-old Madrassa Azizia was set on fire. "I heard people shouting and breaking the main gate of the library. When I came out, they had already entered the library and were ransacking it," says the 25-year-old security guard. The crowd was armed with *bhala* (javelin), *talwaar* (swords) and bricks. *Woh log chillah rahe the 'Jala do, maar do'* (They were shouting, 'kill them, burn them')." Budha is a migrant from Nepal. He had been working at Madrassa Azizia for the last year and a half. "When I requested them to stop, they started attacking me. They punched me and said, '*Sala Nepali, bhago yahan se, nahi to maar denge* (You damn Nepali, run away from here or we will kill you'). Nothing is left in the library, says Budha. They now don't need a security guard. Now I am unemployed."

The madrassa with its library of over 4,000 books was set on fire by rioters in Bihar Sharif, a town in the Nalanda district of Bihar. The *madrassa* (school of Islamic studies) was set ablaze by communal rioters during the Ram Navami procession in the city. PARI visited Madrassa Azizia in early April 2023, a week after communal rioters had attacked not just this *madrassa,* but other places of worship in Bihar Sharif town. Initially, authorities placed the city under Section 144 of the Criminal Procedure Code (CrPC) of 1973, and there was an internet shutdown, but both were lifted after a week. A former student, Syed Jamal Hasan, is walking listlessly saying there were so many books in the library. He started in this school in 1970 as a young boy in Class 3 and studied up to *aalim* (graduation). "I have come to see whether there is anything left," says Hasan. As the 70-year-old looks around, the hall he once studied in as a young man has been gutted. There are blackened papers and cinders of burnt and half-burnt books everywhere. The walls of the library where students and teachers read and researched through the school day are black with smoke and have cracked. The smell of burnt books hangs in the air. The antique wooden cupboards that housed the books have been reduced to ash.

The books included 300 handwritten sets of the complete Quran and Hadith, holy books of Islam. Mohammad Shakir Qasmi, the Principal of Madrassa Azizia, is first generation teacher from his family. He says, "There were 250 *kalmi* [handwritten] books in a cupboard, including books related to philosophy, eloquence, and medicine. Apart from this, admission registers, mark sheets, certificates of the students studying from 1910 were there in the library." Recalling that tragic day, Qasmi says, "As soon as I reached near the City Palace hotel, I saw that the situation in the city was very serious. There was smoke everywhere. The conditions were not such that we could venture out into the city." The Principal was able to enter the *madrassa* early morning the next day. There was no electricity in the entire city of almost three lakh people. "I came alone at four in the morning. When I looked at the library with my mobile torch, I was shocked. I didn't even have the courage to handle myself."

More than half a dozen roadside vendors are busy selling fish near the entrance of Madrassa Azizia. "There is a temple on the west side and a mosque on the east side of the *madrassa*. This is the *behtareen alaamat* (best sign) of *Ganga-Jamuni tehzeeb* (syncretic cultures)," points out Principal Qasmi. "Neither were they troubled by our *azaan* (prayers) nor have we ever been troubled by their *bhajans* (devotional songs). I had not imagined that rioters would spoil our *tehzeeb* (culture). We feel very sad."

Others in the school say that the next day rioters tried to damage other rooms by throwing petrol bombs. More than a dozen shops and godowns were destroyed and looted and this reporter was shown copies of many First Information Reports lodged by the residents. Communal violence is not new to Bihar Sharif. In 1981, a major communal riot was reported but even at that time, the library and *madrassa* were not attacked.

The Madrassa Azizia was founded by Bibi Soghra in 1896 in Patna and was shifted to Bihar Sharif in 1910. Bibi Soghra set it up after the death of her husband Abdul Aziz, a landlord. "She also established the Bibi Soghra Waqf Estate and the income from the land was used for social work – running the *madrassa* for education, a clinic, maintenance of masjids, pensions, food distribution and more," says Umar Ashraf, founder of the *Heritage Times*. This *madrassa* is also part of the project *Taalim-i-Naubalighan* – an adolescence education programme of the United Nations Population Fund (UNFPA), the Bihar Madrassa Board and the Education Department that was started in 2019. Five-hundred boys and girls are enrolled at the Madrassa Azizia. A student who joins here can finish with a post-graduate degree.

"Perhaps this wound (burning down of the madrassa and library) will heal a little, but it will continue to give us pain," says Mokhtarul Haque, administrator of the Bibi Soghra Waqf Estate.

Courtesy: PARI (People's Archive of Rural India)

# Bulldozer Justice in M. P.
# erases Muslim lives

PARTH M. N.

*State directed demolition of homes and shops as retribution for communal violence is a one-sided affair as only minority communities pay the price.*

It's a warm April day in Khargone town of central India. The early morning bustle of residents is suddenly interrupted by the steady hum of advancing bulldozers as they trundle into the crowded and busy Chandni Chowk area of this town in Madhya Pradesh. Nervous residents come pouring out of their small shops and homes. Wasim Ahmed, 35, watches in horror as, in a matter of minutes, the bulldozer's heavy steel blades crush and destroy his shop and the valuable material inside. "I had put whatever money I had raised into my shop," he says.

The bulldozers, ordered by the state government, flatten not just his small shop on April 11, 2022, but around 50 other shops and homes in this largely Muslim-dominated locality in Khargone. This destruction of private property was meant to be retributive justice meted out by the state government of Madhya Pradesh to the "rioters" that had engaged in stone pelting during the Ram Navami festival. But the likelihood of Wasim pelting stores is difficult to establish – a double arm amputee, he can't even have tea without assistance, forget lifting and stoning. "I had nothing to do with the incident that day," says Wasim. He used to be a painter before he lost both arms in an accident in 2005. "One day, I was electrocuted while on the job and the doctors had to amputate both my arms. Even through extreme adversity, I had found a way out [with the shop]," he adds, proud that he didn't waste time feeling sorry for himself. In Wasim's shop, customers would tell him whatever they needed – groceries, stationery, etc – and help themselves. "They would place the money in my pocket or the drawer in the shop and leave," he says. "It was my livelihood for 15 years."

Mohammad Rafique, 73, lost three of his four shops that morning in Khargone's Chandni Chowk area – a crippling loss of Rs. 25 lakhs. "I pleaded, I fell at their feet," Rafique recalls. "They [municipal authorities] didn't even let us show the papers. Everything about my shops is legal. But it didn't matter." The razing of Wasim and Rafique's shops among others selling stationary, chips, cigarettes, candy, cold drinks and such, was a punitive measure ordered by the state government to recover the damages caused during the riots. Later, the district administration would say that the structures razed were "illegal", but the home minister of Madhya Pradesh, Narottam Mishra, had told reporters, "Jis *gharon se patthar aaye hai, unn gharonko hi pattharonka dher banayenge* [We will turn the houses from where the stones were pelted to a heap of rubble]." Before the bulldozers, it was during the riots that some like Mukhtiyar Khan lost their homes. His house was in a predominantly Hindu area of Sanjay Nagar. A *safai karmachari* with the municipal corporation, he was on duty when the violence erupted. "I got a call from a friend and he asked me to rush back and take the family to safety," he recalls. It turned out to be life-saving advice as Mukhtiyar's house is in a Hindu area of Sanjay Nagar. Fortunately, he managed to get back in time and the family escaped to his sister's house in a Muslim locality. When he returned, it was to a charred home. "Everything was gone," he recalls. Mukhtiyar had lived in the locality for all his 44 years. "We [his parents] had a small hut. I saved money for 15 years and built a house for us in 2016. I lived there all my life and always had amiable relations with everyone," he rues. With his home gone, Mukhtiyar now lives on rent in Khargone, paying Rs. 5,000 per month, a third of his salary. He had to buy new vessels, new clothes and even furniture because his house was burnt down along with the material inside. "They didn't think twice before destroying my life. Tensions between Hindus and Muslims have risen particularly in the past 4-5 years. It was never this bad. These days, we're always on the edge." Mukhtiyar is due for compensation of Rs. 1.76 lakh – a fraction of what he lost. But he hasn't received that till this story was published; he doesn't expect the money to come through any time soon. "I want compensation and justice because my house was demolished," he says and adds, "Two days later, the administration did the same thing the rioters did."

Several BJP-ruled states in the past two or three years have become synonymous with "Bulldozer justice." Apart from Madhya Pradesh, states like Uttar Pradesh, Delhi, Haryana and Maharashtra have seen instances of homes and shops owned by people accused of a crime being flattened by a bulldozer. The accused may or may not be guilty. But in more cases than not, the structures belong to Muslims. In Khargone, the state bulldozed only Muslim structures, points out a report shared with this reporter by the People's Union of Civil Liberties (PUCL) who examined the state's demolition drive. They found that nearly 50 structures that were razed ALL belonged to Muslims. "Even though both communities were affected by the violence, all the properties destroyed by the administration belonged to Muslims," the report states. "No notices were given; no time was given to retrieve belongings. The demolition teams led by district officials simply descended on the homes and businesses and destroyed them."

It all started with a rumour, as it often does. During the Ram Navami celebrations, word spread that the police had stopped a Hindu procession near Talab

Chowk in Khargone. Social media amplified it and in no time a militant mob gathered, shouting incendiary slogans as it moved towards the location. Around the same time, Muslims coming out of the nearby mosque after prayers were met by this angry mob. Things turned violent with stones being pelted and the violence soon spread to the rest of the town where far-right Hindu groups targeted Muslim homes and shops. To make matters worse, CNN News18's prime time anchor, Aman Chopra, hosted a debate show on Khargone around the same time, which was titled, "*Hindu Ram Navami Manaye, 'Rafique' Patthar Barsaye.*" Roughly translates to, "Hindus celebrate Ram Navami but 'Rafique' showers them with stones." It is unclear whether Chopra intended to specifically target Mohammad Rafique or he wanted to use a generic Muslim name. But the show had a terrible impact on Rafique and his family. "I couldn't sleep for days after that," he says. "At this age, I can't afford this stress." It's been a year and a half after Rafique's shops were demolished. But he still has a printout of the screen from Chopra's show. The Hindu community for a while, he says, avoided buying cold drinks and dairy products from him after Chopra's show. The far-right Hindu groups had already called for an economic boycott of Muslims. The show made it even worse. Wasim has no savings to rebuild the shop again. For the last year and a half since the demolition, with no shop to run, he has not been able to earn any money. The Khargone Municipal Corporation said they would help him: "Mujhe *bola tha madad karenge lekin bus naam ke liye tha woh* [They said they would help me with compensation but it turned out to be just lip service]." There isn't much a man with no hands can do, he adds.

After Wasim's store was demolished by the state, his elder brother, who runs an equally small store in Khargone has been taking care of him. "I have enrolled my two kids in government school," he says. "The third one is two years old. He too will have to go to a government school. My children's future has been jeopardised. I have been forced to compromise with my destiny."

Courtesy: PARI (People's Archive of Rural India)

# POEMS
PRATISHTA PANDYA

## Bulldozed Hopes and Flowers

Najma's life lay shredded by a bulldozer. As if the riots a few days ago had not done enough. But the wildflowers, she knows, will grow like hope from the vicious claws of these machines. She stood empty-handed on the pavement. A monument of grief. She was no longer trying to retrieve anything from their vicious claws. She couldn't keep the numbers steady in her head and so had stopped counting her losses. From disbelief to fear to rage to resistance to utter despair to numbness – she had traversed many states in a matter of minutes. Now she was just on both sides of the street. Eyes welling up with almost frozen tears and a choking lump of pain in her throat. Her life lay shredded at the feet of a bulldozer. As if the riots a few days ago had not done enough. Nazma knew times were changing for a while now. Not just the way Rashmi looked at her when she went to ask for some starter from her to set curds. Nor was it about a nightmare that visited her regularly since she joined the women protesting at Shaheen Bagh and found herself standing all alone on a small piece of land surrounded by deep trenches. What was changing was also inside her, how she felt about things, herself, her girls, her country. Nazma was afraid. Though being robbed of what they thought was their own was not the first time in the history of the family. She was sure Dadi knew this feeling, tailgated by communal rioters carrying flames of hatred. A little finger tugged at her chunni. She turned around and was greeted with a helpless smile. That is when her thoughts turned wild again...

## Wild smelling flowers

Heavy, ruthless blades
haul and push debris away,
excavate ghosts of history,
demolish mosques, minarets.
They can even uproot an old banyan,
nests and aerial roots and all.
Make way for bullet trains,
remove stumps and boulders,
clear battlefield obstacles,
prepare firing positions.
Iron claws of sharp rippers break
down dense, resistant grounds.
They know how to crush, clear, and
level things up. But when you are done
with all of it You still must deal with
these pollinators, fiery, potent, soft,
love-filled falling out of books
sliding off tongues.

You don't need bulldozers
to tear those defiant books
or to rip the loose tongues off.

But what to do with them,
escaping on the back of chance winds,
riding on the wings of birds and bees,
sliding on river waters, diving
underneath the lines of a poem
pollinating without restraint here,
there, everywhere?

Light, yellow, dry, obstinate dust
encroaches on fields, plants, petals,
minds, and slippery tongues.
See, how they burst out!
Colonies of bright flowers
Wild smelling, holding onto this earth.
Growing like hope from between
the blades of your rippers from under
the tracks of your bulldozers.
See, how they burst out!

Courtesy: PARI (People's Archive of Rural India)

## I cannot write poetry today

July 2023

Don't tell me to have some shame
Don't tell me to rein my tongue
I am stripping off all your poetic conventions
One by one... lines, hemistich, caesura, stanza,
rhythm, meter, rhyme, alliteration,
enjambment...
I am tearing off your bloody Alphabet

from my chest
I am pulling away the cursed metaphors
covering the wounds between my thighs.
Yes, i am roaming your civilized streets
shameless and naked, bleeding....
Oh, shut up!
Don't tell me to keep my voice down.
Hear me...Hear me scream, howl, roar,
explode,
ululate in high pitched trills
Watch me make these raw, wounded,
mangled words lie stretched out
on this pristine ground like naked bodies
of raped women — Kuki-Zomi, Meitei,
Dalit, Christian, Adivasi, Hindu, Muslim...
all next to each other.
Don't tell me how to write poetry today.
*(Burning Manipur leaves ashes of mangled words)*

Courtesy: Indian Cultural Forum

## Witness

These days I force myself to watch
every bit of the horror
that falls on you from the sky,
with an ugly precision.
I watch your farms burn,
your children die,
your schools, tents,
hospitals, memories
and love being blown apart.

I force myself to listen
to the wails of men and women,
the flutter of the dying light
in the eyes of the survivors.
I don't squint my eyes
when I see them pull out
mutilated bodies from
under the debris, or run with
blood-soaked sacks carrying
the dismembered bodies,
still breathing.
I put the volume on
even when the bare-faced war-leaders
come on, justifying massacres,
giving their sins another name.
It is the wedding season in my country
So yes, I watch the grotesque colours
Of *peethi* , *panetar* , and *kumkum*
fill my screen with open eyes.
No, I do not swipe up and select
scenes, shades, songs....
I watch until
the glass screen that separates
me from you cracks,
until my silence is wounded,
guilty and ashamed.
But I refuse to write.
I know the treachery of poetry
the way it folds and unfolds truth
between the layers of its textured fabric,

the way it sings, paints, and embroiders
my shame and your pain,
the way it conjures up beauty
from the most heinous spaces.
Forgive me,
for I shall not write about
this barbaric time in poetry.

———————

Poems by Badri Raina

## The King can do no Wrong

The King was a byword
For showering benefactions,
Until, under the press of those
Who propped his piratical majesty,
His rugged beard began
To match his cruel eyes into
The Instagram of an unsmiling hawk.

Before it was many years old,
His rule began to fray.
He could be seen to rob the wretches,
And enrich the robber barons of the day.

As disaffection came to be writ large
On common subjects' faces,
He drew from his hollow chest
The last of his trusted aces.

Thundering menace at his detractors,
He yelled abominations
Which contravened the agreed
Rules and stipulations.

So, citizens took the matter to
The Commission overhead;
They pondered deeply for thirty days
To nail what the King had said.
On the thirtieth day they heard it right—
The King had never said a word;
It was no menace from the royal mouth,
But a royal fart that had been heard.

The stern Commission concluded
The matter with aplomb.
Justice to the Royal cause was done
The Commission had defused a stinking bomb.

The truth having been dissipated,
The King returned to the helm;
Soon the Commission was rewarded
For the keenest ear in the realm.

§

# Safest Citizen in India of Today

Name the safest citizen
In the India of today—
Is it cop or minister,

Judge or celebrity?

What a dated query you propose—
It is none of the above;
It is nothing that walks on two legs,
It is the holy cow.
No cop, minister, or judge,
No celebrity of any grade,
Dare annoy a cow and be spared
By government or cow brigade.
Indeed, if Indian woman would be safe
From two-legged animals,
Let her learn to be a cow,
And she will be safe as the hills.

And if you do become a cow,
You can be dark from tail to the horn;
For alone among Nature's dark-skinned
creatures,
Only a dark-skinned cow is twice-born.

§

# God and Religion

Tell me not of religion,
O well-meaning friend of mine;
God and religion are as apart
As Milkmaid from brine.

Failing in truthful, honest ways
To be good-natured men,

They devised a fatal instrument,
And called it religion.

Visiting, I once asked God,
"Do you have religion?"
"I kept the gold," he said to me,
"And left the dross to men.
Were they not to quarrel so,
Would I sleep sound in heaven?"

# Seminar on Madness

Madness is a topic much discussed
from ancient times to ours;
Now a crime, now disease,
Now an affliction of lovers.
Sane men keep safe distance
from unaccounted laughter,
wishing to know what it is
that the laughter may be after.

Madness mocks the day's routine,
upsetting useful work;
Often just under a civil skin,
Waiting to go berserk.
So, when just one goes mad, the family
attempts a private cure;
But when there are more, the state appoints
Professional Counsellor.

But when madness pricks the counsellors
of nations near and far,

the only sane thing left to do
is to go to an all-out war.

War lets out the maddened blood
and restores sanities
which in time promise further wars,
putting madness on lease.

## Frozen in Birth

First we are born to man and wife,
Then they give us our names,
Those names then our prison make
Of inflexible religious frames.

But I that a 'Hindu' am
Might well have a 'Muslim' been,
Had the sperm and egg that wrought me
Come from an Aslam and Nasreen.
What sense that we should thus invest
Our lifelong loves and hates
To an instant we had no inkling of,
And consign to that our fates.

If then we remain a dumb zygote
Through all our waking life,
What use a heart, a brain, a tongue,
What use our sentient strife?

Must we in loyalty embrace
What darkness made of us?
Or should our selfhood discriminate
A 'maybe', a 'no', a 'yes'?

Is it our name that renders us
At all times wrong or right?
Or should 'human' mean that we create
Some self-made luminous light

Beyond what thoughtless body heat
And the accident of birth
Confer upon us unbeknown—
Mere creatures of the earth?

Those that gave us 'holy' books
Remade what went before;
Would they have wanted generations
To rest frozen in their Lore?

Courtesy: *Stout and Tender*
published by AuthorsUpFront | Paranjoy

# *Shav-Vahini* Ganga

PARUL KHAKHAR *is well-known in the literary circles of Gujarat. Her Gujarati poem Shav-Vahini Ganga of May 11, 2021, about the devastating sight of Covid-19 dead bodies floating in the Ganges went viral and was translated into several languages. English translation by* SALIL TRIPATHI.

Don't worry, be happy, in one voice speak
the corpses
O King, in your Ram-Rajya, we see bodies
flow in the Ganges
O King, the woods are ashes,
No spots remain at crematoria,
O King, there are no carers,
Nor any pall-bearers,
No mourners left
And we are bereft
With our wordless dirges of dysphoria
Libitina enters every home where she dances
and then prances,
O King, in your Ram-Rajya, our bodies flow
in the Ganges
O King, the melting chimney quivers, the virus
has us shaken
O King, our bangles shatter, our heaving chest
lies broken
The city burns as he fiddles, Billa-Ranga thrust
their lances,
O King, in your Ram-Rajya, I see bodies flow

in the Ganges
O King, your attire sparkles as you shine,
glow and blaze.
O King, this entire city has at last seen your
real face.
Show your guts, no ifs and buts,
Come out and shout and say it loud,
"The naked King is lame and weak",
Show me you are no longer meek,
Flames rise high and reach the sky,
the furious city rages;
O King, in your Ram-Rajya,
do you see bodies flow in the Ganges?

---

# Macabre Dance
## *A sequel to Shav-Vahini*

L K SHARMA

Come ye all Indians,
come and dance with us.
In this exotic land,
we breath and laugh,
we sing and dance.

We were brought here
by *Ma Ganga.*
Here it is all *Changa*!

Come ye Indians, rich and poor,
young and old! Come to
this Land of silver and gold.
We are having the promised
Good Times here.
Come and see. Come and see.

The Supreme Being released
us from earthly bondage
and called on *Ganga Maiyya*
to bless our souls.
The Mother came running,
embraced us all, carried us for
miles and miles and deposited us
in this wonderous Hell.
Hell is swell! Hell is swell!
This is the promised place.
The place you dreamt of in 2014.
You hope that India will be it.

You will join us soon or late.
But why do you wait.
You will not miss Him because
every five years, He will visit us.
His commission granted us
postal ballots. An office here entered
our names and finger-printed
us as we were brought
wrapped in white. It has machines
on which we place a finger and
a light flickers and reaches India.

We are in His Kingdom.
His agencies and cells run a
high-tech office.
We send messages from here.
That's all we do.
The broadband speed will be
Tripled soon. We will then
flood India with billions of
message of gratitude to the One
who made us migrate.

As NRIs, we remain in touch
with the Fatherland. At the next
*Bharatiya Pravasi Diwas,*
we shall be present in spirit.
You want to hang on till the
opening of the Modi Mahal there.
Don't. Come and see
a grander Mahal coming up
here in Hell.

# A knock on the door

Last night a man
knocked at my door.
'Open up!',
he demanded with authority;
I complied;
although I do not deny,
it was dark;
I was perplexed,
but still, I did not remark.
'Your number!' he commanded.
I hastily obliged by giving him
my cell phone number.
But he threw it back;
'Your number!'
Befuddled, I gave him my Aadhaar Card
with my biometrics
but he seemed eccentric,
he defaced it;
'Your number', he said grimly,
throwing it back at my face.
I did not take umbrage,
instead I rummaged
and gave him my voter's card
the identity of my citizenship;
but he was getting angry.

'Your number!' he shouted,
although I had done my best to oblige,
I had absolutely nothing to hide.
'The one that you have earned!'
he said by way of an explanation;
so I gave him my Pan card number
where my taxes are duly deposited.
But now he was furious;
he clasped a handcuff to my wrist,
holding me so close,
I could not resist.
'Your prisoner number!' he shouted.
'But I am not a prisoner', I protested.
'*You are all numbered*'.

Courtesy: Mainstream

# For My Sister, Gauri Lankesh

*Gauri Lankesh, journalist, was killed in Bangalore on September 5, 2017. Eight years later the accused, when released on bail, got a rousing welcome and were garlanded by a Right-wing Hindu group. A BJP leader Jeevraj said Gauri Lankesh would have been alive if she had not written against the RSS.*

September 2017

Tonight, I write the saddest lines,
They killed my sister, last night.
As she came back from work,
Parked the car
To open the gate to her house,
They pumped three bullets
Into her forehead,

And there she lay
Bleeding, oh! so forlorn.

They sped away on their motorbike,
I know they will come again,
I do not write these lines in vain;
They killed Kalburgi,
They killed Dabholkar,
They killed Pansare,
And called it a Law&Order Game.

Tonight I write the saddest lines
As my sister lay bleeding;
She had gone from village to town
Recording the voices of the people
And their feelings,
The sun had burnt her skin
From every pore of her body
The love of her people had poured in,
Tonight that love mingled with her blood
Gushed out on the stones of the street,
But after their murderous feat,
They called her a 'bitch'
Even in her death;
We are to see worse, yet.

They tell me to be silent,
They tell me to write poems that are pretty,
But I tell you
When the blood is pouring

onto the streets, of my sister,
You may very well,
Call us both a litter.

I will not succumb to the venom
You have spewed,
The feud you have created
Between the people,
This fear, This anger, This hatred,
You are creating shards
Of the fabric of society,
Which was once a homespun khadi;
Creating a clamour about beef,
The *mandir*, And the *tiranga*;
Oh! do take a bath in the Ganga.

You have electoral power
And the barrel of the gun;
Have your merciless fun;
But in this darkest hour
I will cling to my words
True to my salt;
You killed my sister
Whose only fault
Was to speak and write, fearlessly.
Tonight I write the saddest lines,
You killed my sister, Gauri.

Courtesy: Mainstream

# Second Partition



We fought for freedom
but they decided,
our very own homeland
would be divided.
No one knows of the
mayhem and madness
that did descend;
take this as my testament:
the knives at the nape of necks,
the rapes of women,
their jumping into wells,
followed by blood-thirsty yells.

The people sleep-walked
with their belongings,
then just dropped them,
unable to carry further;
mothers abandoned their babies
hoping they would find them again;
a line drawn, had torn
and turned our world insane.

In the caravan I sat,
my eyes were red with crying;
then the other caravan stopped,
just for a moment
we both looked at each other,
their eyes too were red.

Red is the colour of blood
and there was a flood;
in that instant we both realized
we had been caught
on the rack of history;
why had they decided
to partition our minds and bodies
will remain a mystery.

I was compelled to leave my home
which housed in the garden,
the grave of a *pir*,
to whose spirit my mother
always lit a lamp;
but after Partition
my eyes are still damp.
The memory of that time wells,
scars do not heal.

Why do you not see the pain
of the bulldozed people in Nuh;
the women raped in Manipur,
even those felled by bullets on a train,
must we still go down that lane?

Will we ever learn
that red is the colour of blood
both yours and mine, and of the eyes
that cry, ours and thine.

Courtesy: Mainstream

# Are You A Hindu?

I sigh,
As the years pass from the green to the golden
Of my country, that travels
From a colonial past,
To some kind of modern.

But I wince,
As the young and idle, scream near mosques,
To find more and more temples,
For a lost and lonely Ram,
Who couldn't find a temple in their hearts.

I wince,
When a frail old man in a skull cap,
Is mocked by young men in rowdy swagger.
As they pull at his grey beard,
Can't they see their grandfather?

I wince,
As millions take a reverent dip,
In a holy river, by sin made unholy.
Chaos, stampedes and VIPs,
A civilization falling, and not so slowly.

I wince,
As three-hundred-year-old graves
Are sought to be desecrated,
By people who are goaded,
Into hatred, contrived, ill-fated.

I wince,
As more and more people shout,
And others become more and more silent,
A nation that loses equilibrium,
The rulers smile and the police turn violent.

I wince,
No money, no food, no medicine,
No education, no skill, no job,
Pushes the poor man into
Religion, caste and Hindu-Rashtra?

I wince,
For how long we will be divided,
By our food, our clothes, our God?
Yet when riots kill a loved one,
We shed the same tears of blood and salt.

I wince,
For we'll fight about 'us' and 'them'
Till vultures claw us both to death.
And will only in death we really know,
They were 'us' and we were 'them'?

# The Lost Stars of a Nation

You used to tell me that my eyes did shine
With little wet stars each time the Anthem
played. Could you now push away
the dark fog my country's lost in and
find those precious stars again?

But you chose your God
And told me he's not mine.
Then you chose your hearth
And told me it's not mine.
You said you were a native
And I an outsider, ungainly
With an awkward gait struggling
For eons I walked my own country

Then I invoked my God and race
As a revenge to you and yours
I burned in self-righteous flames
And you chose a King you thought was yours
Because he said he'd banish me
You smiled and sealed my fate
He set fire to all that was mine
I burned in fear, and you in hate

We made insurmountable mountains
Of our puny little differences
We dug deep rivers
Of unnavigable distances.

One piece of the loved land
A mother who was yours and mine
We picked up sinful swords
To hack, lynch and defile
Now both our homes are in flames
And pestilence frightful us befalls
And dark death is partial, neither
To your kingsmen nor to my Gods
As the bodies in white are carried
With screaming eyes and tired shoulders
How much really is the wailing difference
Between funeral, cremation or burial?
You and I are just expendable pawns
Who never mattered in your King's game
When we cry and when we mourn
Our anguish is just the very same
Our life and death are the same
And one and same must be our poor God
Why then did we not choose a King
Who could be equal for one and all?

Can you look beyond the black fog
And find the lost stars in my eyes
Can you gather them together
And paint them in my country's skies?

For you are my brother my friend my playmate
With you, I've such long and pious ties
And maybe when the Anthem plays someday
Dancing wet stars will shine again in our eyes.

# Father Stan Swamy

An unworthy piece of drift wood
I carve alone through the night
My anxious chiselling begets
Neither any good nor right

Many masks have I donned
This, the scariest of them all
A mask to stay silent
No matter what befalls

A Poet Teacher Priest
Incarceration of a saint
He's not me or mine
Let there be no complaint
They sing songs of him in jungles
Indeed a well lived life!
But in this country even love
Now bears a heinous price

Water denied to the ailing old
The innocent shackled and broken
But don't the sins of a cruel nation
Come back to haunt its children?

Midnight children burn.
Rape, arrest, broken spine
Of a country I once loved
But seems no longer mine

My fourteen years of childhood
Right from wrong, they taught
Never said their God was greater
Never asked me to 'Convert'

But I must carve my deathly mask
And shroud myself in silence
They say my religion is in danger,
So I must partake in the violence

# My Mother's Fault

You marched with other seven-year-old girls,
Singing songs of freedom
at dawn in rural Gujarat,
Believing that would shame the British
and they would leave India.
Five years later, they did.
You smiled.

When you first saw Maqbool Fida Husain's
nude sketches of Hindu goddesses,
And laughed, when I told you that
some people wanted to burn his art.
'Have those people seen any of our
ancient sculptures?
Those are far naughtier,' you said.

Your voice broke,
On December 6, 1992,
As you called me at my office in Singapore,
When they destroyed the Babri Masjid.
'We have just killed Gandhi again,' you said.
We had.

*Aavu te karaay koi divas* (Can anyone do
such a thing any time?)
You asked, aghast,
Staring at the television,
As Hindu mobs went, house-to-house,

Looking for Muslims to kill,
After a train compartment
in Godhra burned,
Killing 58 Hindus in February 2002.

You were right, each time.

After reading what I've been writing
over the years,
Some folks have complained that
I just don't get it. I live abroad: what
do I know of India?
But I knew you; that was enough.

And that's why I turned out this way.

## Leader frustrates Lover

No area of life or literature has remained unaffected by the populist Leader. He has wormed his way into mass psyche. Dreams, romance, love affairs, and personal relationships, all are scuttled by the turbulent political situation. In the New India, poets write on the blood-soaked daily newspaper (Gulzar). Couples are attacked by right-wing vigilantes in public places. In the privacy of a room, a lover is incapacitated by the thought of a repressive regime. Watching a community threatened distracts her from love for an individual. She is deaf to the call when a Prufrock-like young Indian K. Anand Kak desperately wants to make love. The disappointed lover cries about the Leader's intrusion into his personal life. The activist, in a disturbed state, resists Kak's cowardly erotic moves. Kak pleads with her:

## Come to me, abandon your Cause

Like you, I too lament the state we are in.
We are engaged in a macabre dance, amusing
ourselves to death amid a deafening din.
But how will we get to meet unless you
end your obsession with the nation.
You live with India, day and night.
Possessed by the idea of India.

You tell me where India is going. You
take me through the day's depressing
developments. I want to take you in a
rose garden. I talk of us; you talk of
India. I am up against a country.
Your heart beats for a cause, not for me.
Your views about India are very strong,
feeling for me very weak. You feel
anguished about the nation and want
me to feel the same.

You like me. Want to see me every night.
I come without fail. You welcome me
but cannot make up your mind as to how
far can you go! You switch TV channels,
doom-scroll, and chat about the Leader's
irresistible rise and unlikely fall. You
never strike a chirpy note. Our nights
are laden with words and gloom.

You talk of India, its ills and descent
into hell. You say this is not the India
you had seen or dreamt of. India is
regressing. Going back to the medieval
age. New India is mythological India.
You fear a new Mahabharat, a grand
battle within the family.

Masses are fed imagined history and
myths by millions of hired internet

nutters. There is an astounding rise
of unreason. Non-issues dominate
faux debates that publicise the hate
merchants, opening and scratching
healed wounds.

The past is virulent for a nation as for
an individual. The Leader invokes the
past. His army fights over memory and
seeks to avenge a Mughal emperor's
bigotry by indulging in bigotry. It ignores
the depredation by the British rulers.
His vigilantes invoke patriotism to drain
away knowledge from society and damage
universities, centres of liberal democracy.

The deafening chants of nationalism
drown the cries of injustice, poverty
and protests the Government's
misadventures and dismal performance.
Welcome to the Mumbo Jumbo Nation.
March of modernity stopped. Progress
nullified. Intellect and scientific temper
derided. Dissent suppressed. Dissenters
silenced. The concept of truth obliterated.
The idea of India destroyed. Mendacity
rules. Paranoia and mistrust envelope
us in this communal cauldron bubbling
with hatred. Built by freedom-fighters,
India is being demolished by those who
had kept away from the freedom struggle.

Churchill had forecast who will rule
independent India. Some Indians too
feared that India was not ready for
universal franchise. India got too
much democracy too early. They say
had Britain been a democracy in the
time of Robin Hood, that outlaw
would have been the Prime Minister!

For long independent India was ruled
by those who and whose fathers had
fought for freedom and gone to British
jails. These liberals ignored the threat of
sectarianism. Communal leaders took
advantage of the liberal ethos and spread
their tentacles to destroy secular ethos
and promote their version of Hinduism.

The Hindu right-wing failed to
grab power so long as Indians
remembered the tragedy caused by
religious extremism and polarisation.
The fanatics waited in the wings,
knowing that human memory is short.
India's secular fabric developed holes,
giving an opportunity to leaders using
cadres to oppress a minority and incite
the majority by making it feel besieged.
They fight the faith of a frightened
minority and fragment society.

They proved that liberal democracy was fragile and could be pushed on the path of terminal retreat. We had taken the idea of India for granted. The bubble in which the liberals lived was small and got punctured easily.

In the Republic of Fear, children are groomed to be vigilantes. The power of rumour to destroy dissenters and institutions and create an ugly society is established. Mass consciousness is poisoned.

Language has been distorted. Words given new meanings. Insidious and invidious confront us. Mobs march waving flags as sticks. Menace the Other, lynch the nation.

We are at war, struck by weapons of mass disinformation. Suffocated by smoke of the digital battlefield. No decaying corpses. Decaying women and men stare and cry, seeking safety from deafening digital shelling.

An ancient faith hijacked and turned into a political weapon. Hindu saints watched it all. Said nothing to defend

their faith and explain true Hinduism
to those claiming to follow this faith.

You say religious right-wingers and
fake nationalists are ruining India.
Secularism buried under 20 million
paid tweets. People's courts punish
those promoting inter-faith harmony.

As to the Gandhian legacy, an MP
applauds Gandhi's assassin. A woman
in saffron robes enacts the murder of
the Mahatma and praises his killer.
She is hailed by her saffron-dressed
followers. Her video showing a pistol
and flowing blood is liked by many.
Some pray at the Godse Temple!
Such weird scenes are to be seen to
be believed. Video wars are fought
with viral lies and fake news.
Indians now live in Absurdistan.
It has become the new normal.
The Deep State watches and rules.

Fear stalks the infantilized nation.
Officials fall in line. As per orders,
they wreck vengeance on the innocent
to settle scores with the critics of the
Leader. Those asked to commit crimes
for political gains are fully protected and
allowed to go scot-free.

Business leaders and Bollywood stars
turned out to be men of low character.
Big A B or C shake their hips in public
and shake with fear in private. They
seal their lips and look the other way
when their few fearless colleagues are
trolled by vigilantes and threatened by
the despotic Government.
*Maha Nayaks* masquerade as heroes,
fight the reel villains and sell snake
oil for a fee. Filmmakers make films
to please the Leader.

Order vanished. Laws redundant. Judges
know which side their bread is buttered.
Politicized police have been given a new
charter of duty. State-sponsored vigilantes
wield the weapon of religion. They have
tasted blood. Private armies march
through the night.

Conspiracism has won. Manipulation
is the key to power. We cannot think.
We are drugged. Drunk on hate, we
laugh and kill, kill and laugh and
indulge in mass hysteria.

The itch to be violent has gone virulent.
A riot can be engineered at a moment's
notice. Green fields become killing fields
when visited by women in the morning.

At night, the TV studios become boxing
arenas. The power-drunk anchor jumps
up and down shrieking, striking hands
in the air, demanding drugs, to launch
a million tweets praising his ugly show.
Bear-baiting and public executions gone
out of fashion. Humans enjoy dogfights
among humans. They watch the idiot box
and enrich the channels that spread hate.

Clowns play politicians. Politicians clown.
They fool and amuse to win poll after poll.
Their failure of intent has caused a disaster.
All-consuming polarisation has destroyed
social harmony as well as internal security.

The crapification of the Indian mind is
beyond treatment. A novelist needling
politicians with her luminous prose, is
derided as activist-writer. Let us be
hyphenated at the hips!

Poets and politicians are drawn to
the power of words. Poets use these
to express, wonder and find answers.
Politicians use these to beguile and
mobilise people. Poets say what
others cannot or do not.

Some say poetry is a luxury enjoyed by the educated middle classes and schools should not teach poetry because it is irrelevant. "Poetry, though heavenly born, consorts with poverty and scorn". Poetry makes nothing happen! A poet says so. I say no. Poetry makes things happen, things that are not seen.

Poetry makes you live, helps you cope with sorrow. It provides a healing touch. It is way of trying to come to peace with the world. This "charming nymph is neglected and decried". What is worse, studied as text. You believe "the blood jet is poetry and there is no stopping it." As a poet, you sense what is coming long before it does, as animals sense a tsunami or an earthquake. So, you know where India is headed.

A culture war precedes a religious war. It will take decades to recover what we lost in a few years. Our civilization is losing its resilience. The genie is out. It can't be pushed back into the bottle. The lie outlasts the liar. The toxic political culture will not let a sensible leader emerge. No one will be able to make this country governable.

Future looks grim. Post-truth politics
has ushered in a pre-fascism phase.
and fascism has had a good trial run.
I call India Prozac Nation and get
away with it since semi-literate
nationalists think it is a compliment.
India turned upside down. Bigotry,
misogyny, sectarianism, hatred and
violence have become all pervasive.

You believe protest poems will make
a difference, change the world. Words
are weapons but the Pope has few
battalions and the Leader knows it.
Writers have been maligned
and marginalized. Logicians have
no role. A semiotician in India must
look both sides before crossing a road.
A philosopher bolts back on seeing a
mob on the street.

Intellectuals who alert the nation
have been rendered toothless. In
future, books will appear with titles
such as *The not so Strange Death
of the Liberal India.*

Conflict has paid a rich political
dividend. Those who engineered
a moral panic will keep the conflict

running to demonise the
Other. The people do not flock to
a Messiah during peaceful, normal
times. Perennial conflict is needed
to keep the Leader in power.

You are not a born poet. This cruel,
Violent, divided and fearful nation
turned you into a poet. You enrich
your poems with politics. I see you
writing *Notes from a Dead Nation.*

You smell evil. Recite *Second Coming.*
" *Things fall apart; the centre cannot
hold. The best lack all conviction while
the worst are full of passionate intensity.*"

Things have indeed fallen apart.
The beast that was to come,
arrived and we welcomed it!

Your protest poems, infused with
lyrical anguish, boil with rage.
Political is personal and personal
is political. I say the same to those
asking me not to take it personally
and not let my blood boil.

You light a candle, but no light can
dispel this darkness. That Yellow Fog
was benign. The mental fog is dense.

All have been hit by organised rage.
You and I remain on the same page.

Contrary to the mantra recited often,
our sacred *Janani Janmabhoomi,*
the motherland, is no Heaven. It has
turned into Hell that many of its sons
leave and many more want to leave.

Abandon your cause. Please shift your
focus from national affairs to our affair.

Forget Him, think of me.
In this darkness, you spot the
Divider-in-Chief who injects the daily dose
of hateful rhetoric, raising fear and insecurity.
As a teller of lies and super-spreader of hate,
he competes with Trump.

He sells hyper-nationalism that fuels
bigotry, hatred and violence. Comes
from the same state that produced
the Great Unifier. Ironic!

He imitates Vivekanand and Tagore
with make-up and sartorial props.
His stylist will get a national award.

He shows off hyper-masculinity, like
the British rulers who got themselves
photographed with a dead tiger under

their feet. He boasts of his chest size
and carries on his decivilizing mission.

Efforts to legislate minds and control
thought have succeeded. While the
crude barriers to the movement of
protestors are seen by the world, the
ban on the movement of ideas gets
less attention.

Voters like his display of masculinity
and posturing. They go sleepwalking to
the polling booths under the influence
the witches' brew of fear and hope.
We get the leaders we get.

The finely attired Leader struts on the
world stage. Builds tall iron and stone
pillars of identity and turns them into
sites for exhibition of nationalism and
tourism. He wants to be remembered
through grand monuments.

A mass psychologist, who interviewed
the Leader several years ago, said he
had met a text-book fascist. Scholars
are not read. So, the Leader climbed
the power ladder and rose to the top,
fulfilling his life's ambition.

The academic later warned that one
entire generation of Indians will have
to pay the price for the havoc being
caused by the political adventure
kick-started through polarisation.

Moderation and restraint are banished
from discourse. Patience for nuance is
lost. Hope is derived from rumours.

Scholars calculate the human costs of
tragic transformation that historians
will record years from now. Books will
appear on the descent of the nation and
the spell of mass hysteria that enfeebled
India and Indians.

The scholar who alerted the nation has
met Indians to whom India feels like a
foreign country. Constant social strife is
ruining their mental health. Their pain
is proportionate to the elation felt by
the vigilantes going after their victims.

You say the Leader intensifies our
anxieties and weaponises these against
us. A health expert says the endemic
continuous traumatic stress will cause
a mental health crisis. Fear aggravates
the malady.

GDP-obsessed economists pooh-pooh
the idea of the Gross National Happiness.
Some political scientists dare to say that
democracy cannot survive the loss of a
sense of identity and purpose.

Any internal security expert will tell you
that powerlessness increases depression
and makes people more vulnerable
to extremism and prone to it.

Psephologists write on two narratives
going on in this divided nation, one
backed by populism, rhetoric, lies and
state power. The other backed by facts
and reason, rendered ineffective by a
vicious campaign against "intellectuals".

The talented Leader manipulates mass
behaviour. Through dramatic gestures
and words, he makes people angry or
ecstatic, as per his requirement of the
moment. A blatant persuader. He has
gauged our stupidity and pliability.

He may not have gone to a university
but understands mass psychology and
India's religious and social fault lines
better than academics. He thinks big
and has global ambitions. The religious
card has got him a large following of

long-distant nationalists and the
Hollywood Hindus.

The Leader is a 21st century man even
though he learnt to wear trousers late.
His wardrobe is the envy of film stars.
He owned a digital camera before it
was invented and knows all about
camera angles. His mentor calls him
the best event manager.

He understands data science better
than any IITian. He is smarter than
an algorithm in tracking our hopes
and fears. The toolkit containing the
two lets him control the hearts and
minds as he plays the right notes.

His ability to invent false narratives
makes him a literary genius. He tells
tales to conquer the soul of the nation.
Just as the British did with stories of
their supposed sense of justice and
fair play!

He uses simple messages to bewitch
simple people. Rhymes to entertain
the masses. Uses innuendo to say the
unsayable. Delivers his message
without risking legal action. He

commands and controls social media
that gets users addicted to lies.

In conjuring up enemies of the nation,
he gave lessons to Trump. He demonizes
the Other and reaps political dividends.
Unleashes divisive politics, branding
half the people as enemies. Polarisation
divides all but pays him richly.

He came to power by appealing to the
worst instincts of voters and expands
his empire by turbocharging these.
The bigots feel empowered to act.

The mantra of *beg, borrow and steal*
lets him enlarge his constituency. He
wins some opponents by offering pelf
and power and some by threatening to
fix them. He says in public: "I have
everyone's birth-chart", which forces
others to flock to him out of fear. Once
in his party, their crimes are forgotten.

You say he seduced India by envy and
hate and pushed it into the infamous
company of failing democracies. Corralled a
corrupt populace, lapdog media and obliging
oligarchs who keep him aloft. He returns the
favour and enriches his selected cronies.

The Leader parrots the Sanskrit saying
"the world is one family" but makes
each community see itself as different
from the Other and the Other as the
Other.

He makes us believe the world is illusory.
Nothing is as shown, and everything is
the opposite of what we are told. He
convinces the multitude that facts are
fiction and lies are truthful.

Ignorance is a virtue. Deception is
state policy. We have entered the
Age of Humbug and Hypocrisy.
A smart operator propped up by
bots rules our *Andher Nagri.*

You say the Leader is lucky since the
Big Power has turned Islamophobic.
It is no longer keen to destabilise
India which it used to be during the
times of Nehru and Indira. The Big
Power now sees India as an ally needed
to counter China. The Big Power
applauds the Leader for his
majoritarianism. The Western press,
taking the cue from America, used to
run down India and never report
its achievements. It turned friendly
when American foreign policy changed

and the US corporations began to see
India as an opportunity.

Democracy is dead. Leader is elected
again and again in mobocracy. Mobs
approve of kleptocracy and crony capitalism.
A demagogue kills democracy with
ease starving it of secularism.
Communal hatred keeps him in power.
Capitalists nourish him. Eminent persons
want to enjoy his patronage. The poor
hope he will give the promised gifts.
The megalomaniac's writ runs and runs.

Tragedies will be written on repression
used to control distress when the Leader
failed to manufacture consent. Studies
will appear on the dangerous power
of crowds and mass emotions.

These will explain the outbreak of
tribalism and analyse how and why
people came under great pressure to
take political sides and see things in
terms of black and white.

In all this you are right, but I alert you.
You are a single woman. They will
trace you and chase you. Do not talk about him.
Never sing songs against him or for democracy.

Erase from your mind the words freedom
and civil liberties.

Do not think. Thinking is banned for
reasons of national security. And even
after you stop thinking, be vigilant.
You will be damned because of your
region, religion, caste or diet.

Do not phone any friend to express
anger about the wretched state of
the nation. Walls have ears. Walls
have eyes to read your thoughts and
transmitters that send your sound bites
to the Agency.

Beware! The IT Cell is watching you.
It has listed you as an anti-national
involved in an international conspiracy
to spread rumours of rapes to defame
India. It magnifies the demand that you
leave India and go away to Pakistan.

You are vulnerable, not being one of
His Maidens who hailed Him and
secured rewards and personal safety.

India is no place for you. Your poems
have attracted the attention of the cyber
goons. You cannot escape the clutches
of the ghoulish machine of the IT Cell.

My messages to you will be published
to portray you as a fallen woman.
Pouted lips on photoshopped face will
go viral projecting you as a pouncing
vixen.

Your photos will be morphed to retail
your "ignoble" past. This is the least
you must expect, if not an attack on
the street or raids by official agencies.

They have finished Gauri Lankesh
and other rationalists. India is no
place for non-believers. If you want to
live in India, you must believe in Him.

You must stop shouting political
slogans to protect your sanity
and self. I fear for you. India
is not what it was. Nor are its police
or courts. Bollywood and advertising
industry are held to ransom by His devotees.

Literature can critique and condemn
the powerful. Not to talk of Orwell
and Auden; Shakespeare, Milton,
Wordsworth, Byron and Shelley, all
wrote on politics. Dante even paid
for it. Shelley was not allowed to visit
India because of his political views.

You, I and million others know
who is responsible for the state India
is in. You feel so disturbed by what
he does to India that you even use
the four-letter word that I cannot
repeat before you.

I detest him for what he does to us.
He has no health warning inscribed
on his forehead. His noise ruins our
love life. He robs me of your time.

He hijacks you to the world of pain
and away from me. Because of him,
you sing no love lyric to me.
You shed tears not for me but for the
nation. But for the dreadful thoughts
about him, your lips would feel mine!

* * *

You ask me how we can keep gazing at
each other and avoid looking at India.
I do feel guilty for feeling romantic and
being in your room instead of the war
trench dug in every house where families
fight at dining tables over a politician,
the elephant in the room.

The reality of India that disturbs you will
kill my romance. I live an anomalous
co-existence, night after night.

Come with me and be my activist-lover!
Not a common tribe. Considering what
we are going through, it is fine. As a
lover in India of 2021, you are who you
ought to be. I understand but resent it.

I go apocalyptic on hearing you. I share
you anxiety. But I banish all thoughts
that are not about us. I think of only you.
Nation is too big and abstract for me.

It is seen differently by different groups.
Some see it in Gandhi's spinning wheel.
Others in a postal stamp. Bigots call it
Hindu Nation, cleansed of the Other.

Fanatics see it as saffron or green. Chefs
call it Turmeric Nation. Real estate goons
see India as a project site with forests to
be cleared and ponds filled up with rubble.
They see India as the next Las Vegas.

Our motto *Truth Alone Triumphs* is
what India should be about but is not.
Tagore warned us against nationalism.
Like Gandhi, he gets trolled by Hindu
nationalists. Patriotism is the last refuge
of scoundrels.

They attack the nation in the name of
nation. Their nation is a map on paper,

a figure of imagination that they invoke
to beat the Other. They paint the nation
as Goddess and masquerade as her
worshippers to mobilise fools
and win polls.

Their Mother India is fierce. She kills to
protect her devotees. A film imagines a
different Mother India played by Nargis
who ploughs the field to nourish her family.
She bears the burden with courage and
fortitude. She is just and fair.

A poet sees Mother India as a poor frail
woman with dry and dishevelled hair and
a sad sickly face, unable to feed or protect
her sons and daughters. The poet is called
names by the so-called nationalists.

*   *   *

These images do not matter. Unlike you,
I am not obsessed with nation. I try
hard not to care what state India is in.
I do see the fascists and barbarians at
the gates. I repeat your sentences about
the current situation. But I focus on you.
I wish you will do the same and are for
me, not for the nation.
There are sorrows other than India.
I have no sorrow other than love.

You are more precious than India.
What is India to me? You are everything.
My sweetheart comes before the mother.
They say if the nation is in such deep
distress, how do I sing a Love Song.
They should know the most famous
Love Song was published during the
War. There is a crisis now but there
was a far bigger crisis then. Pain intensifies
my love for you. Share my pain to lessen it.
Stop thinking. Feel me all over.
Here, here and here!
I do not want an anguished citizen
wailing about the nation. I want a
woman to behold and to hold.

Recite your poem, if you prefer that to
kissing me. I will listen to you on our
dismal state and devious rulers. How
long will we go on doing that and not
what couples on the Marine Drive
do every evening? You hear music in
light and see light in music. So, surely,
you must see above my spindly legs and
below my balding head. I hope one night
you would want more than my ears.
One night, when your mind gets tired
and heart gets hot, you will shut your
eyes and see me. That night, India

would cease to matter. You will turn
to me, touch me and grab my all.

On that blessed night, you would feel
the whole of me and I would feel the
real you. On that holy night, you
will discover joy that you have never
known in your life that remained
satiated with ideas and starved of emotions.
What a real joy it will be to be going
where I have been wanting to go
all the way with you, wanting to go
and waiting to go to blissful heaven!

Excerpted from *The Love Song of K. Anand Kak*